# The Stranger

JACQUES FERRANDEZ

# The Stranger

BASED ON THE NOVEL BY ALBERT CAMUS

TRANSLATED BY SANDRA SMITH

PEGASUS BOOKS

NEW YORK  LONDON

THE STRANGER

Pegasus Books Ltd.
80 Broad Street, 5th Floor
New York, NY 10004

Copyright © 2013 by Gallimard

Translation copyright © 2016 by Sandra Smith

First Pegasus Books hardcover edition June 2016

ISBN: 978-1-68177-135-9

10 9 8 7 6 5 4 3 2 1

Printed in China
Distributed by W. W. Norton & Company, Inc.

This translation is dedicated to
the memory of Jacques Beauroy,
esteemed French diplomat,
historian, mentor, and friend.

# The Stranger

PART ONE

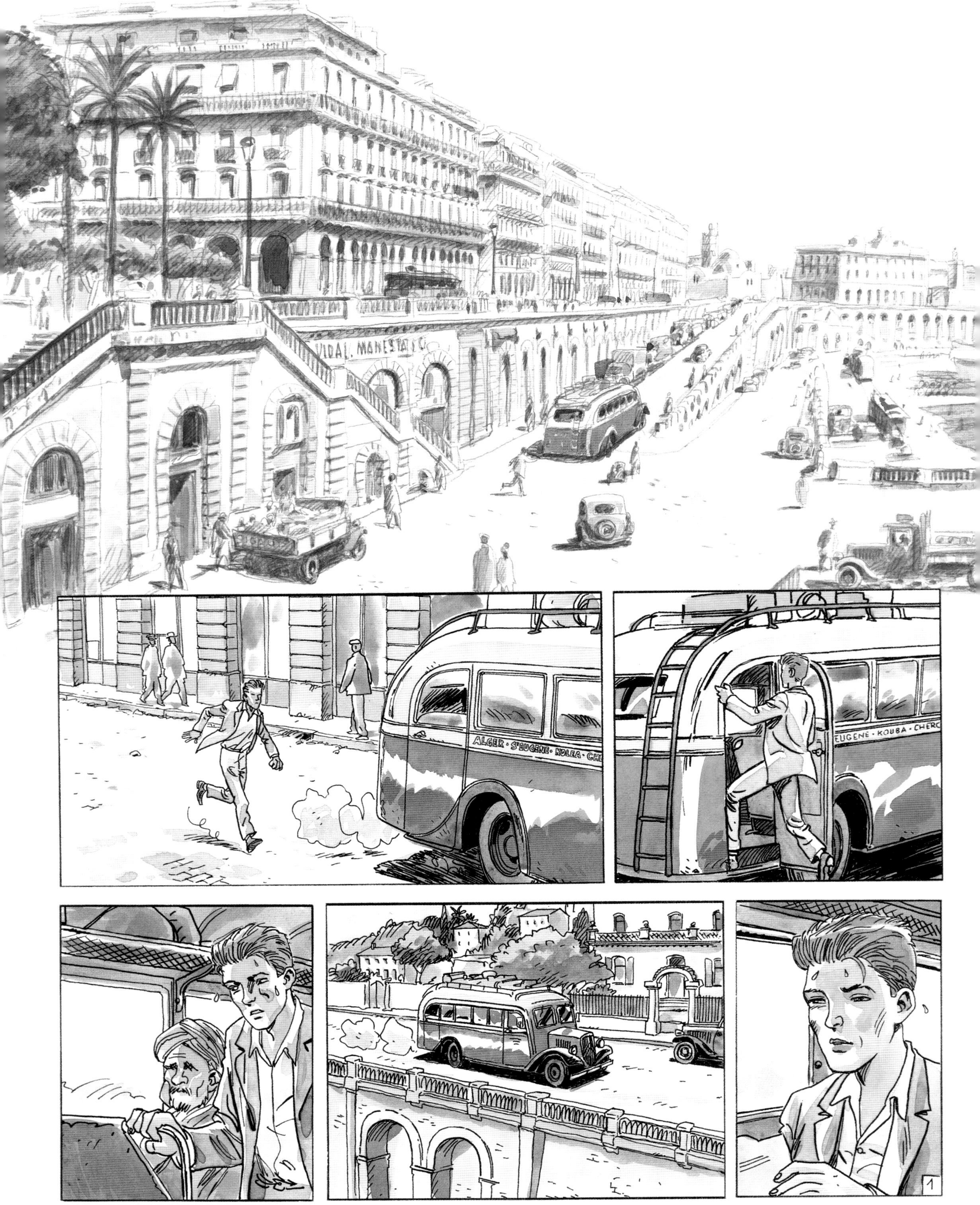
ALGER · S^t EUGENE · KOLEA · CHE
EUGENE · KOUBA · CHERC

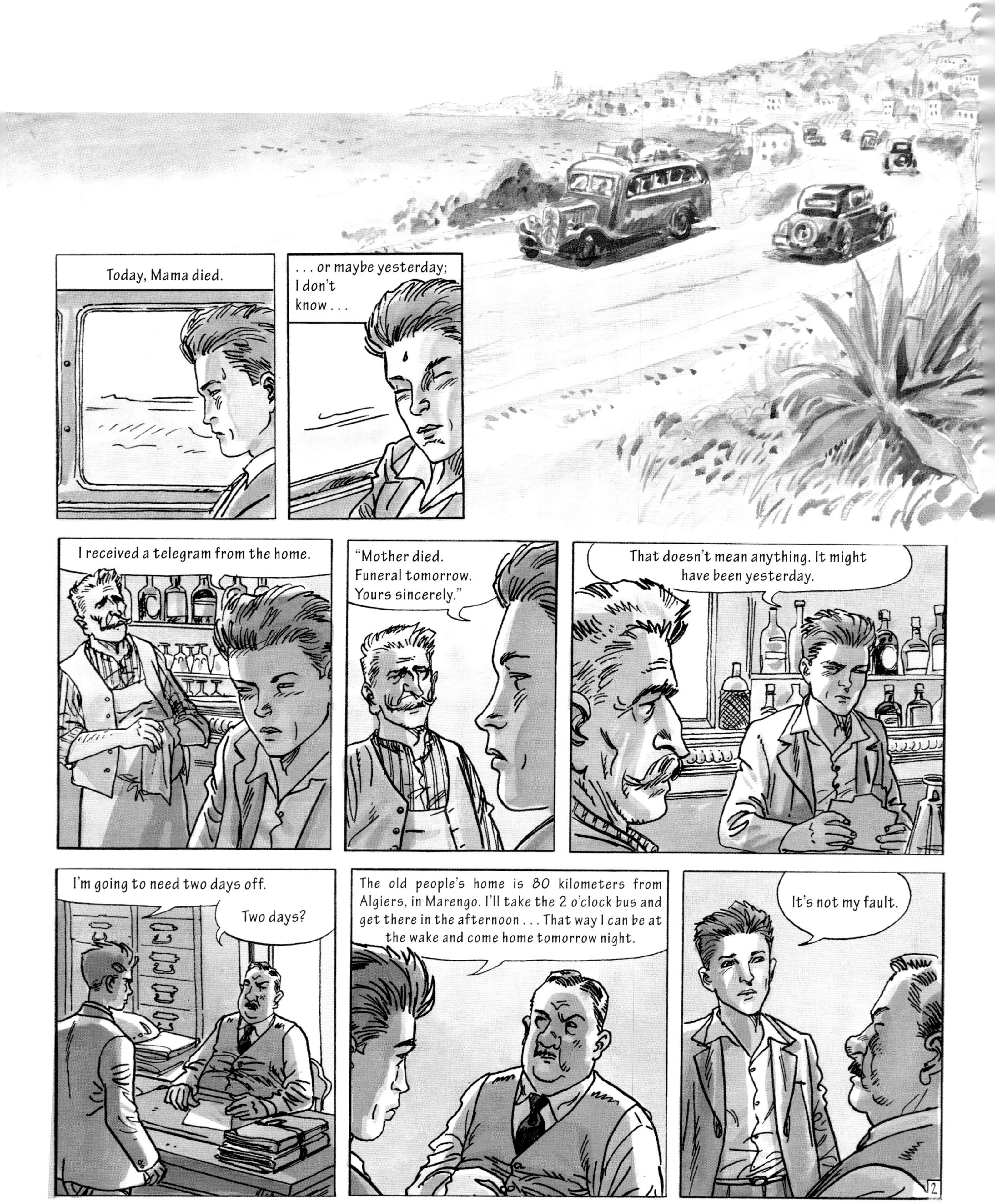
Today, Mama died.
. . . or maybe yesterday; I don't know . . .
I received a telegram from the home.
"Mother died. Funeral tomorrow. Yours sincerely."
That doesn't mean anything. It might have been yesterday.
I'm going to need two days off.
Two days?
The old people's home is 80 kilometers from Algiers, in Marengo. I'll take the 2 o'clock bus and get there in the afternoon . . . That way I can be at the wake and come home tomorrow night.
It's not my fault.
2

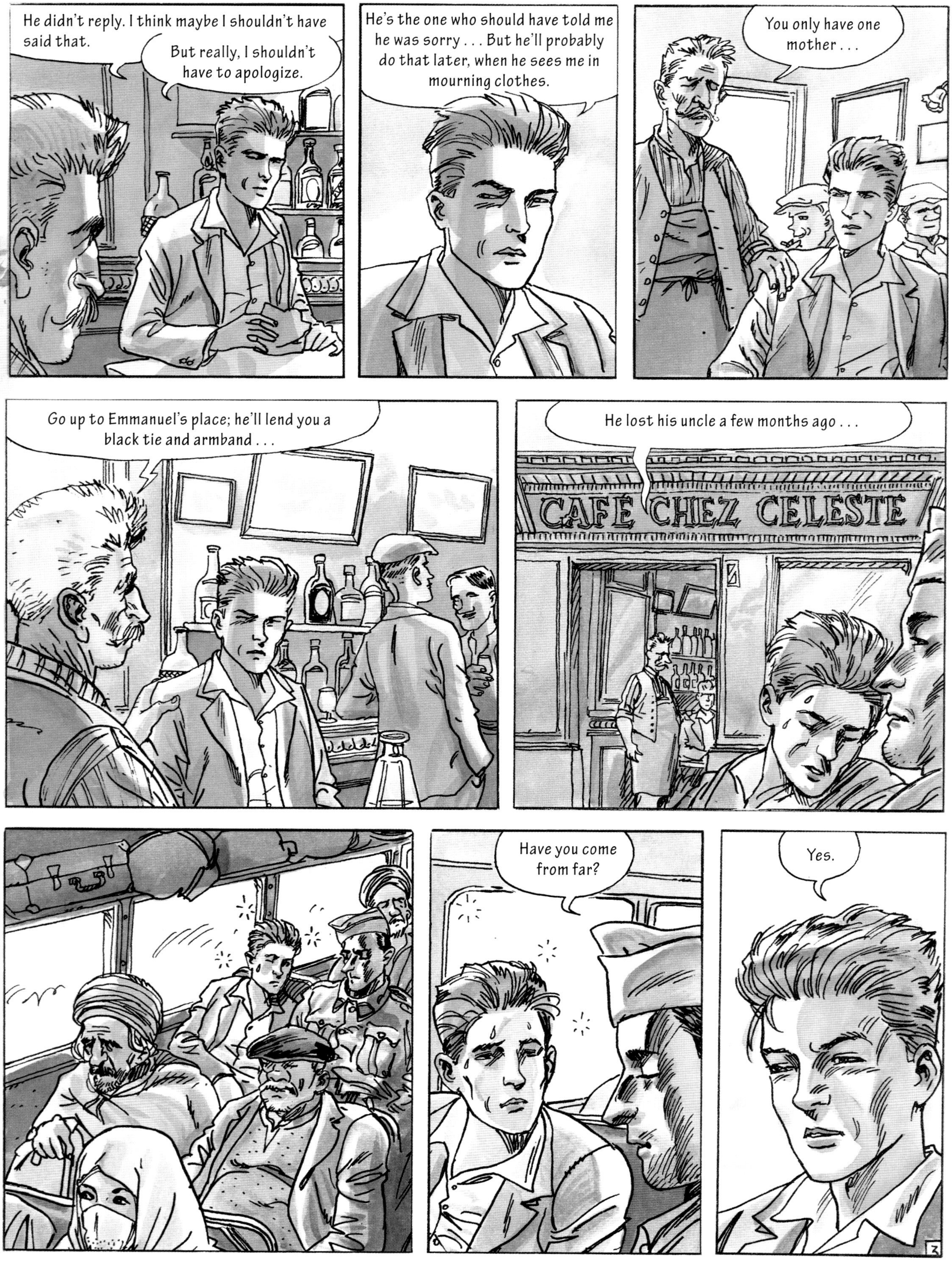
He didn't reply. I think maybe I shouldn't have said that.
But really, I shouldn't have to apologize.
He's the one who should have told me he was sorry . . . But he'll probably do that later, when he sees me in mourning clothes.
You only have one mother . . .
Go up to Emmanuel's place; he'll lend you a black tie and armband . . .
He lost his uncle a few months ago . . .
CAFÉ CHEZ CELESTE
Have you come from far?
Yes.
3

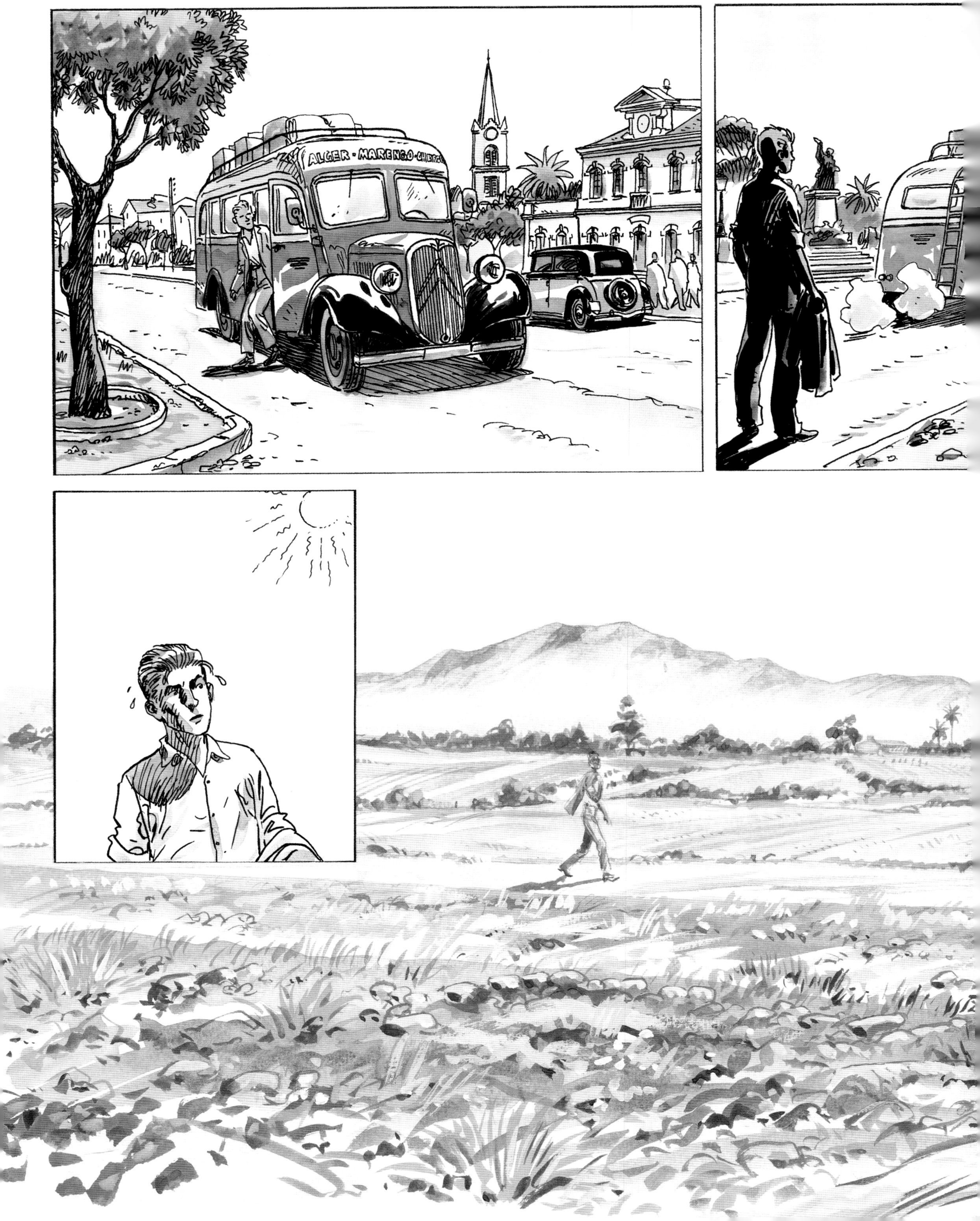
ALGER · MARENGO ·

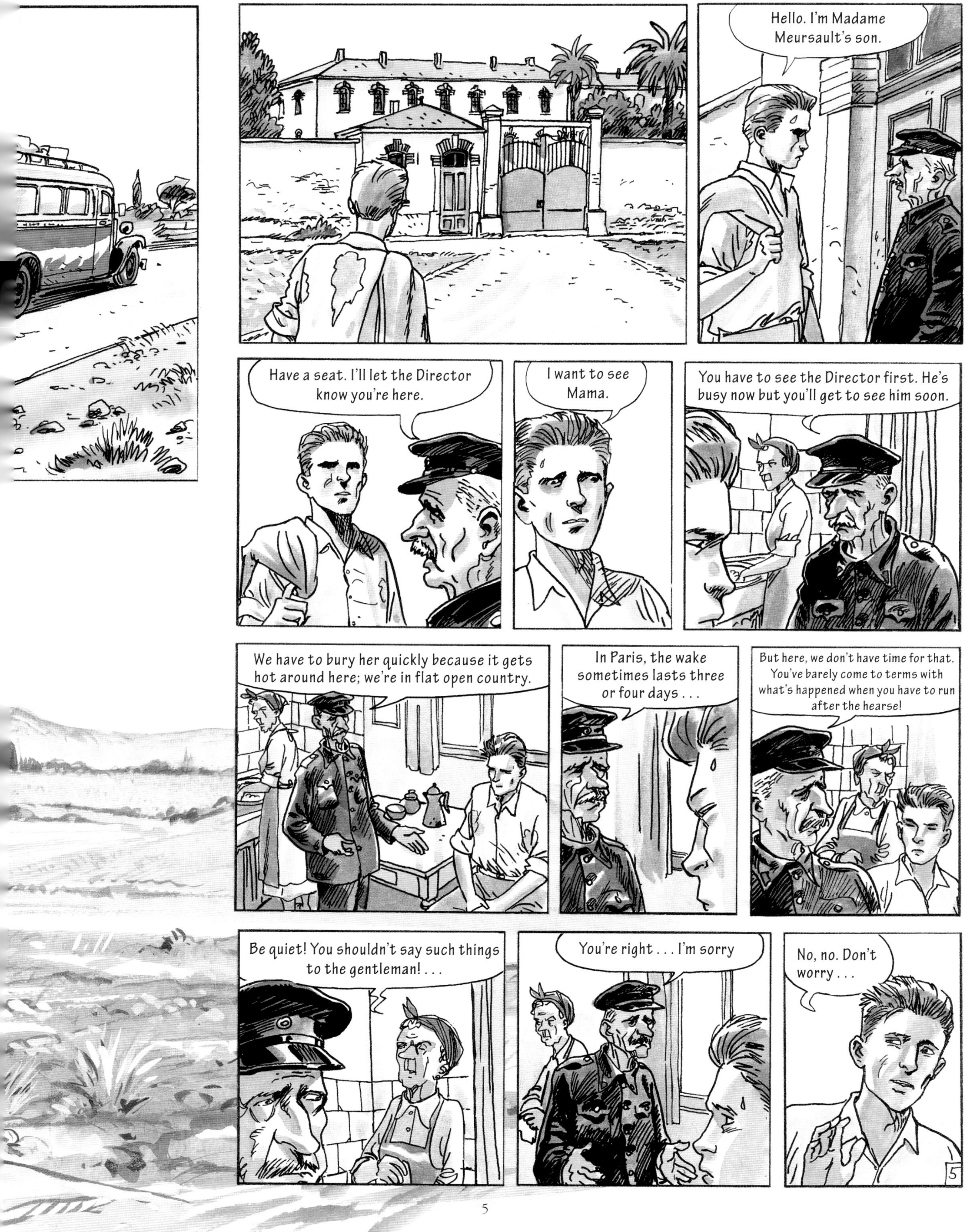
Hello. I'm Madame
Meursault's son.
Have a seat. I'll let the Director know you're here.
I want to see Mama.
You have to see the Director first. He's busy now but you'll get to see him soon.
We have to bury her quickly because it gets hot around here; we're in flat open country.
In Paris, the wake sometimes lasts three or four days . . .
But here, we don't have time for that. You've barely come to terms with what's happened when you have to run after the hearse!
Be quiet! You shouldn't say such things to the gentleman! . . .
You're right . . . I'm sorry
No, no. Don't worry . . .
5

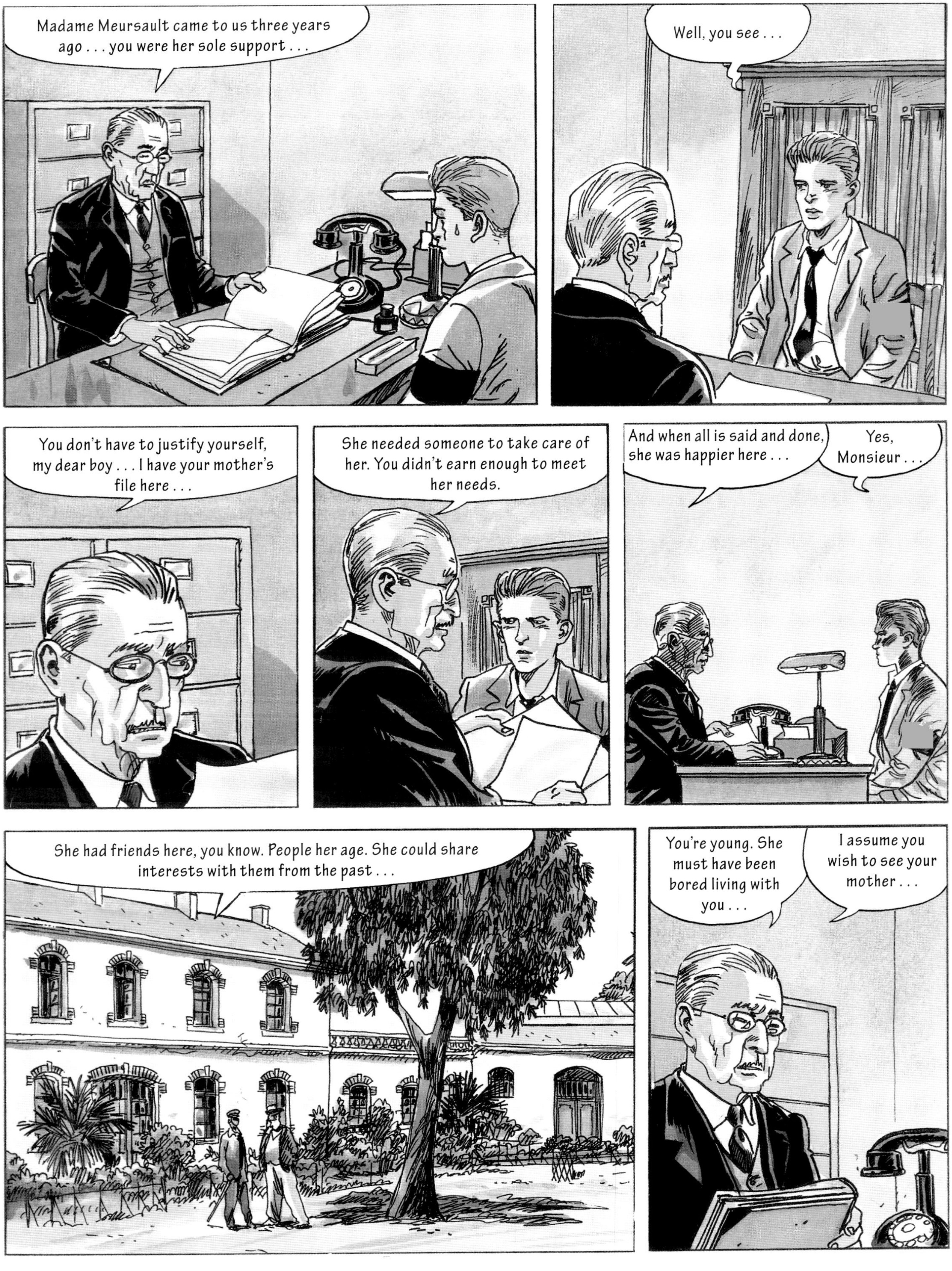
Madame Meursault came to us three years ago . . . you were her sole support . . .
Well, you see . . .
You don't have to justify yourself, my dear boy . . . I have your mother's file here . . .
She needed someone to take care of her. You didn't earn enough to meet her needs.
And when all is said and done, she was happier here . . .
Yes, Monsieur . . .
She had friends here, you know. People her age. She could share interests with them from the past . . .
You're young. She must have been bored living with you . . .
I assume you wish to see your mother . . .

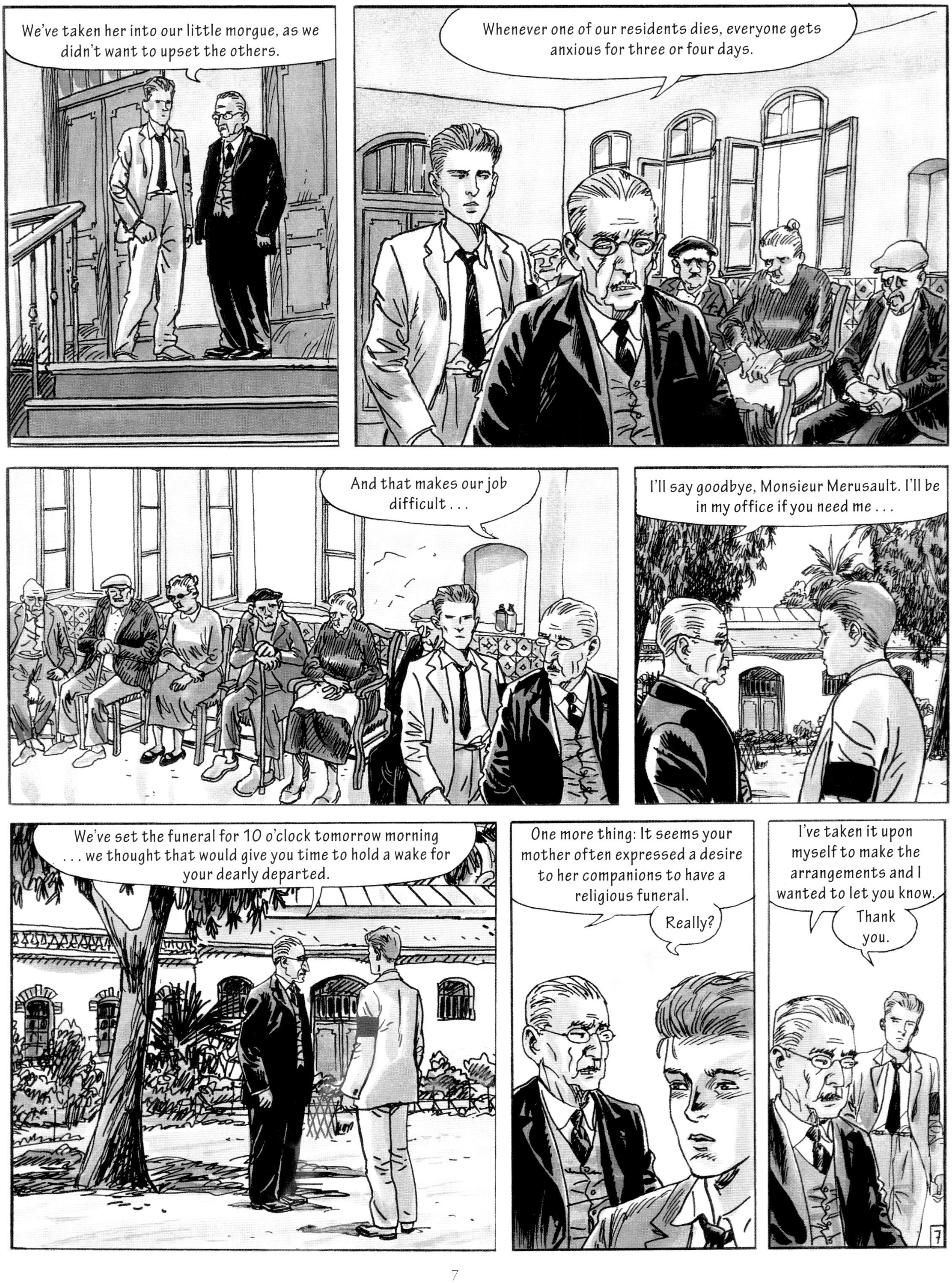
We've taken her into our little morgue, as we didn't want to upset the others.
Whenever one of our residents dies, everyone gets anxious for three or four days.
And that makes our job difficult . . .
I'll say goodbye, Monsieur Merusault. I'll be in my office if you need me . . .
We've set the funeral for 10 o'clock tomorrow morning . . . we thought that would give you time to hold a wake for your dearly departed.
One more thing: It seems your mother often expressed a desire to her companions to have a religious funeral.
Really?
I've taken it upon myself to make the arrangements and I wanted to let you know.
Thank you.
7

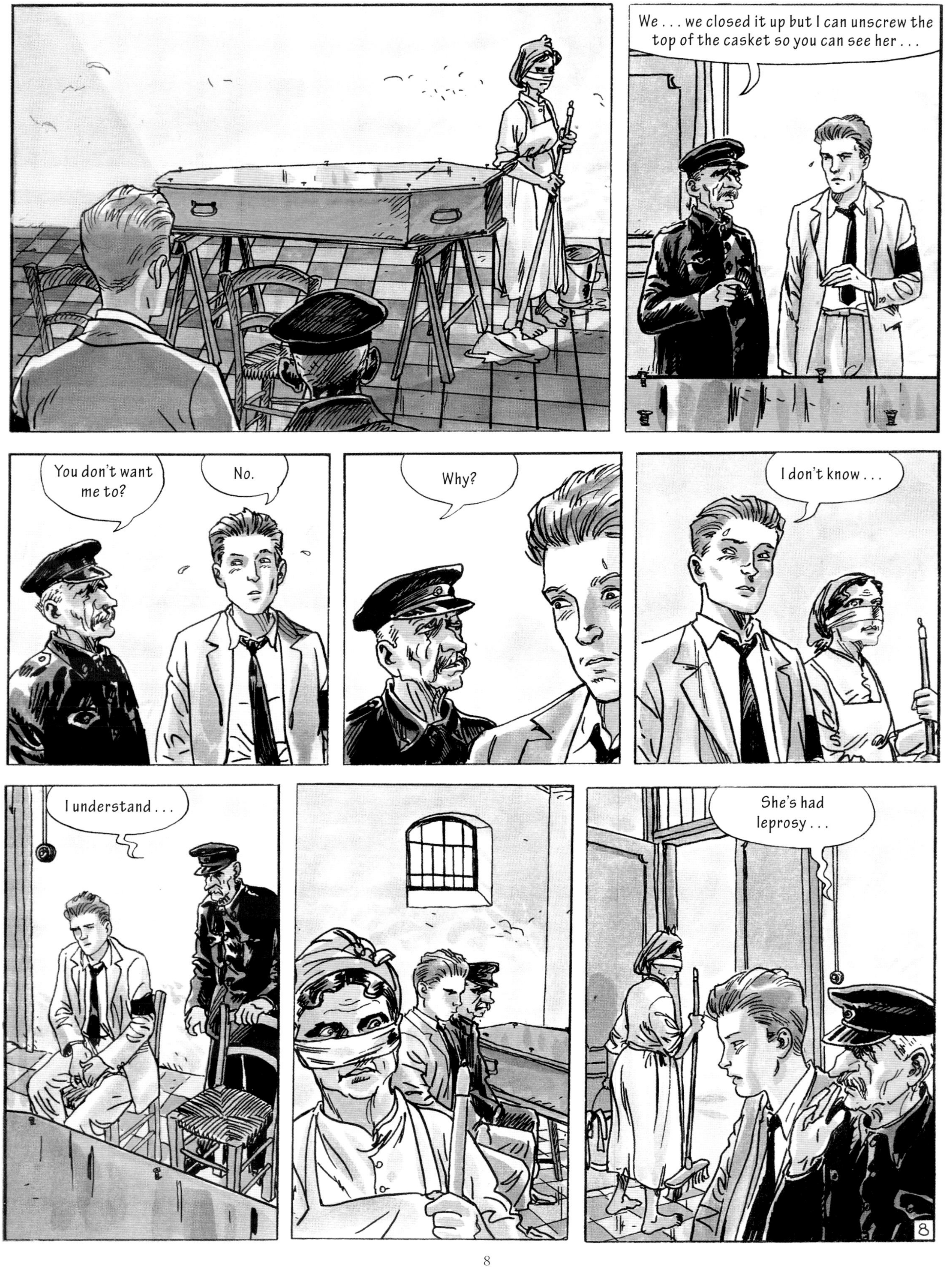
We . . . we closed it up but I can unscrew the top of the casket so you can see her . . .
You don't want me to?
No.
Why?
I don't know . . .
I understand . . .
She's had leprosy . . .
8

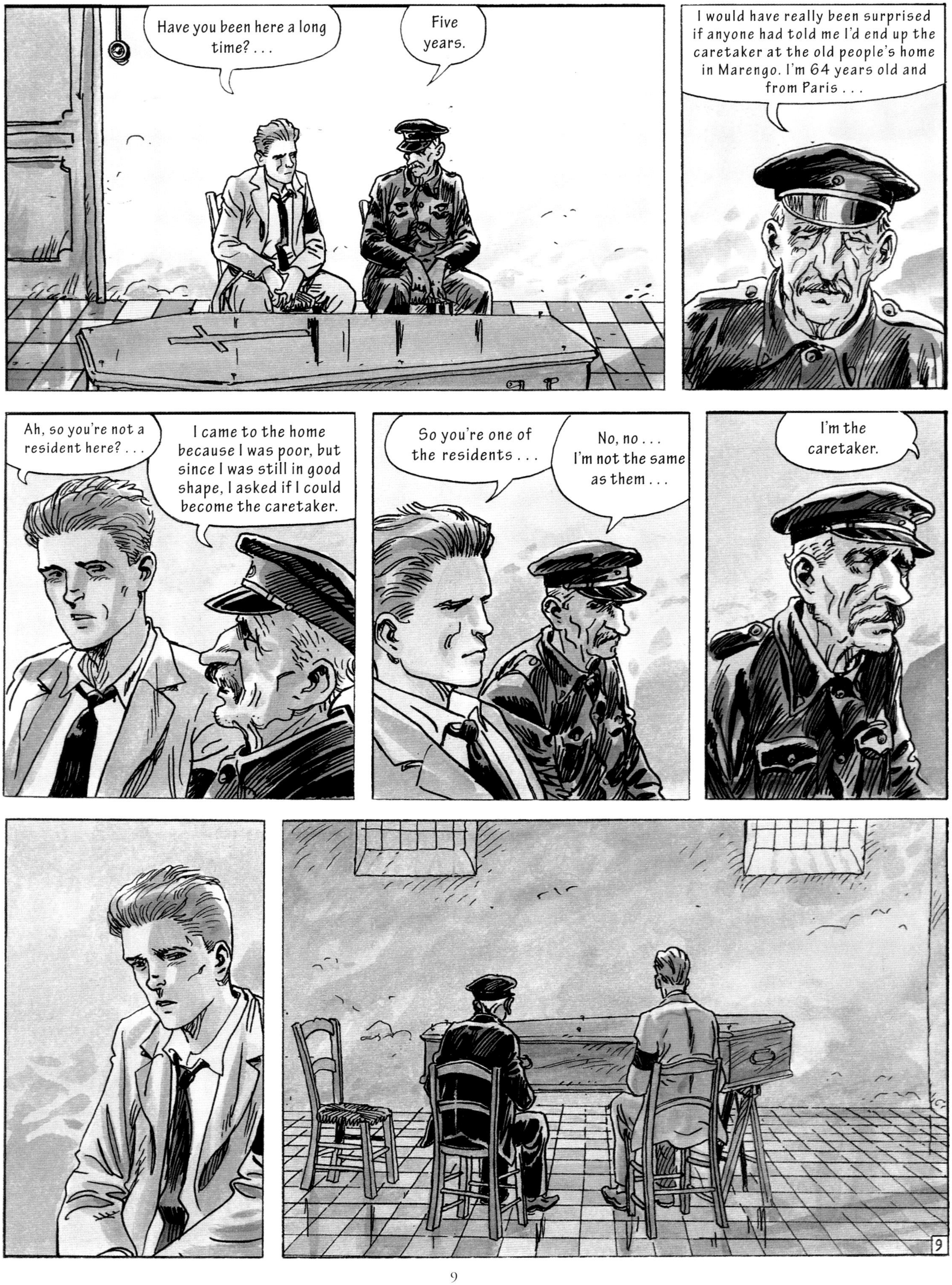
Have you been here a long time? . . .
Five years.
I would have really been surprised if anyone had told me I'd end up the caretaker at the old people's home in Marengo. I'm 64 years old and from Paris . . .
Ah, so you're not a resident here? . . .
I came to the home because I was poor, but since I was still in good shape, I asked if I could become the caretaker.
So you're one of the residents . . .
No, no . . . I'm not the same as them . . .
I'm the caretaker.
9

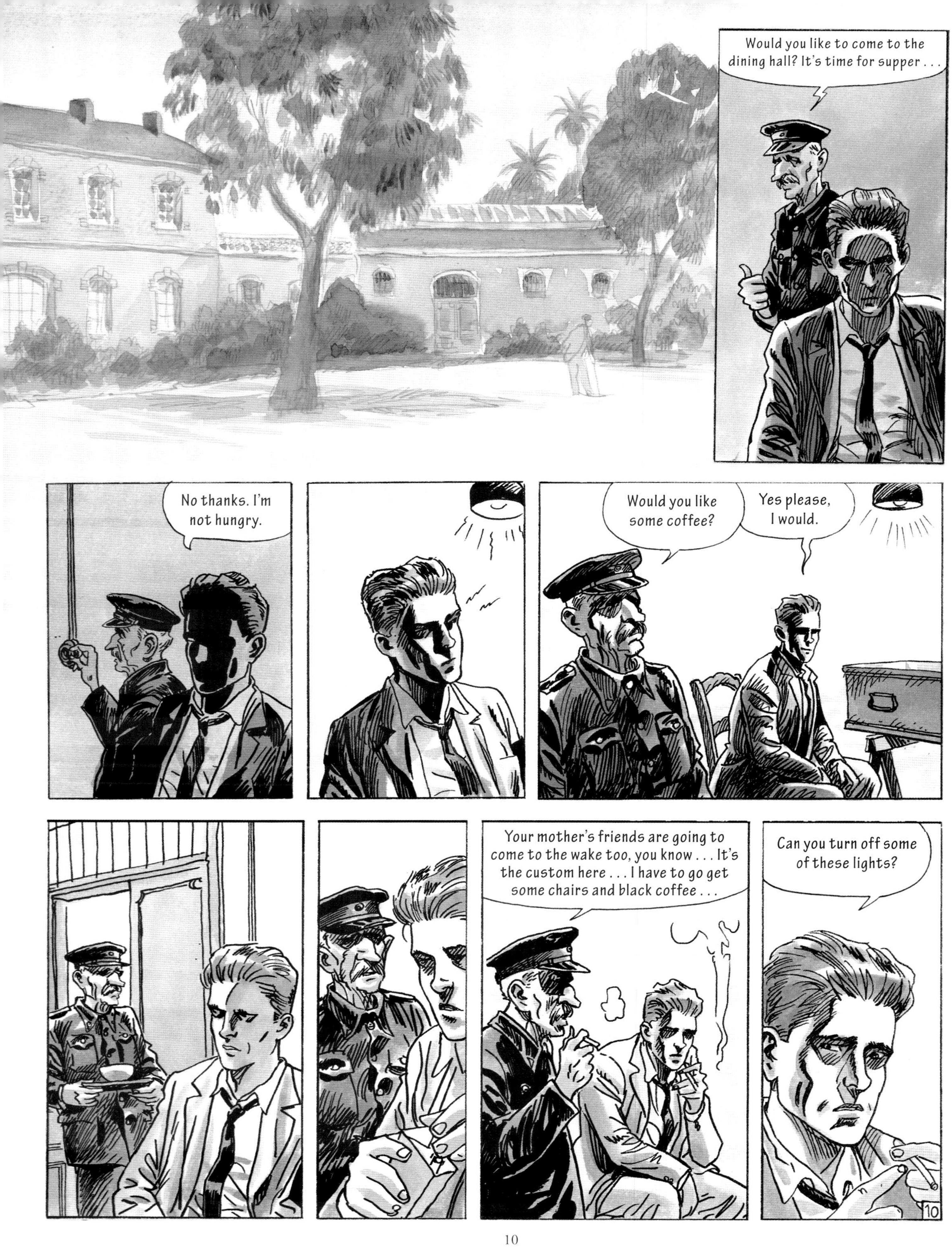
Would you like to come to the dining hall? It's time for supper . . .
No thanks. I'm not hungry.
Would you like some coffee?
Yes please, I would.
Your mother's friends are going to come to the wake too, you know . . . It's the custom here . . . I have to go get some chairs and black coffee . . .
Can you turn off some of these lights?
10

Not possible... They're either on or off... It's all or nothing...

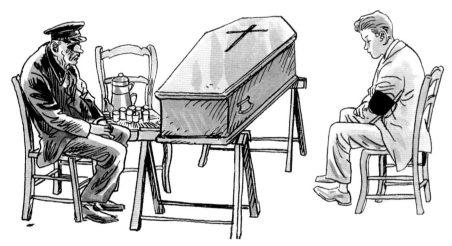

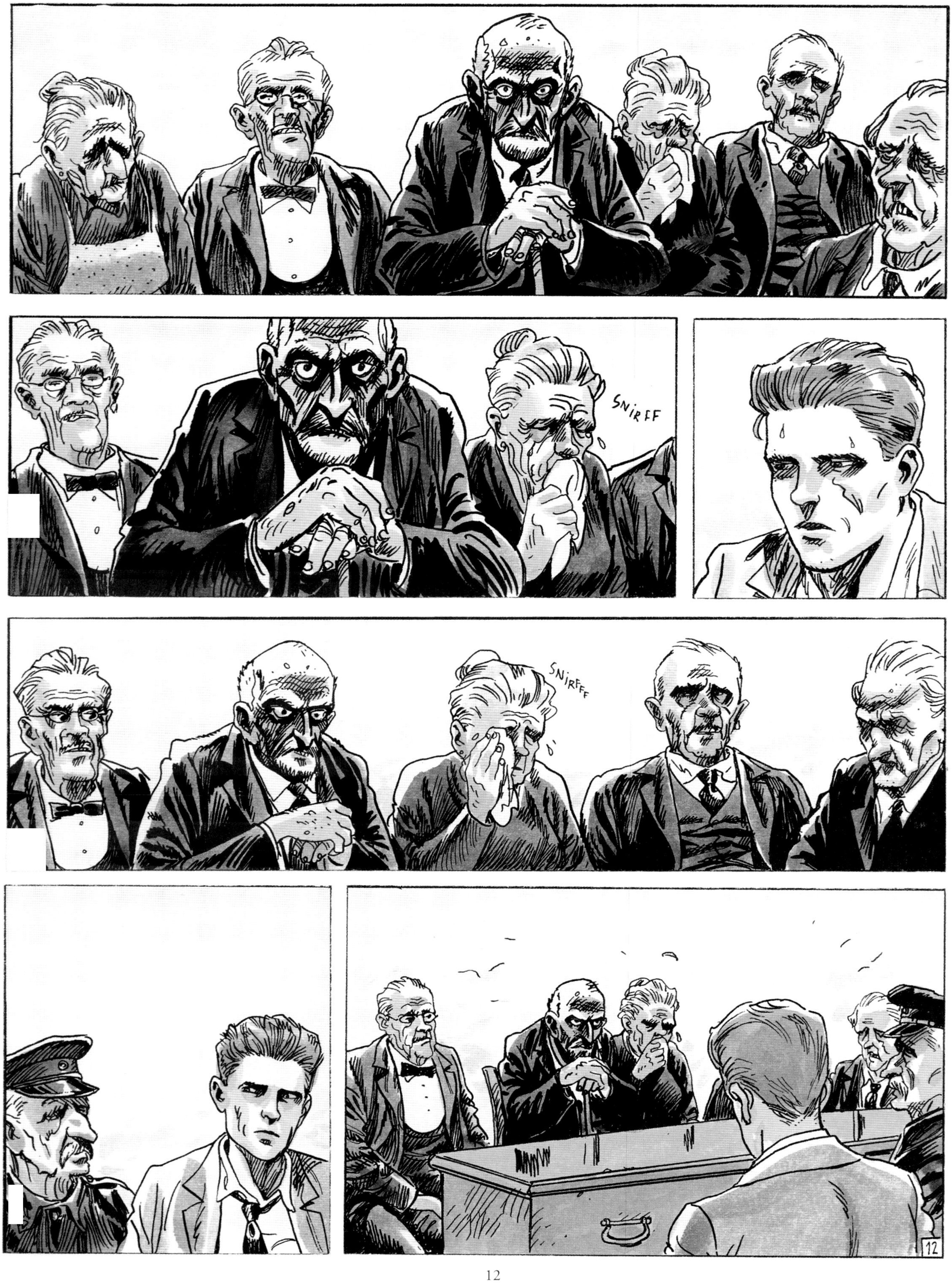
SNIRFF
SNIRFFF
12

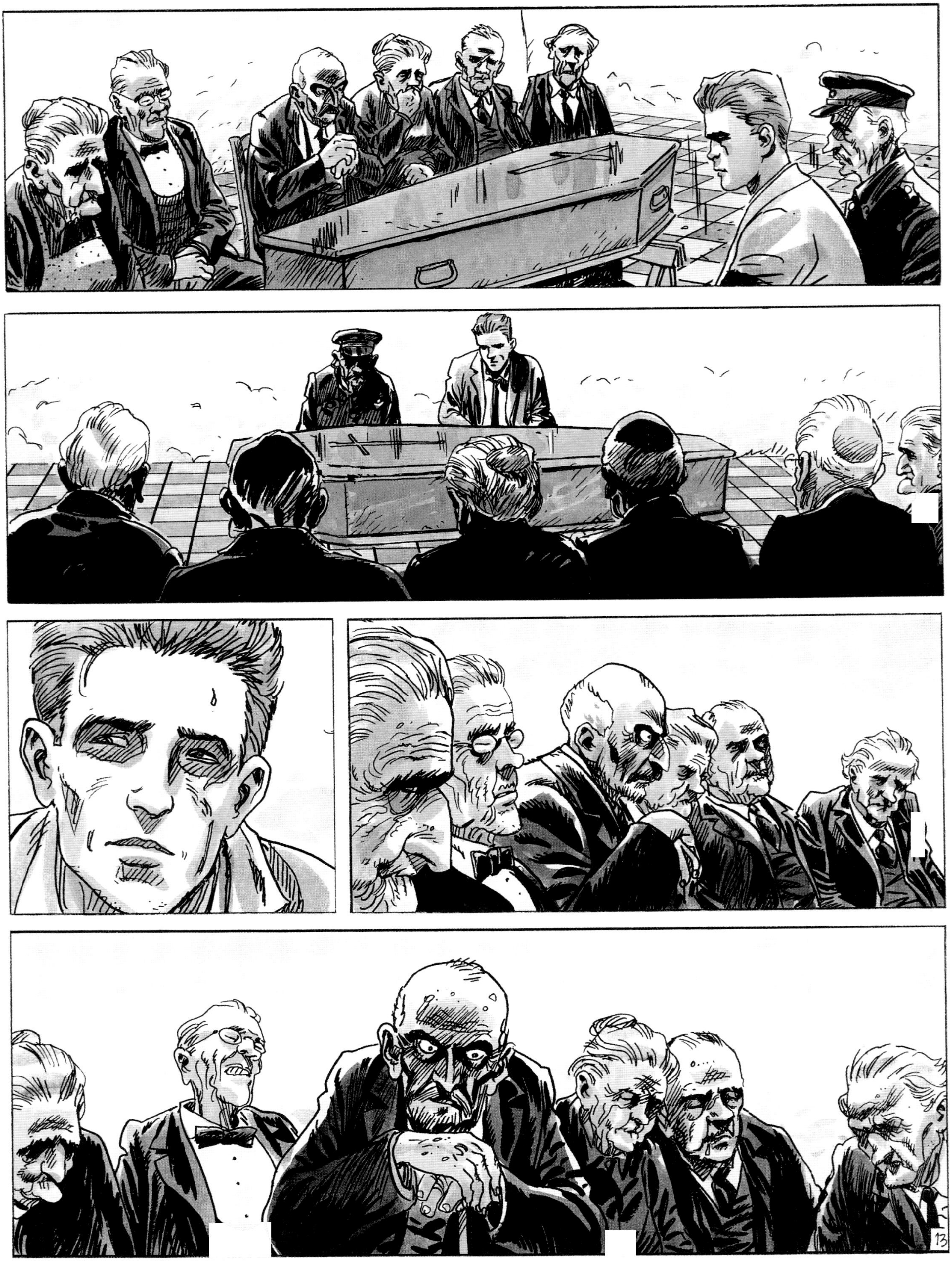
13

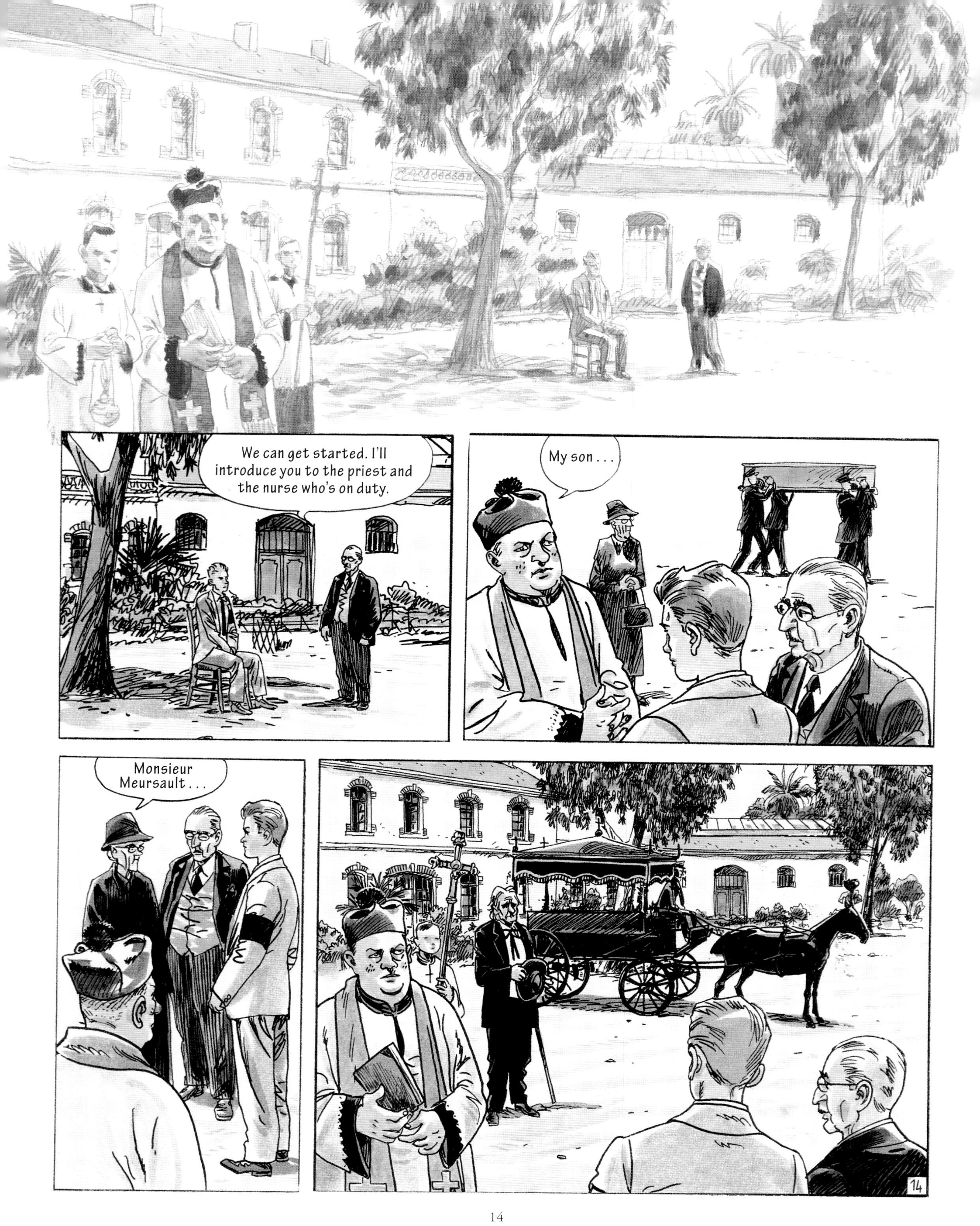
We can get started. I'll introduce you to the priest and the nurse who's on duty.
My son . . .
Monsieur Meursault . . .
14

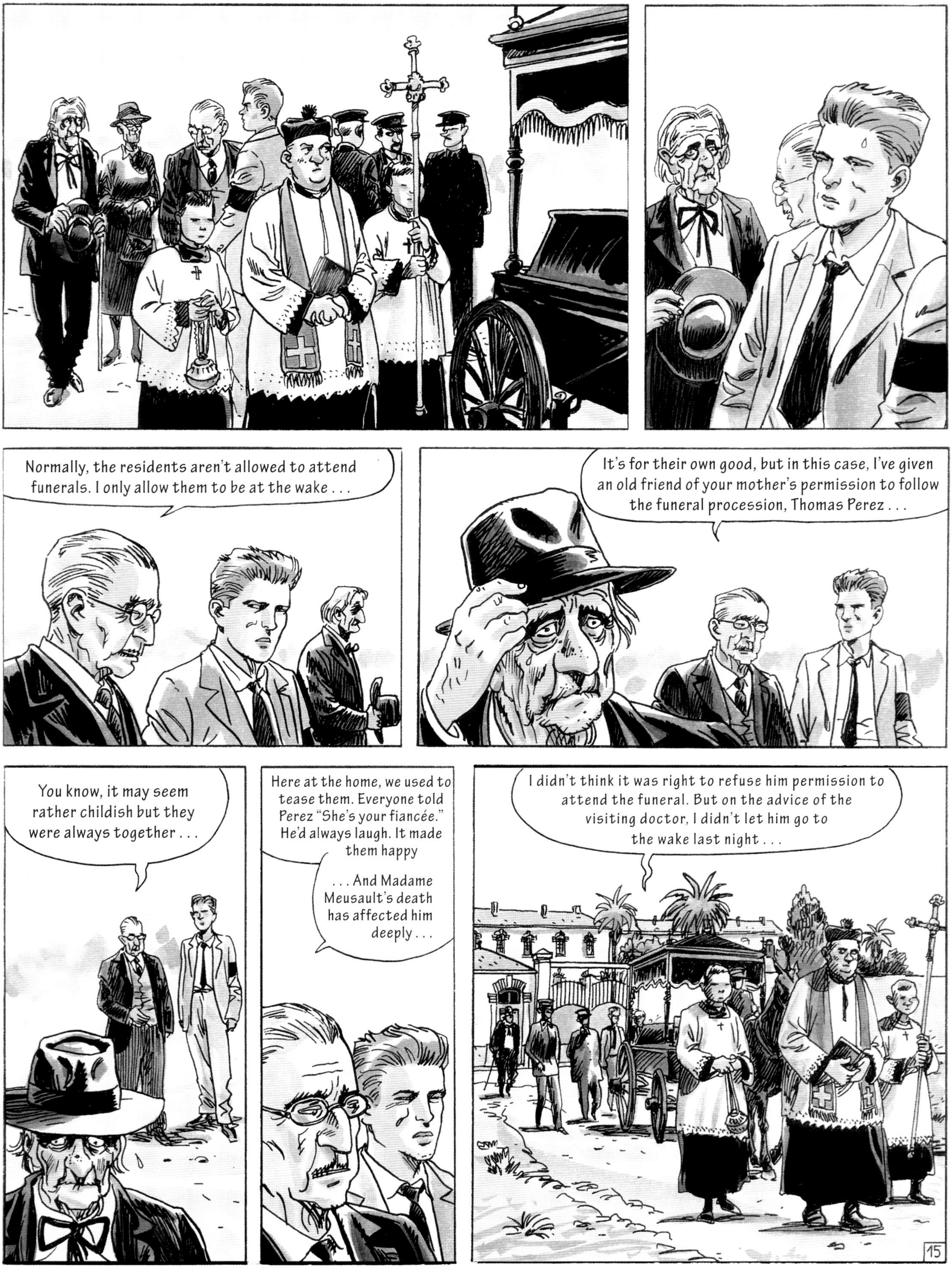
Normally, the residents aren't allowed to attend funerals. I only allow them to be at the wake . . .
It's for their own good, but in this case, I've given an old friend of your mother's permission to follow the funeral procession, Thomas Perez . . .
You know, it may seem rather childish but they were always together . . .
Here at the home, we used to tease them. Everyone told Perez "She's your fiancée." He'd always laugh. It made them happy
. . . And Madame Meusault's death has affected him deeply . . .
I didn't think it was right to refuse him permission to attend the funeral. But on the advice of the visiting doctor, I didn't let him go to the wake last night . . .
15

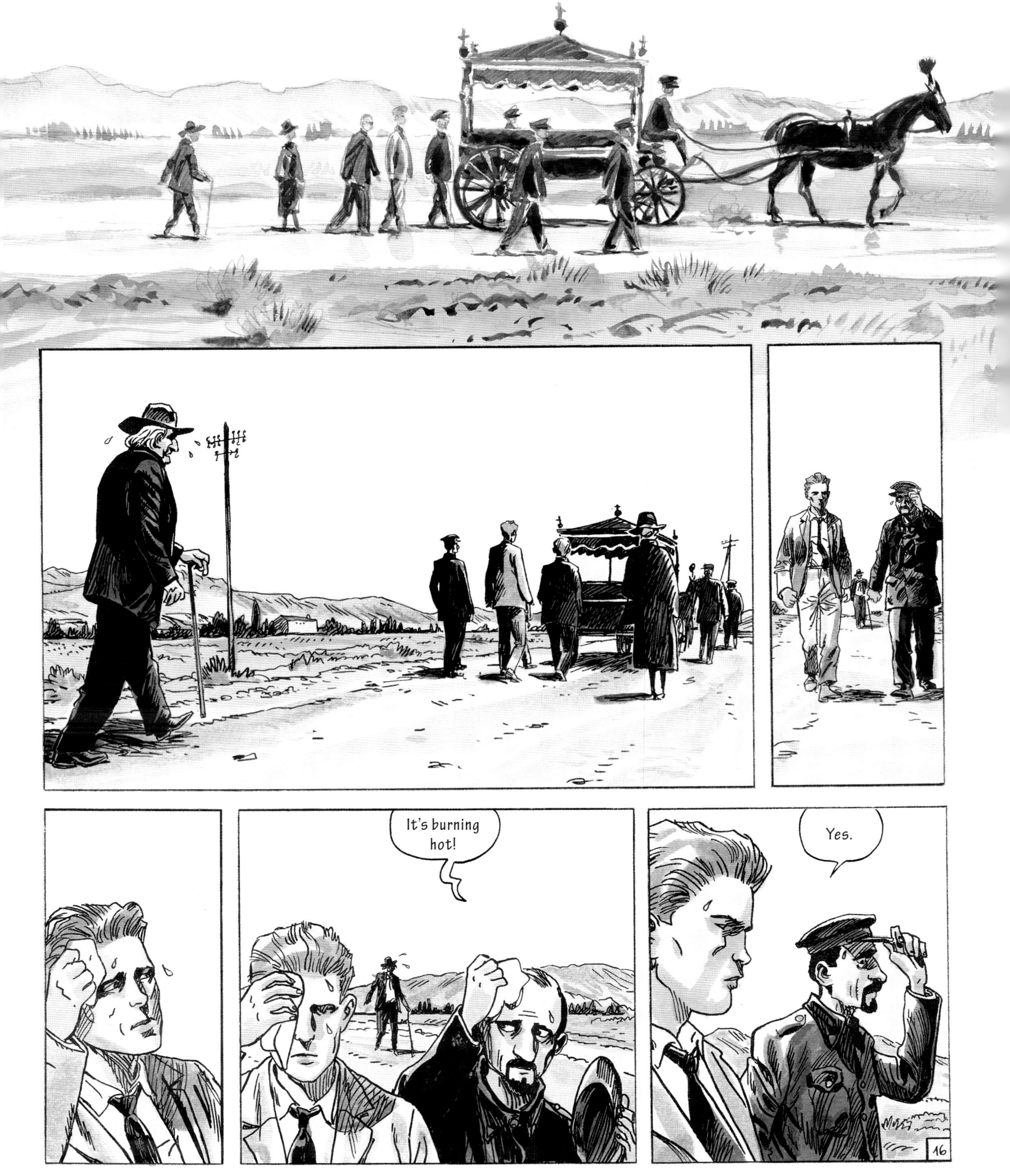
It's burning hot!
Yes.
16

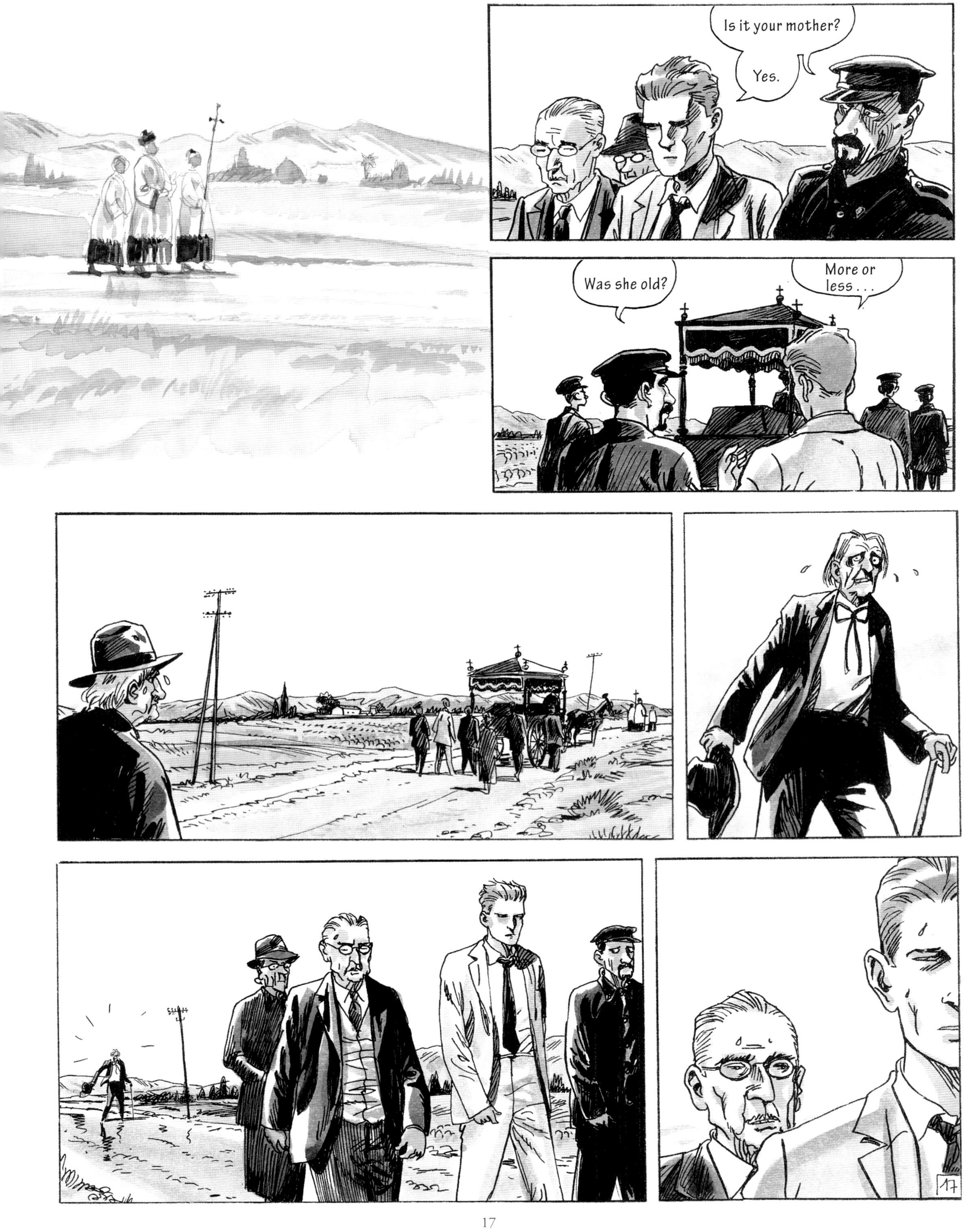
Is it your mother?
Yes.
Was she old?
More or less . . .
17

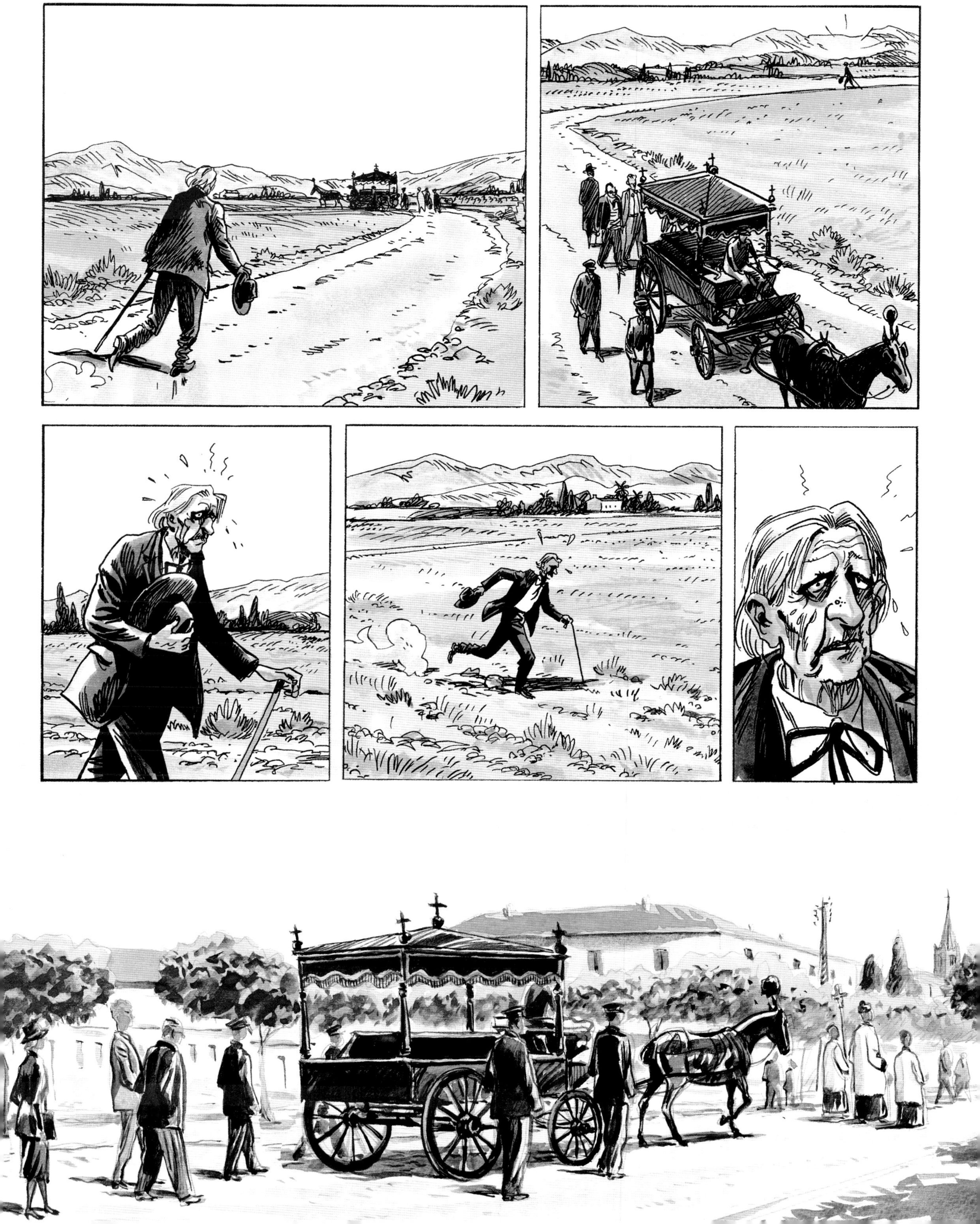

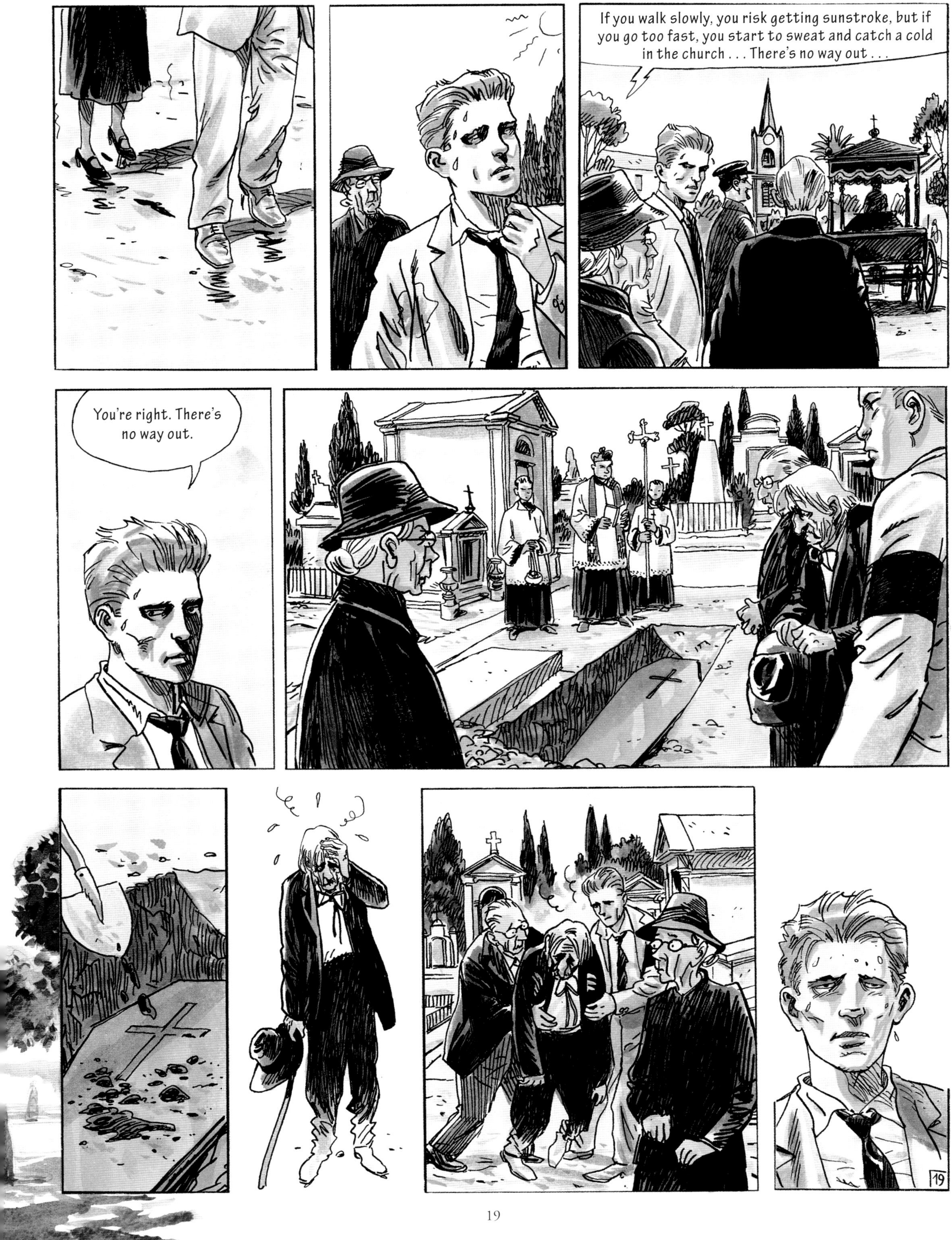
If you walk slowly, you risk getting sunstroke, but if you go too fast, you start to sweat and catch a cold in the church . . . There's no way out . . .
You're right. There's no way out.
19

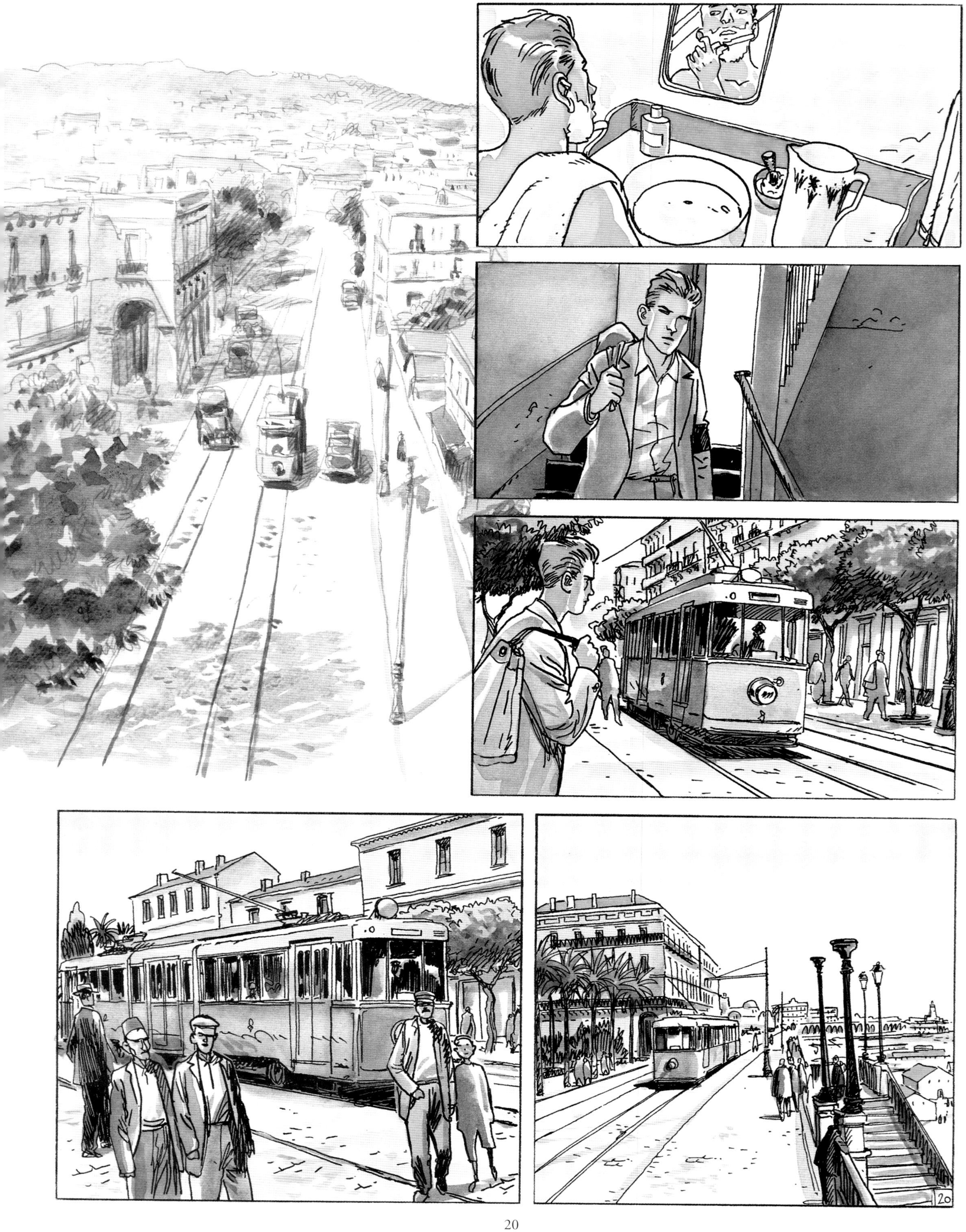

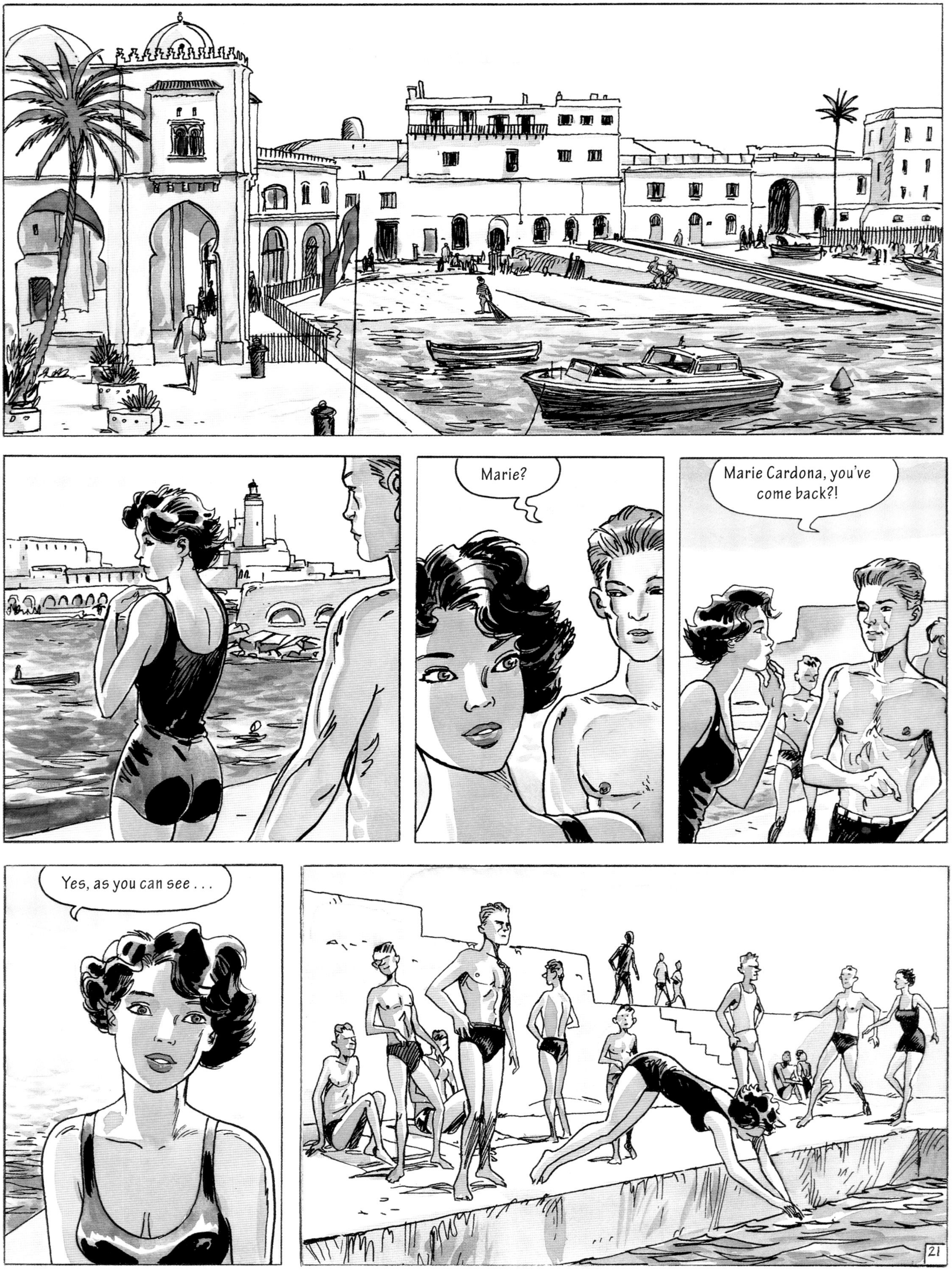
Marie?
Marie Cardona, you've come back?!
Yes, as you can see . . .
21

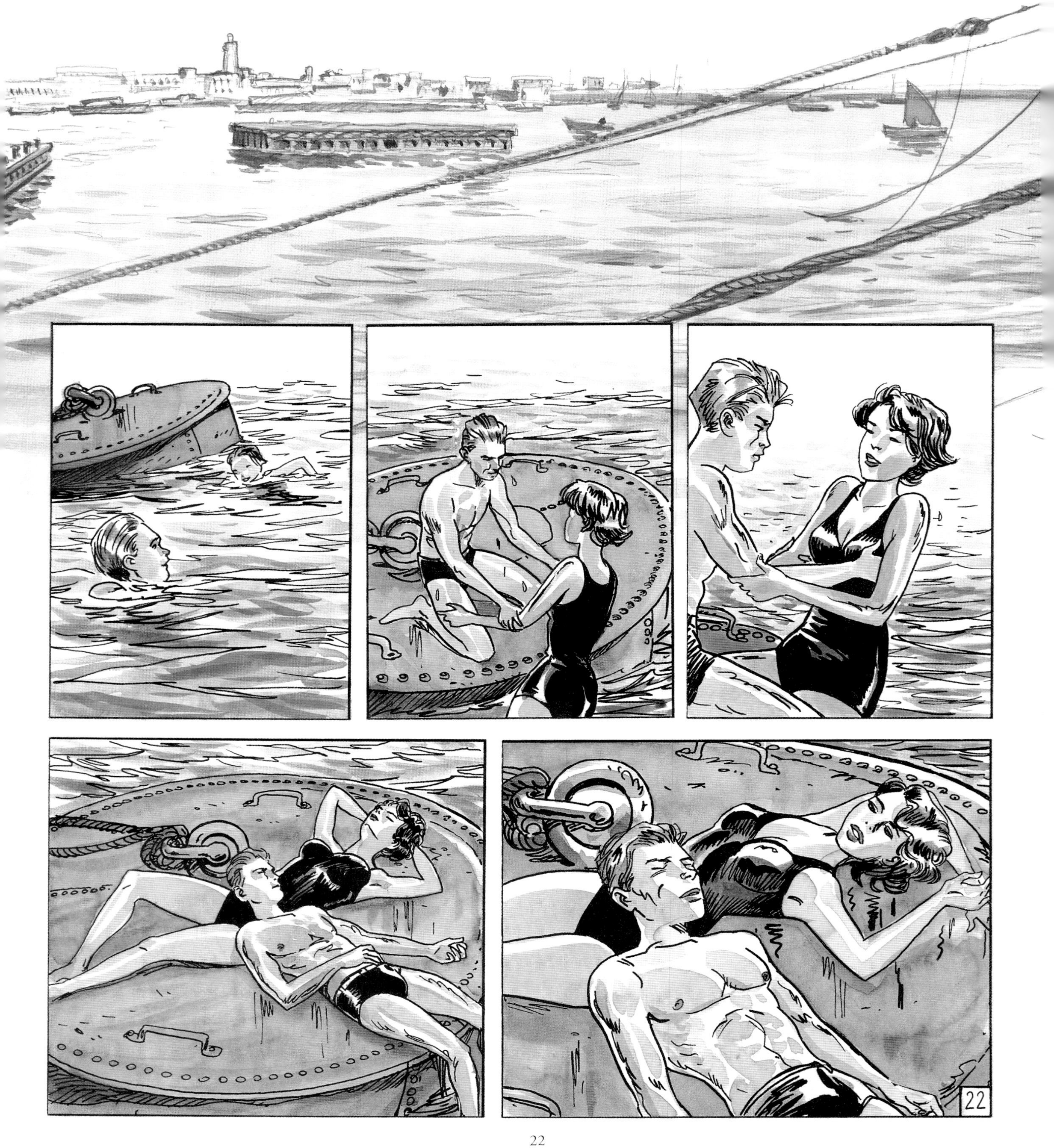

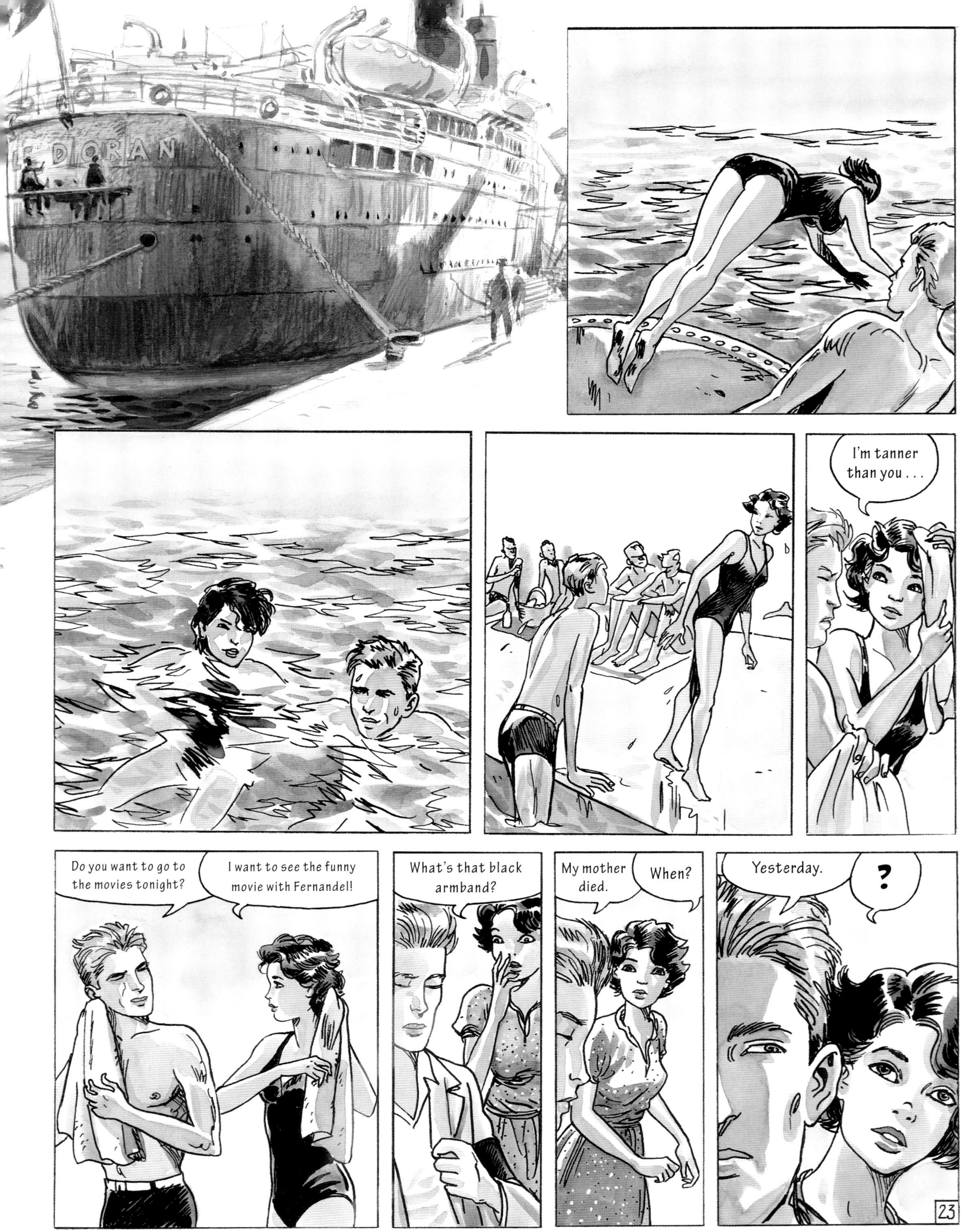
DORAN
I'm tanner than you . . .
Do you want to go to the movies tonight?
I want to see the funny movie with Fernandel!
What's that black armband?
My mother died.
When?
Yesterday.
?
23

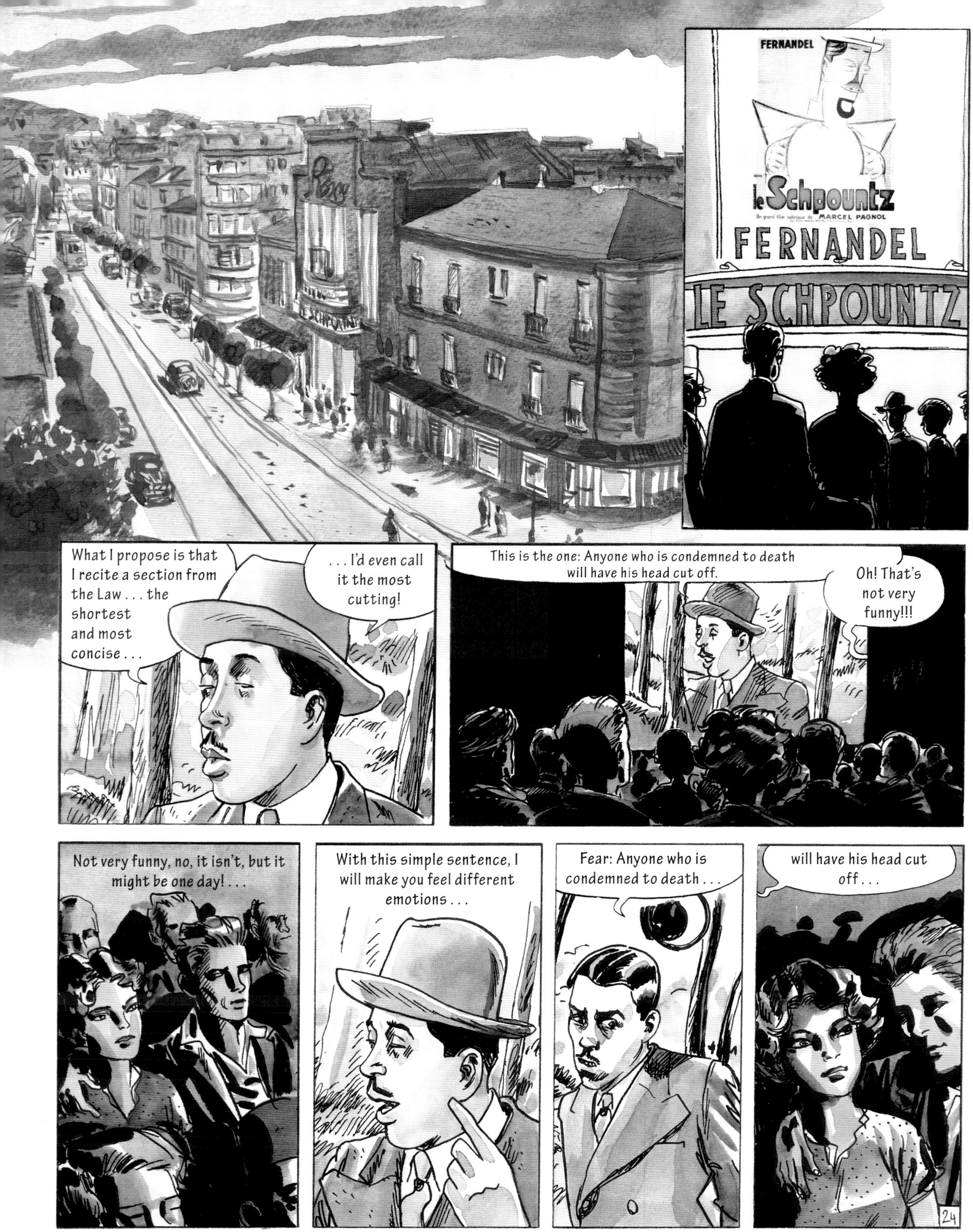
FERNANDEL
le Schpountz
Un grand film satirique de MARCEL PAGNOL
FERNANDEL
LE SCHPOUNTZ
What I propose is that I recite a section from the Law . . . the shortest and most concise . . .
. . . I'd even call it the most cutting!
This is the one: Anyone who is condemned to death will have his head cut off.
Oh! That's not very funny!!!
Not very funny, no, it isn't, but it might be one day! . . .
With this simple sentence, I will make you feel different emotions . . .
Fear: Anyone who is condemned to death . . .
will have his head cut off . . .
24

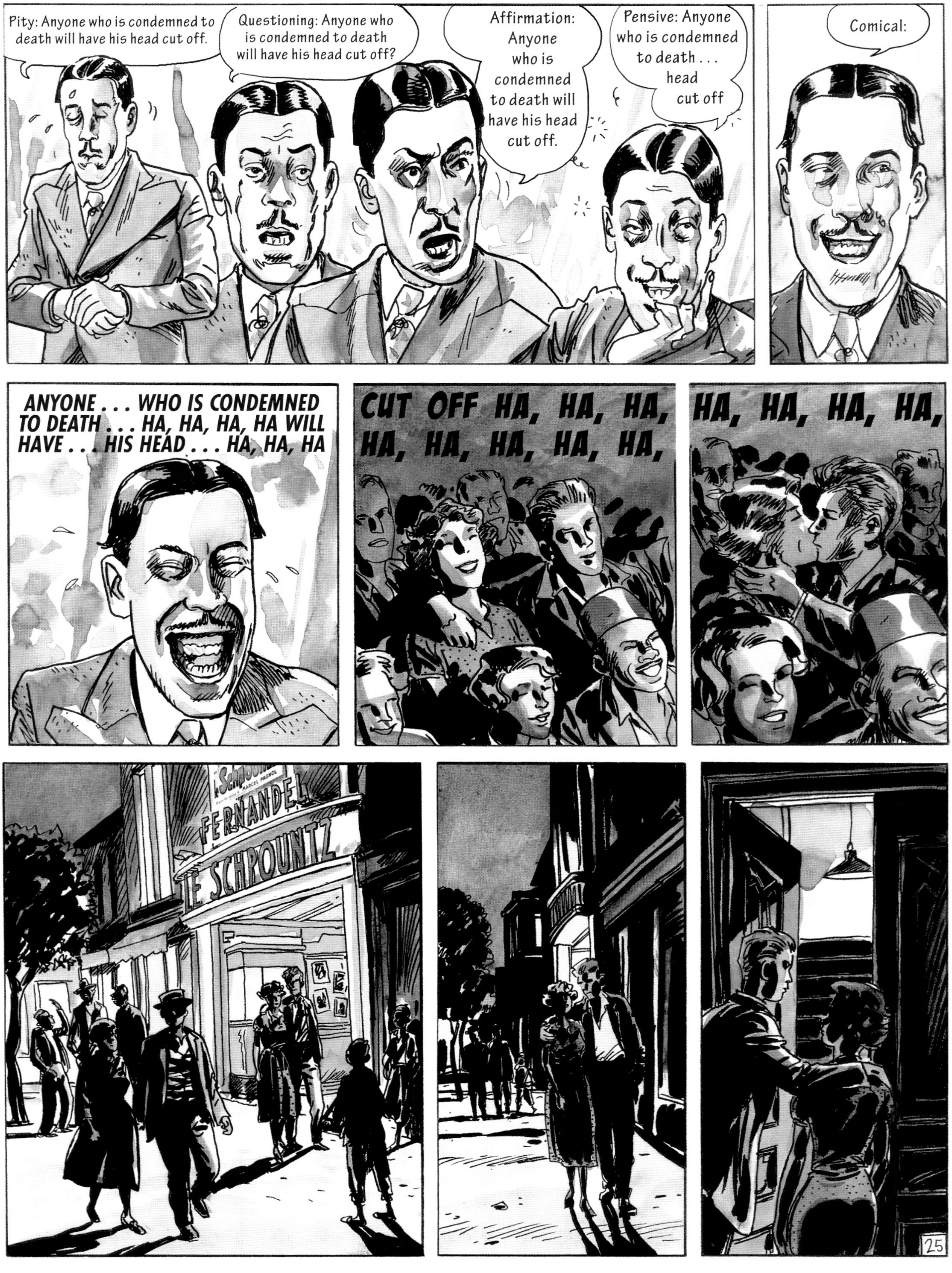
Pity: Anyone who is condemned to death will have his head cut off.
Questioning: Anyone who is condemned to death will have his head cut off?
Affirmation: Anyone who is condemned to death will have his head cut off.
Pensive: Anyone who is condemned to death . . . head cut off
Comical:
ANYONE . . . WHO IS CONDEMNED TO DEATH . . . HA, HA, HA, HA WILL HAVE . . . HIS HEAD . . . HA, HA, HA
CUT OFF HA, HA, HA, HA, HA, HA, HA, HA,
HA, HA, HA, HA,
FERNANDEL
LE SCHPOUNTZ
MARCEL PAGNOL
25

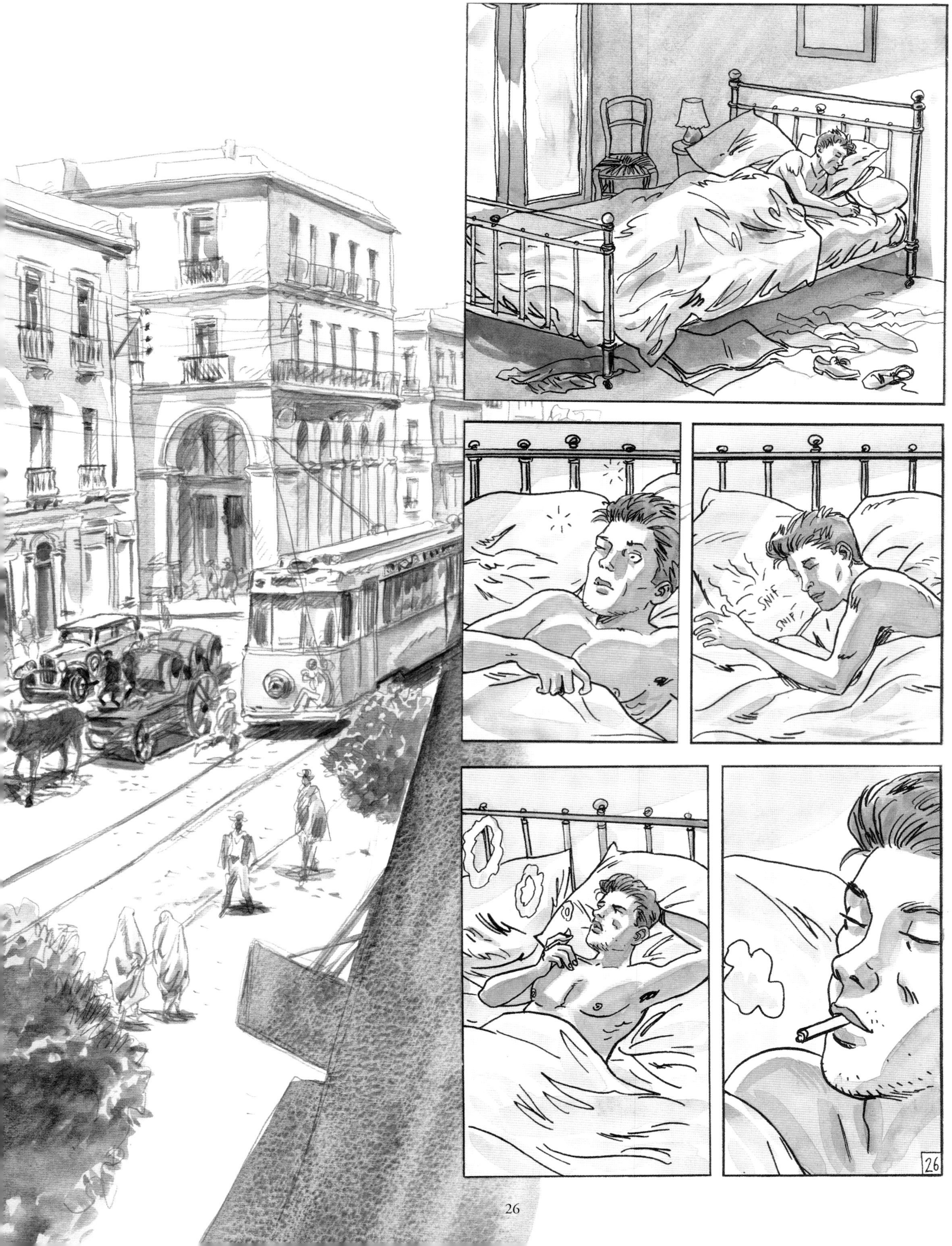
SNIF
SNIF

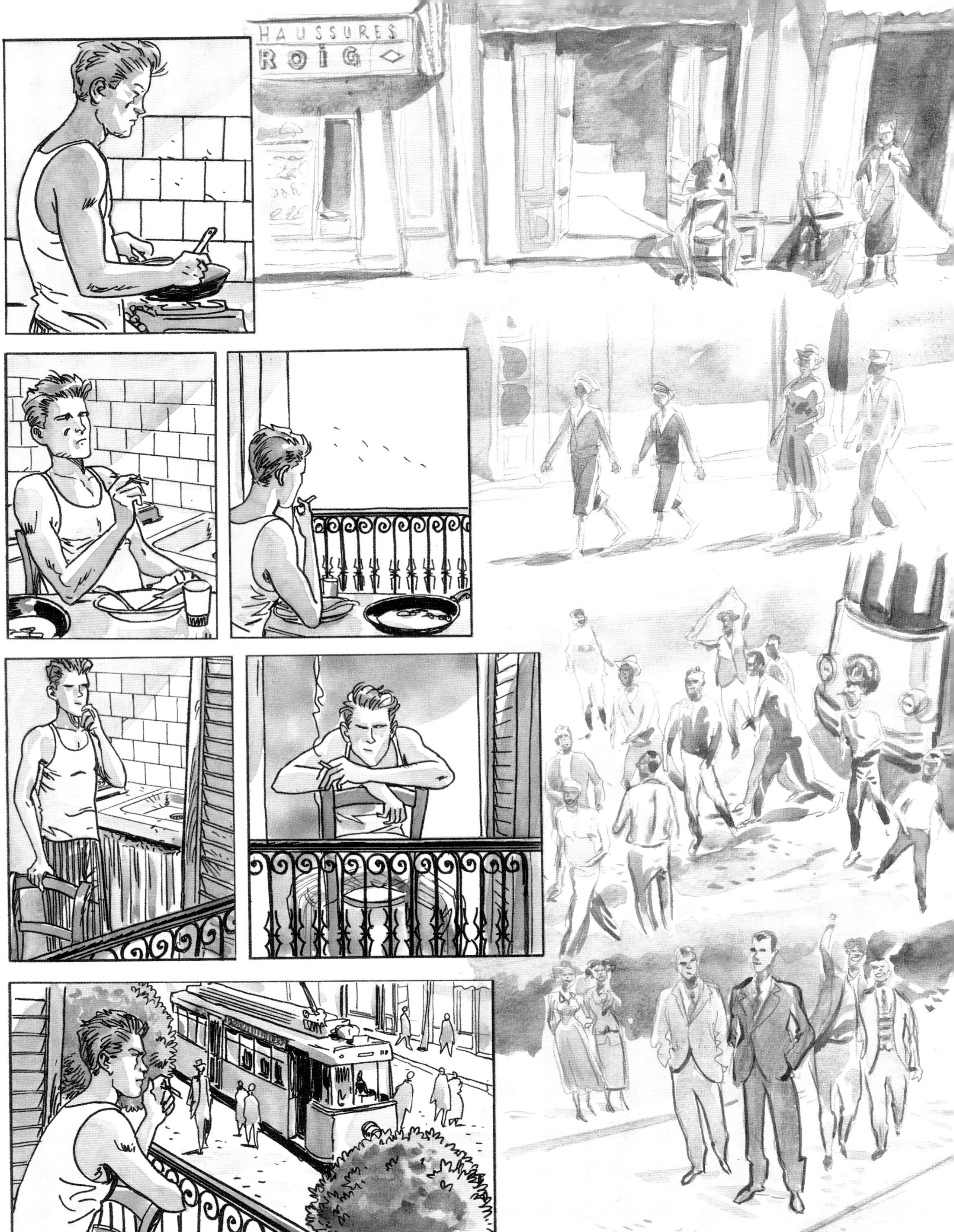
HAUSSURES
ROIG

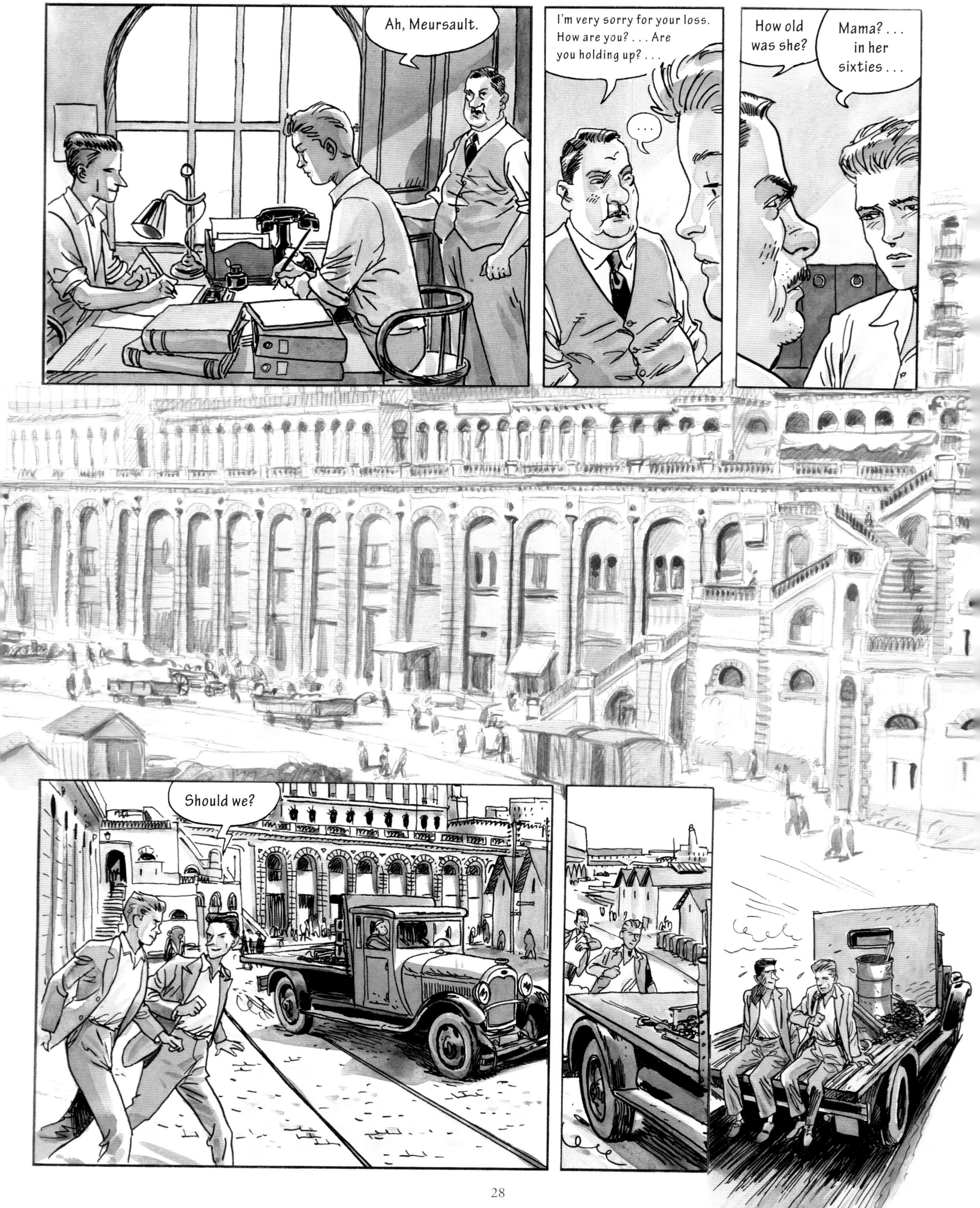
Ah, Meursault.
I'm very sorry for your loss. How are you? . . . Are you holding up? . . .
. . .
How old was she?
Mama? . . . in her sixties . . .
Should we?

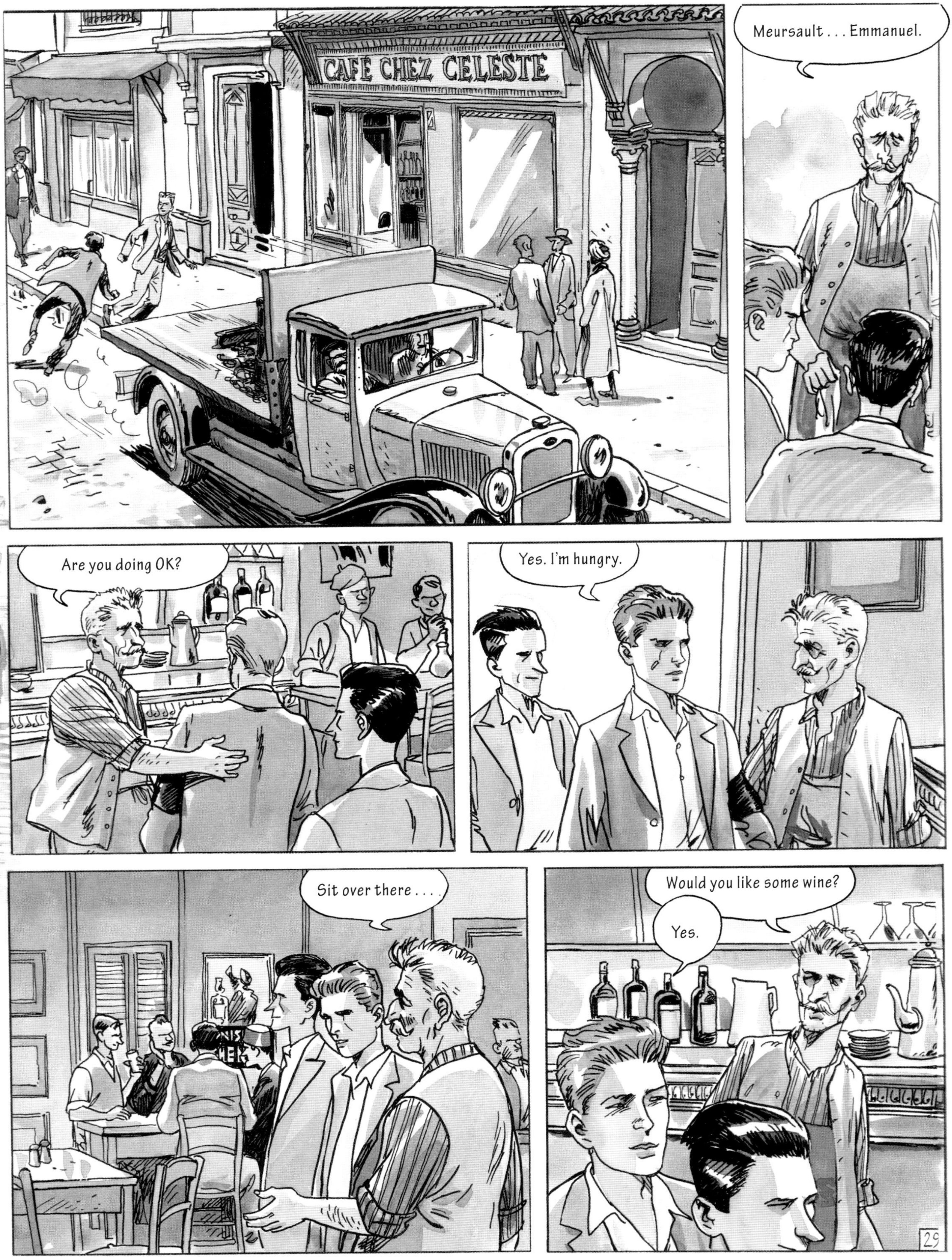
CAFÉ CHEZ CELESTE
Meursault . . . Emmanuel.
Are you doing OK?
Yes. I'm hungry.
Sit over there . . . .
Would you like some wine?
Yes.
29

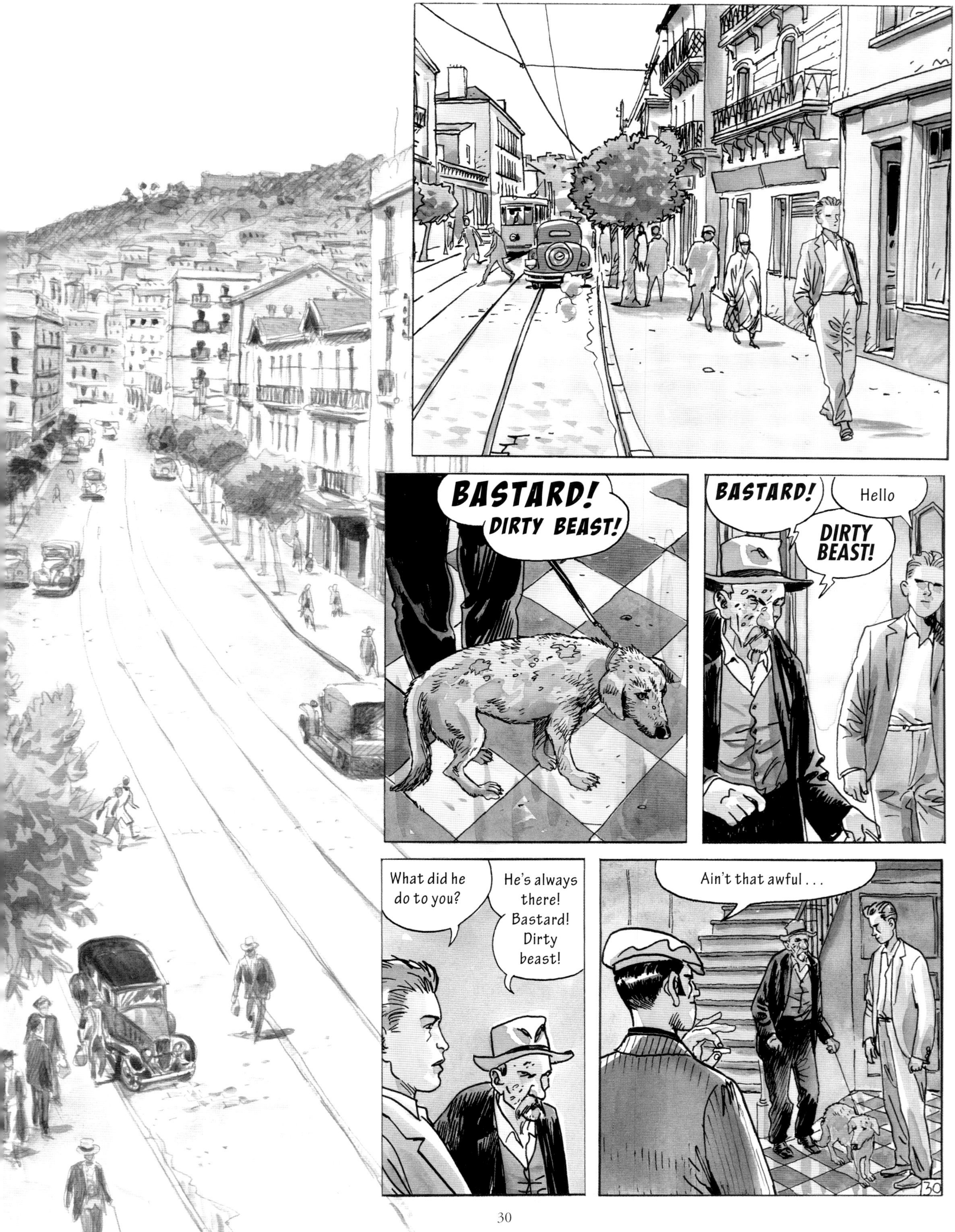
BASTARD!
DIRTY BEAST!
BASTARD!
Hello
DIRTY BEAST!
What did he do to you?
He's always there! Bastard! Dirty beast!
Ain't that awful . . .
30

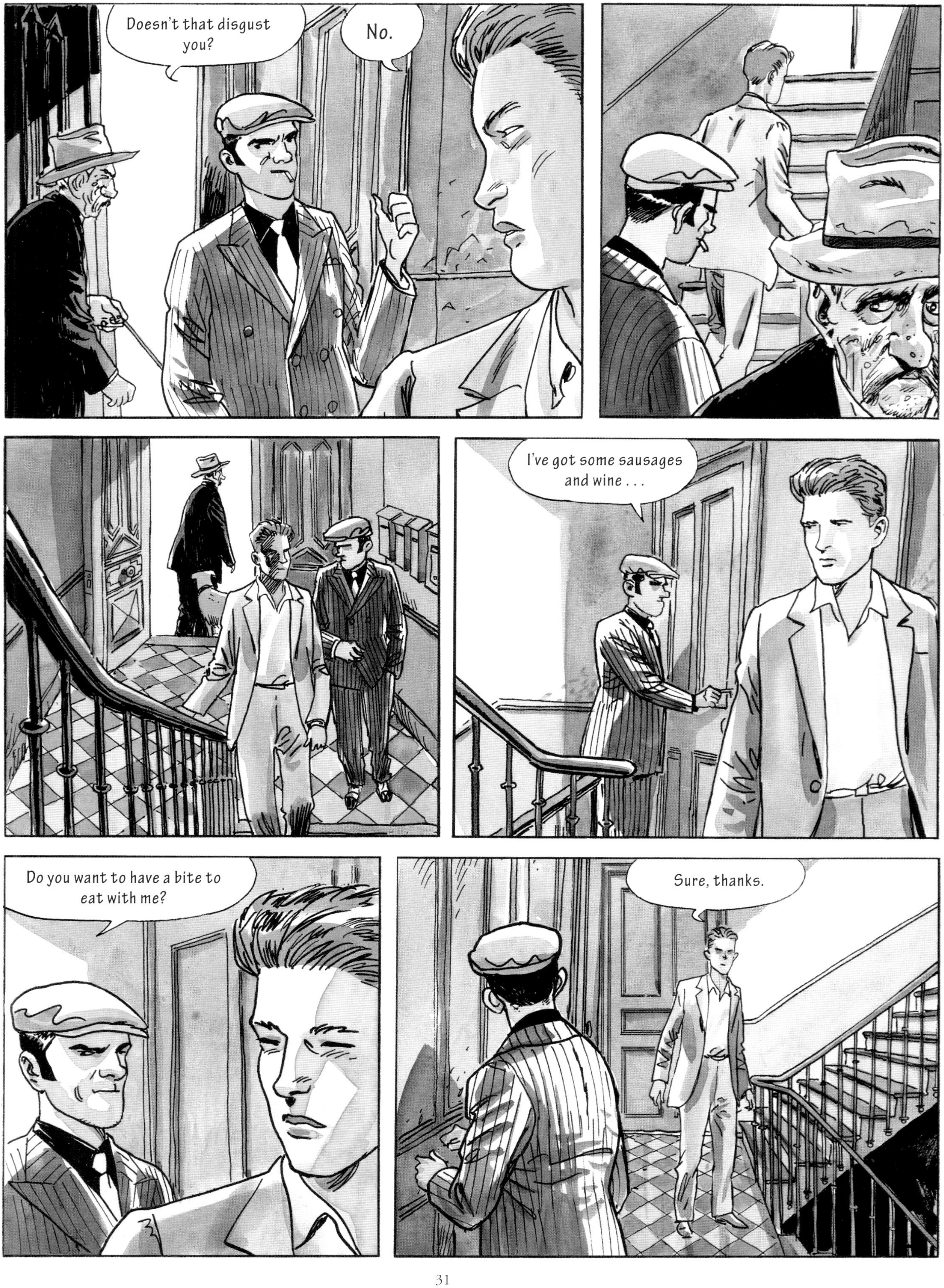

Doesn't that disgust you?
No.
I've got some sausages and wine . . .
Do you want to have a bite to eat with me?
Sure, thanks.

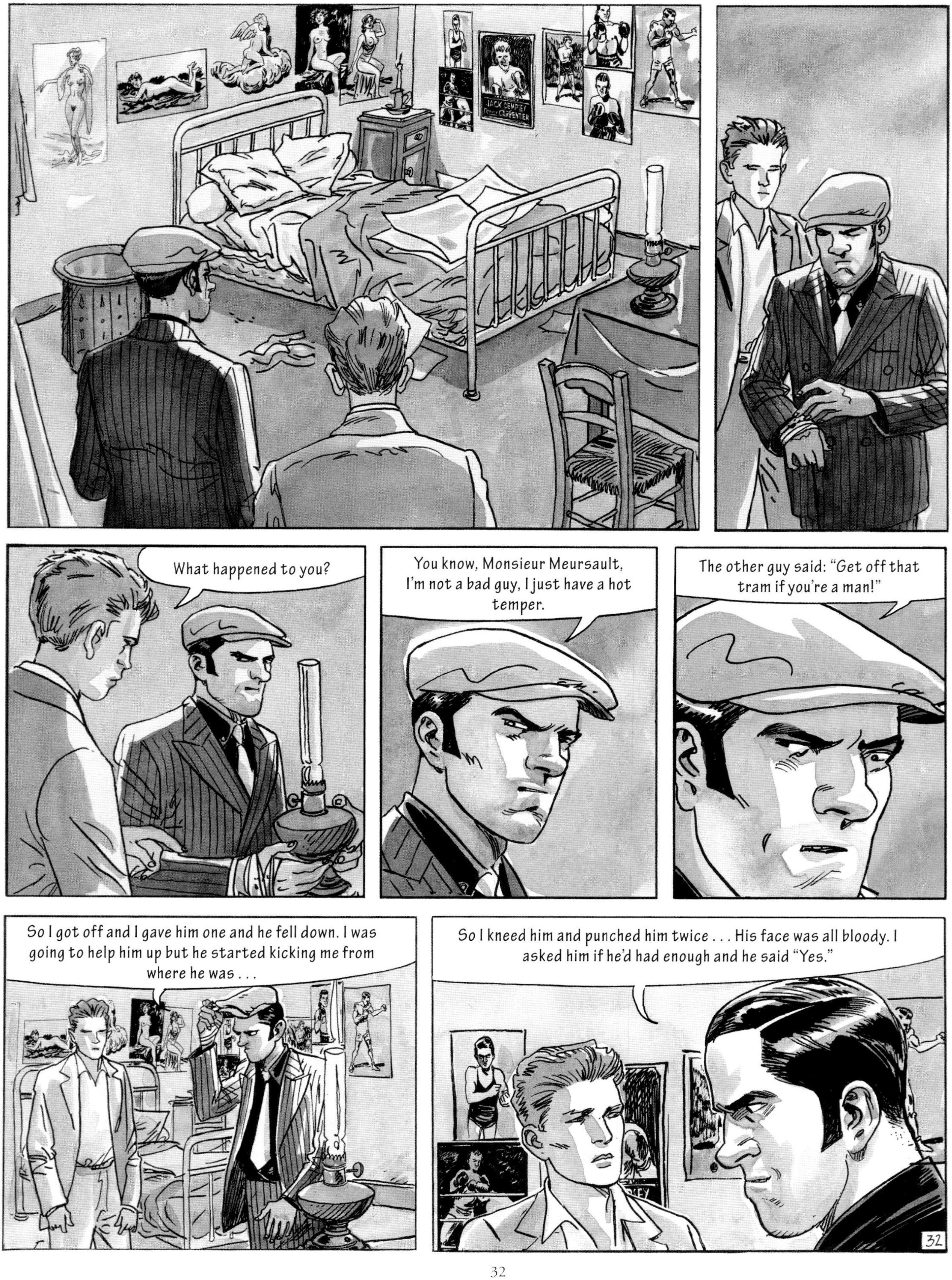
What happened to you?
You know, Monsieur Meursault, I'm not a bad guy, I just have a hot temper.
The other guy said: "Get off that tram if you're a man!"
So I got off and I gave him one and he fell down. I was going to help him up but he started kicking me from where he was . . .
So I kneed him and punched him twice . . . His face was all bloody. I asked him if he'd had enough and he said "Yes."
32

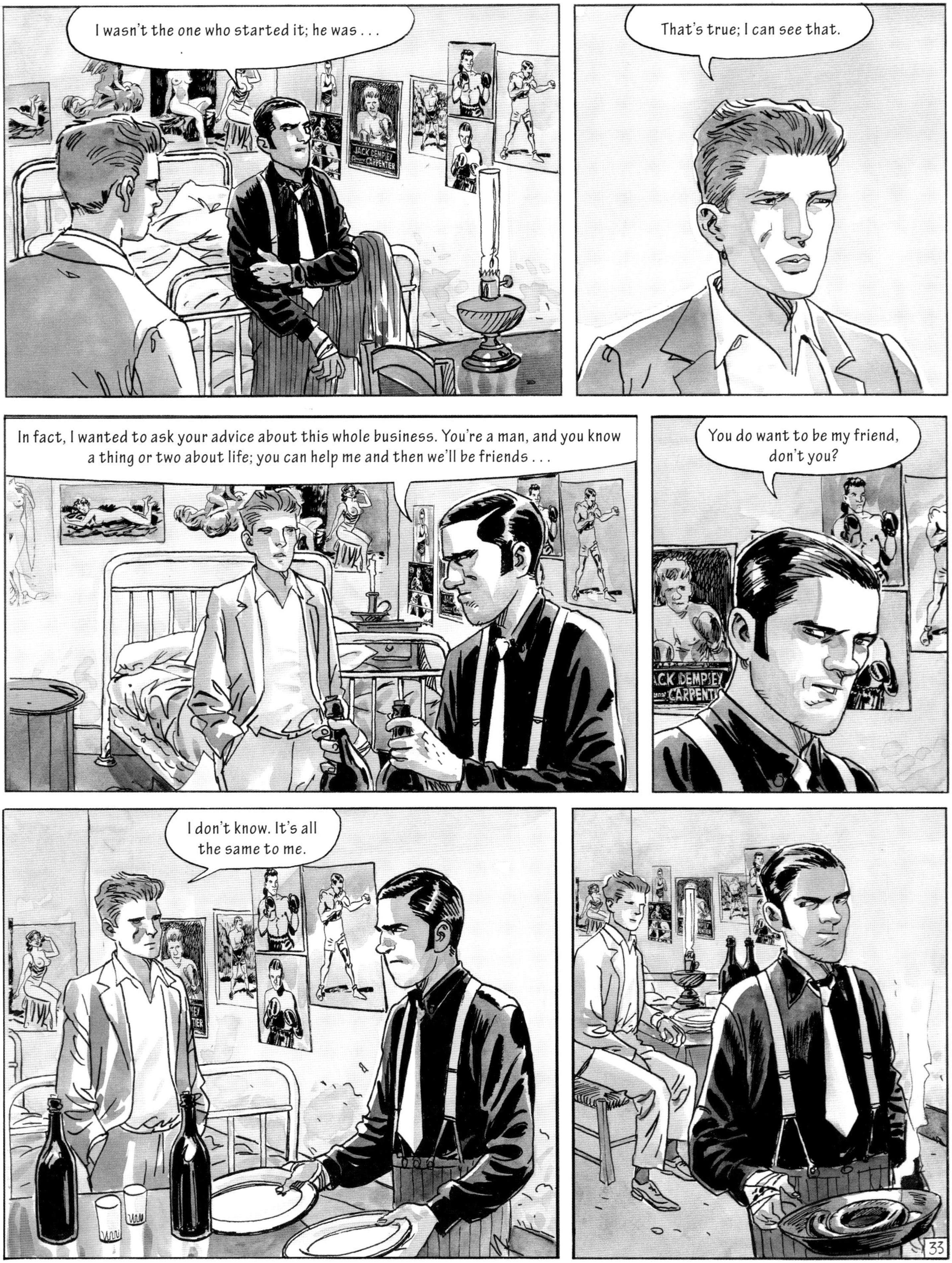
I wasn't the one who started it; he was . . .
JACK DEMPSEY
CARPENTIER
That's true; I can see that.
In fact, I wanted to ask your advice about this whole business. You're a man, and you know a thing or two about life; you can help me and then we'll be friends . . .
You do want to be my friend, don't you?
I don't know. It's all the same to me.
33

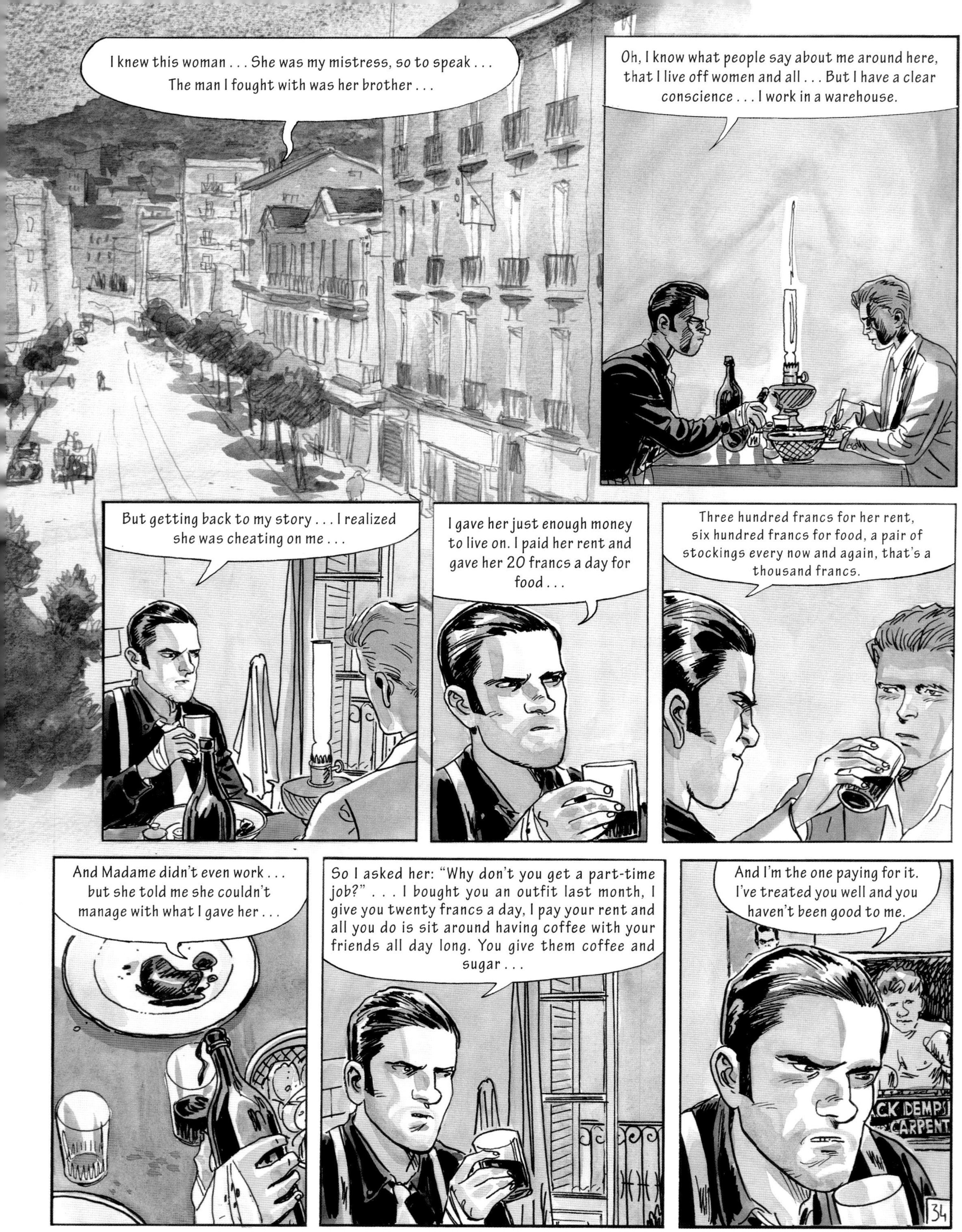
I knew this woman . . . She was my mistress, so to speak . . . The man I fought with was her brother . . .
Oh, I know what people say about me around here, that I live off women and all . . . But I have a clear conscience . . . I work in a warehouse.
But getting back to my story . . . I realized she was cheating on me . . .
I gave her just enough money to live on. I paid her rent and gave her 20 francs a day for food . . .
Three hundred francs for her rent, six hundred francs for food, a pair of stockings every now and again, that's a thousand francs.
And Madame didn't even work . . . but she told me she couldn't manage with what I gave her . . .
So I asked her: "Why don't you get a part-time job?" . . . I bought you an outfit last month, I give you twenty francs a day, I pay your rent and all you do is sit around having coffee with your friends all day long. You give them coffee and sugar . . .
And I'm the one paying for it. I've treated you well and you haven't been good to me.
CK DEMPS
CARPENT
34

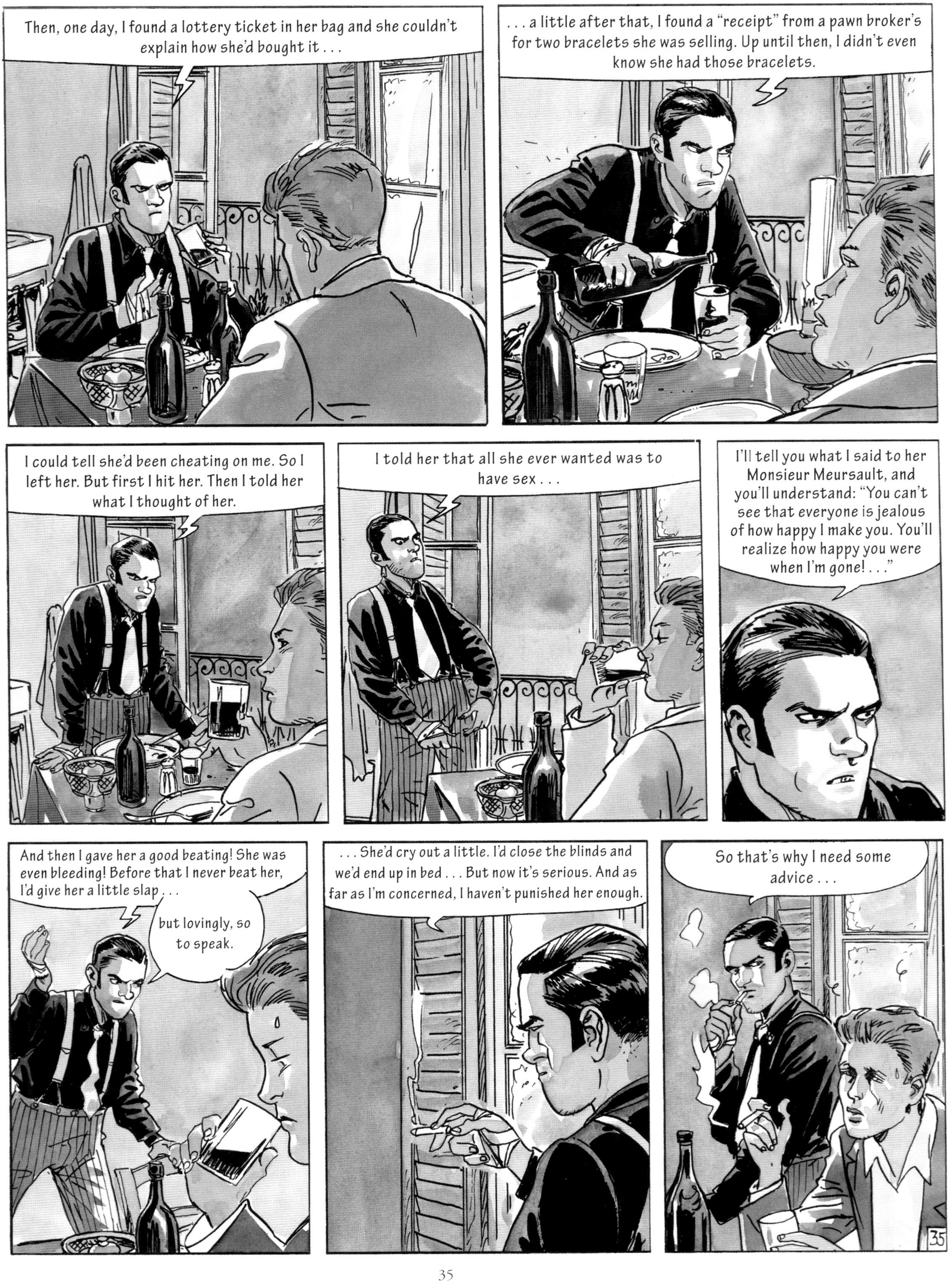
Then, one day, I found a lottery ticket in her bag and she couldn't explain how she'd bought it . . .
. . . a little after that, I found a "receipt" from a pawn broker's for two bracelets she was selling. Up until then, I didn't even know she had those bracelets.
I could tell she'd been cheating on me. So I left her. But first I hit her. Then I told her what I thought of her.
I told her that all she ever wanted was to have sex . . .
I'll tell you what I said to her Monsieur Meursault, and you'll understand: "You can't see that everyone is jealous of how happy I make you. You'll realize how happy you were when I'm gone! . . ."
And then I gave her a good beating! She was even bleeding! Before that I never beat her, I'd give her a little slap . . .
but lovingly, so to speak.
. . . She'd cry out a little. I'd close the blinds and we'd end up in bed . . . But now it's serious. And as far as I'm concerned, I haven't punished her enough.
So that's why I need some advice . . .
35

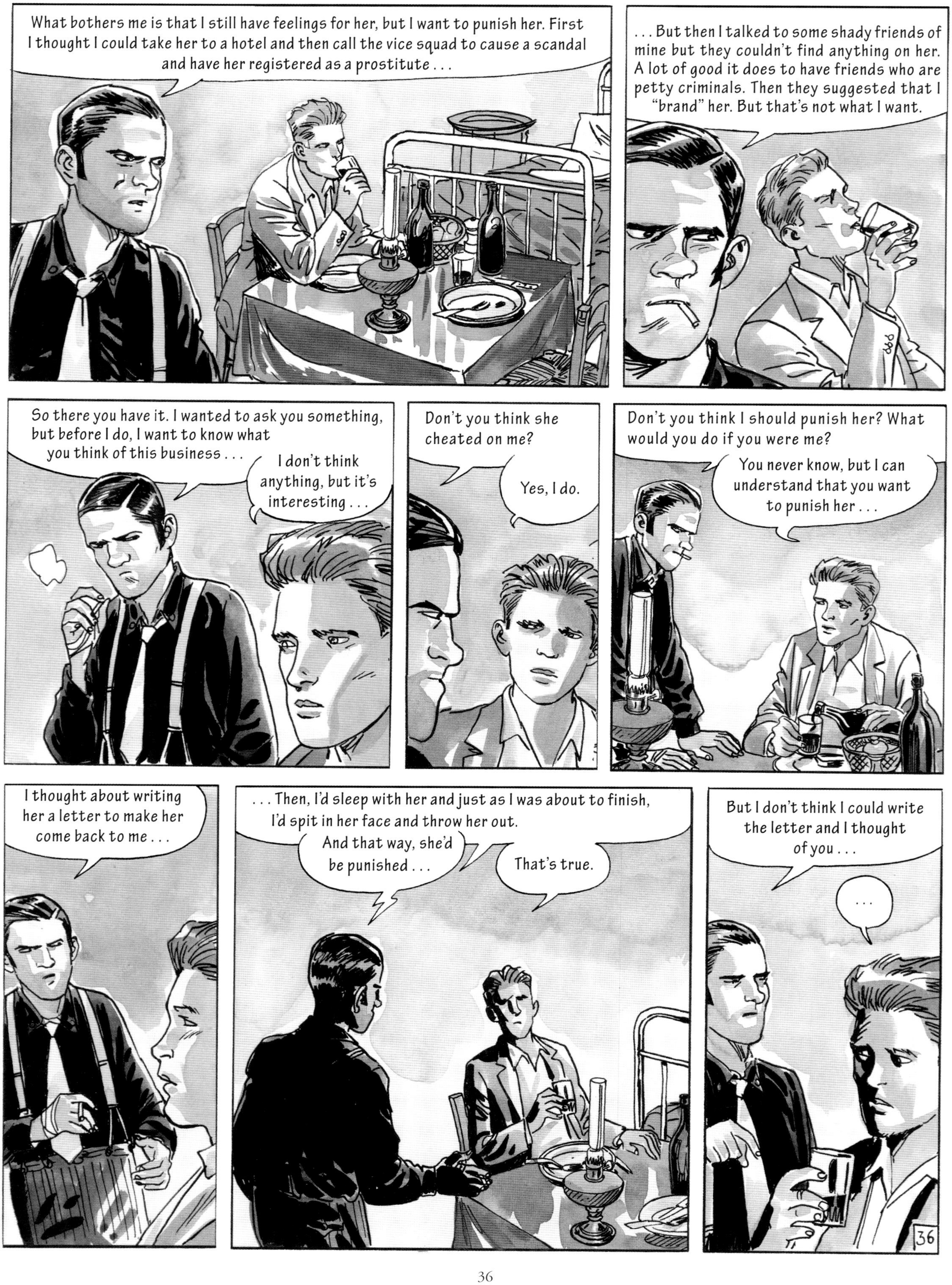
What bothers me is that I still have feelings for her, but I want to punish her. First I thought I could take her to a hotel and then call the vice squad to cause a scandal and have her registered as a prostitute . . .
. . . But then I talked to some shady friends of mine but they couldn't find anything on her. A lot of good it does to have friends who are petty criminals. Then they suggested that I "brand" her. But that's not what I want.
So there you have it. I wanted to ask you something, but before I do, I want to know what you think of this business . . .
I don't think anything, but it's interesting . . .
Don't you think she cheated on me?
Yes, I do.
Don't you think I should punish her? What would you do if you were me?
You never know, but I can understand that you want to punish her . . .
I thought about writing her a letter to make her come back to me . . .
. . . Then, I'd sleep with her and just as I was about to finish, I'd spit in her face and throw her out.
And that way, she'd be punished . . .
That's true.
But I don't think I could write the letter and I thought of you . . .
. . .
36

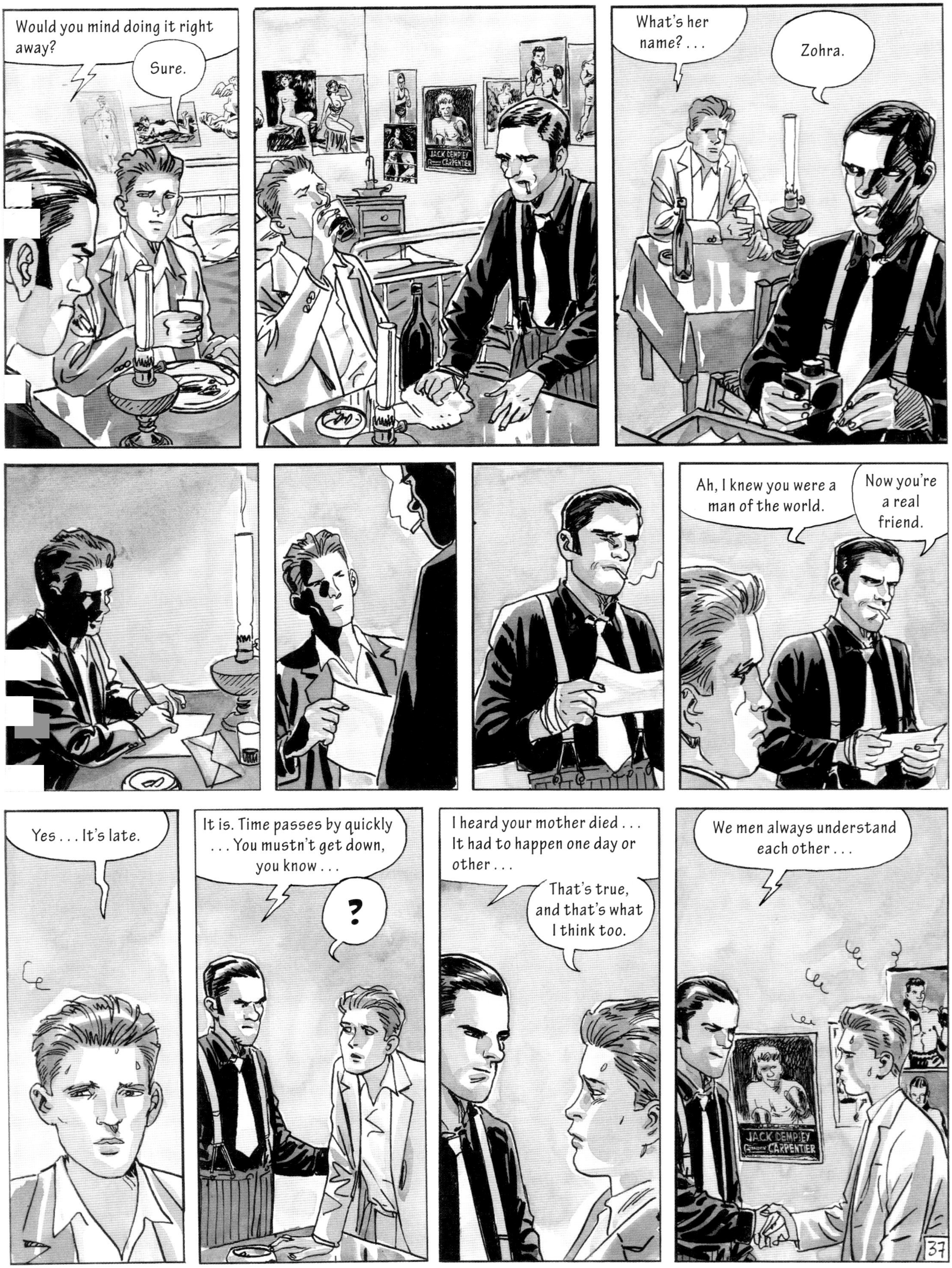
Would you mind doing it right away?
Sure.
JACK DEMPSEY CARPENTIER
What's her name? . . .
Zohra.
Ah, I knew you were a man of the world.
Now you're a real friend.
Yes . . . It's late.
It is. Time passes by quickly . . . You mustn't get down, you know . . .
?
I heard your mother died . . . It had to happen one day or other . . .
That's true, and that's what I think too.
We men always understand each other . . .
JACK DEMPSEY CARPENTIER
37

I'll teach you a game . . .

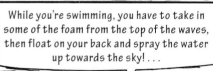

While you're swimming, you have to take in some of the foam from the top of the waves, then float on your back and spray the water up towards the sky! . . .

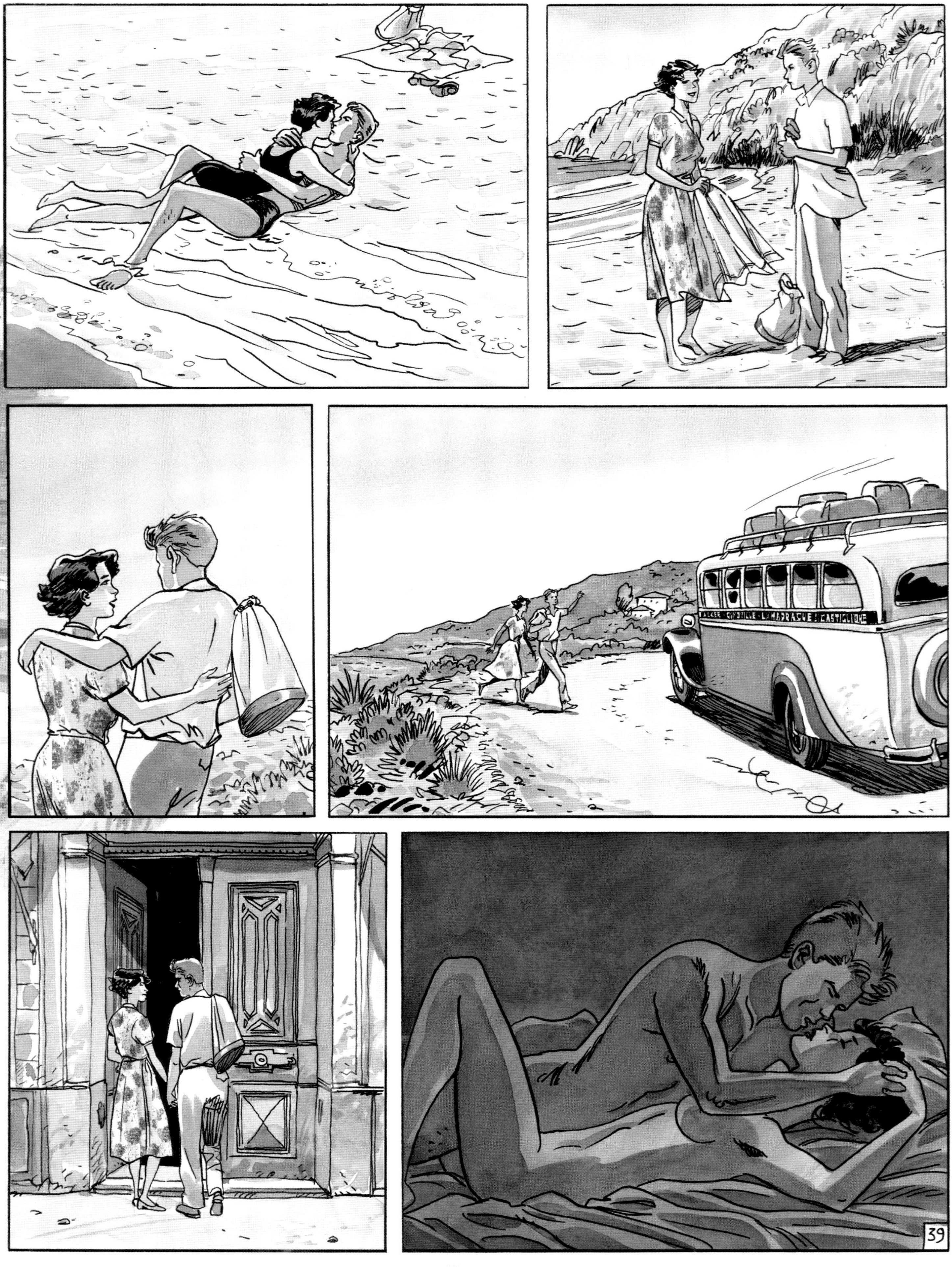
LA MADRAGUE - CASTIGLIONE

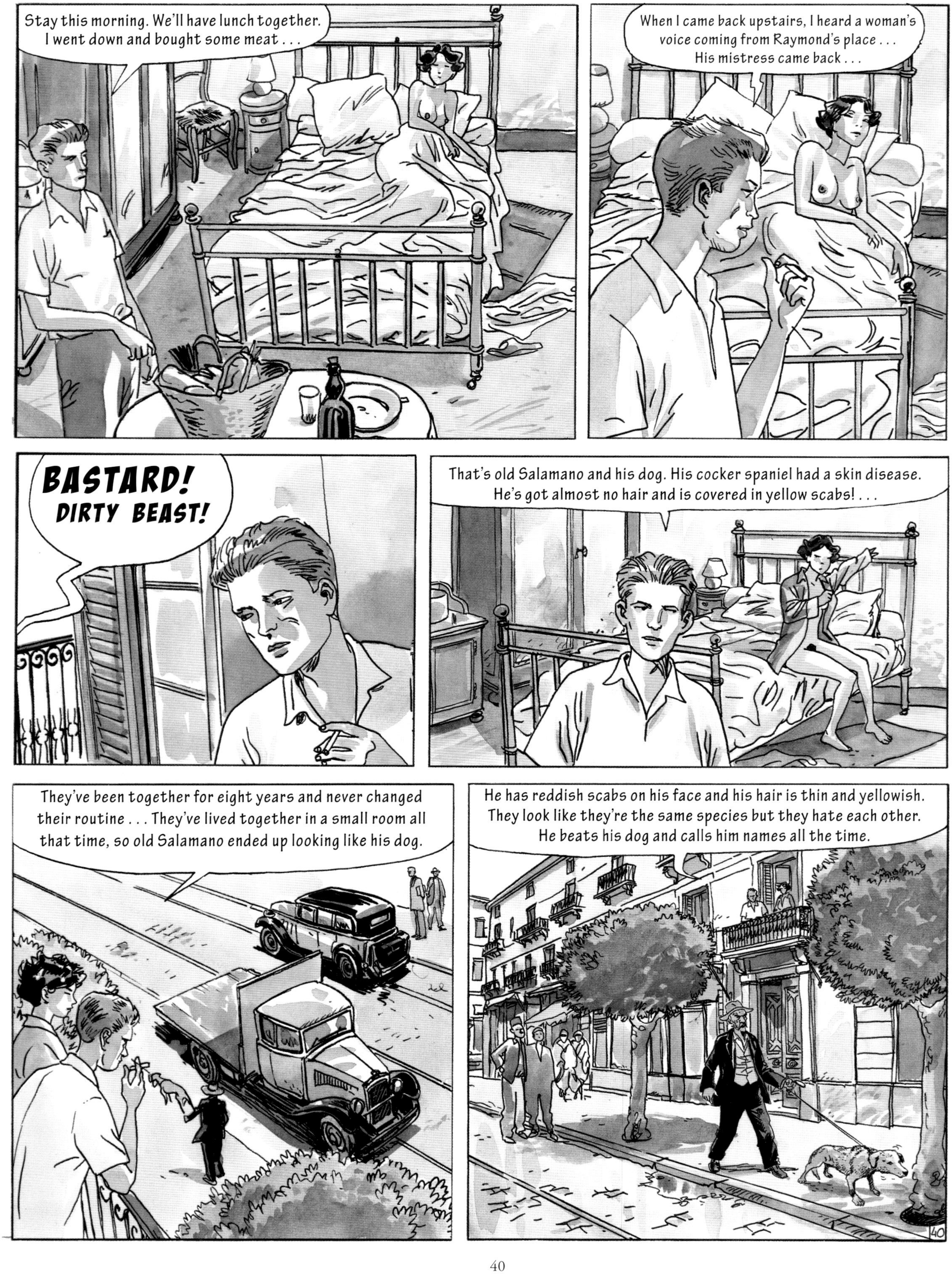
Stay this morning. We'll have lunch together. I went down and bought some meat . . .
When I came back upstairs, I heard a woman's voice coming from Raymond's place . . . His mistress came back . . .
BASTARD! DIRTY BEAST!
That's old Salamano and his dog. His cocker spaniel had a skin disease. He's got almost no hair and is covered in yellow scabs! . . .
They've been together for eight years and never changed their routine . . . They've lived together in a small room all that time, so old Salamano ended up looking like his dog.
He has reddish scabs on his face and his hair is thin and yellowish. They look like they're the same species but they hate each other. He beats his dog and calls him names all the time.
40

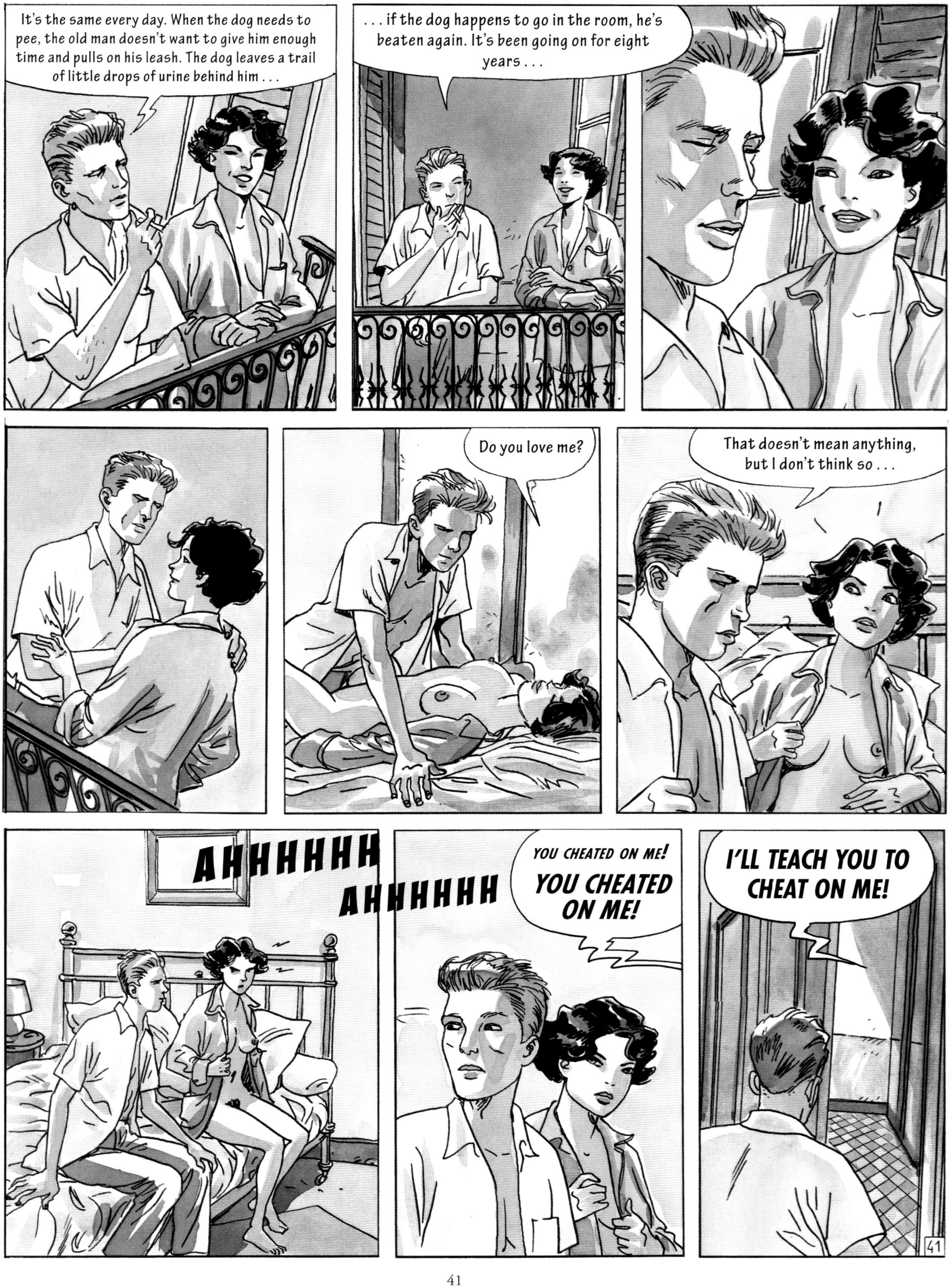
It's the same every day. When the dog needs to pee, the old man doesn't want to give him enough time and pulls on his leash. The dog leaves a trail of little drops of urine behind him . . .
. . . if the dog happens to go in the room, he's beaten again. It's been going on for eight years . . .
Do you love me?
That doesn't mean anything, but I don't think so . . .
AHHHHHH
AHHHHHH
YOU CHEATED ON ME!
YOU CHEATED ON ME!
I'LL TEACH YOU TO CHEAT ON ME!
41

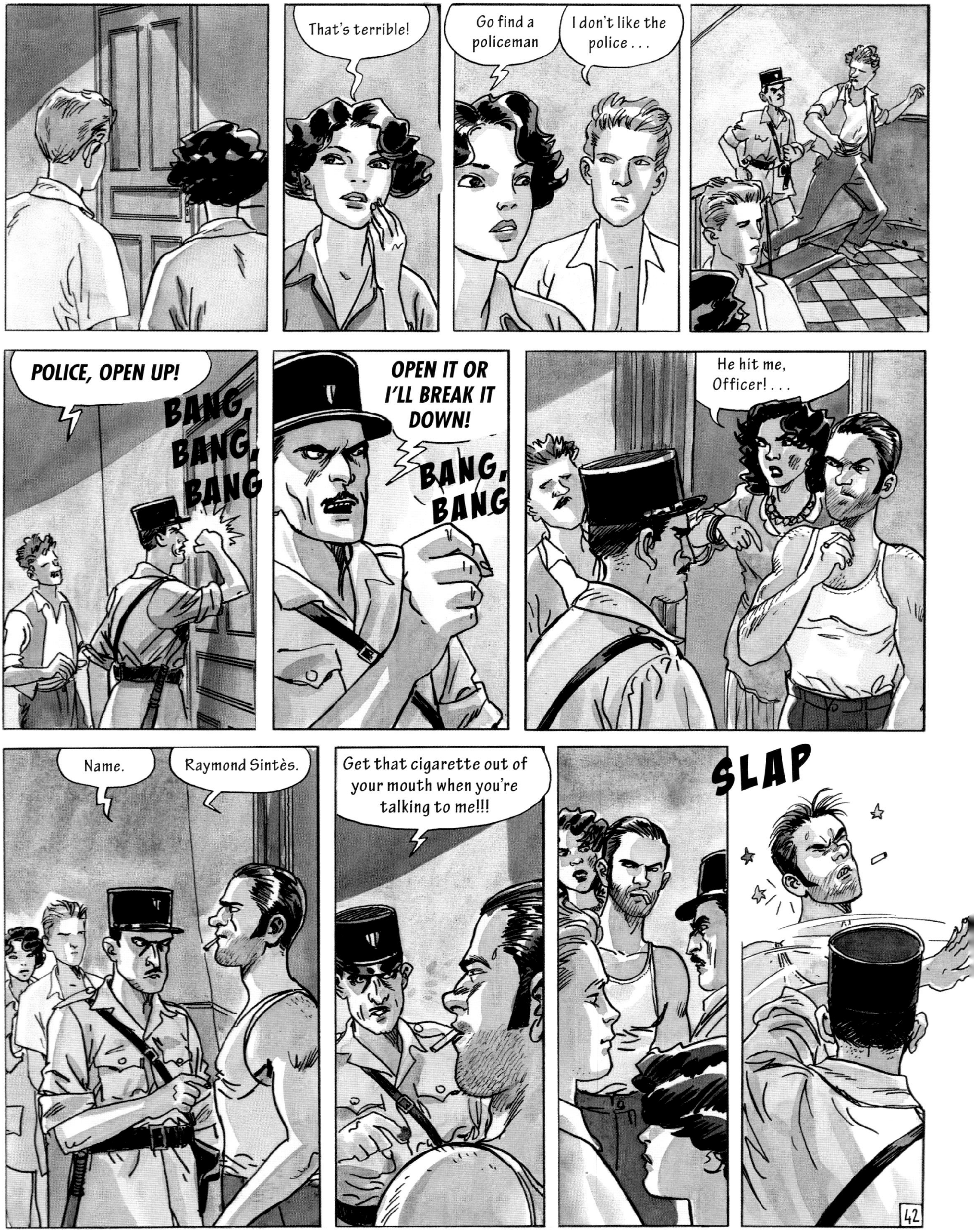
That's terrible!
Go find a policeman
I don't like the police . . .
POLICE, OPEN UP!
BANG, BANG, BANG
OPEN IT OR I'LL BREAK IT DOWN!
BANG, BANG
He hit me, Officer! . . .
Name.
Raymond Sintès.
Get that cigarette out of your mouth when you're talking to me!!!
SLAP
42

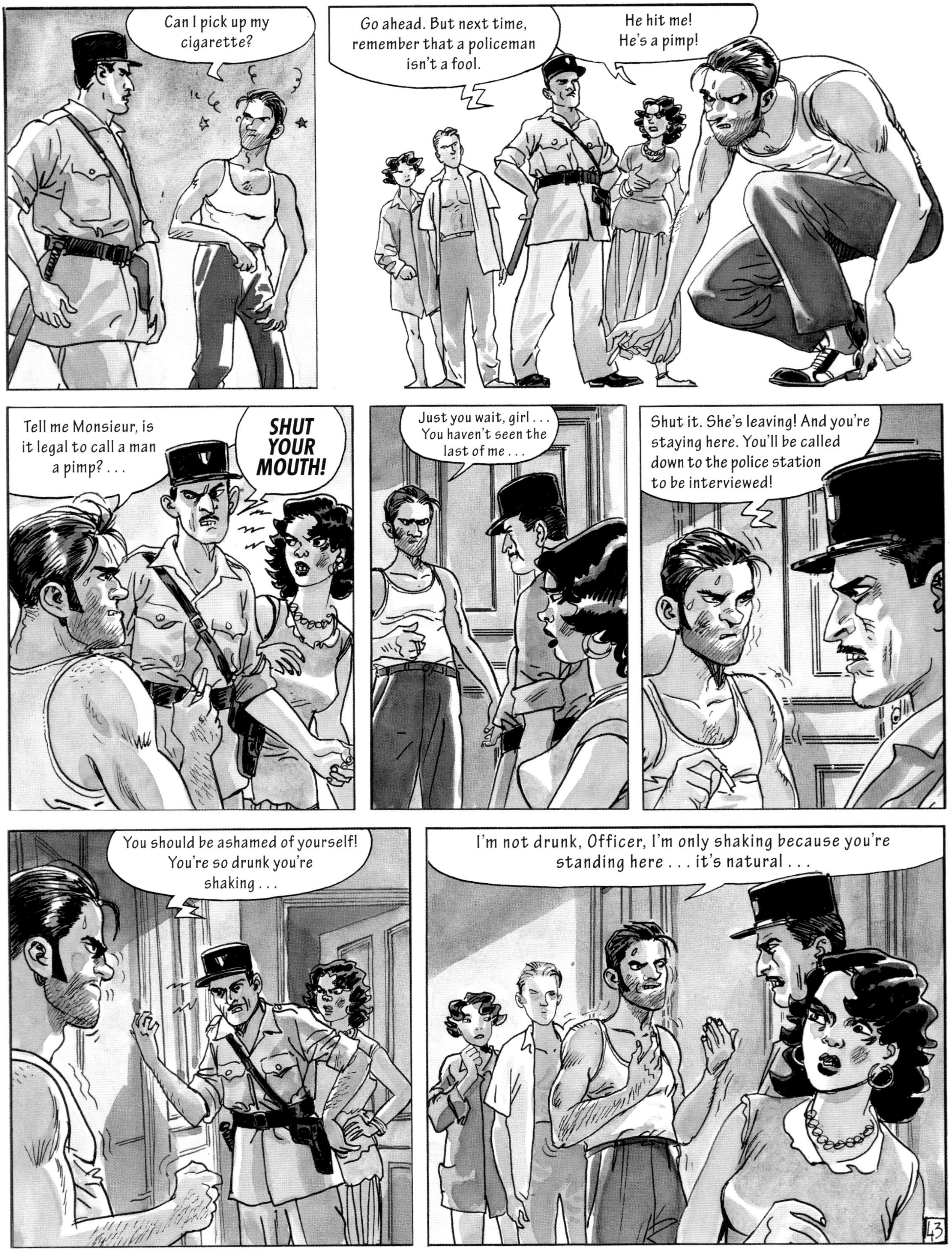
Can I pick up my cigarette?
Go ahead. But next time, remember that a policeman isn't a fool.
He hit me! He's a pimp!
Tell me Monsieur, is it legal to call a man a pimp? . . .
SHUT YOUR MOUTH!
Just you wait, girl . . . You haven't seen the last of me . . .
Shut it. She's leaving! And you're staying here. You'll be called down to the police station to be interviewed!
You should be ashamed of yourself! You're so drunk you're shaking . . .
I'm not drunk, Officer, I'm only shaking because you're standing here . . . it's natural . . .
43

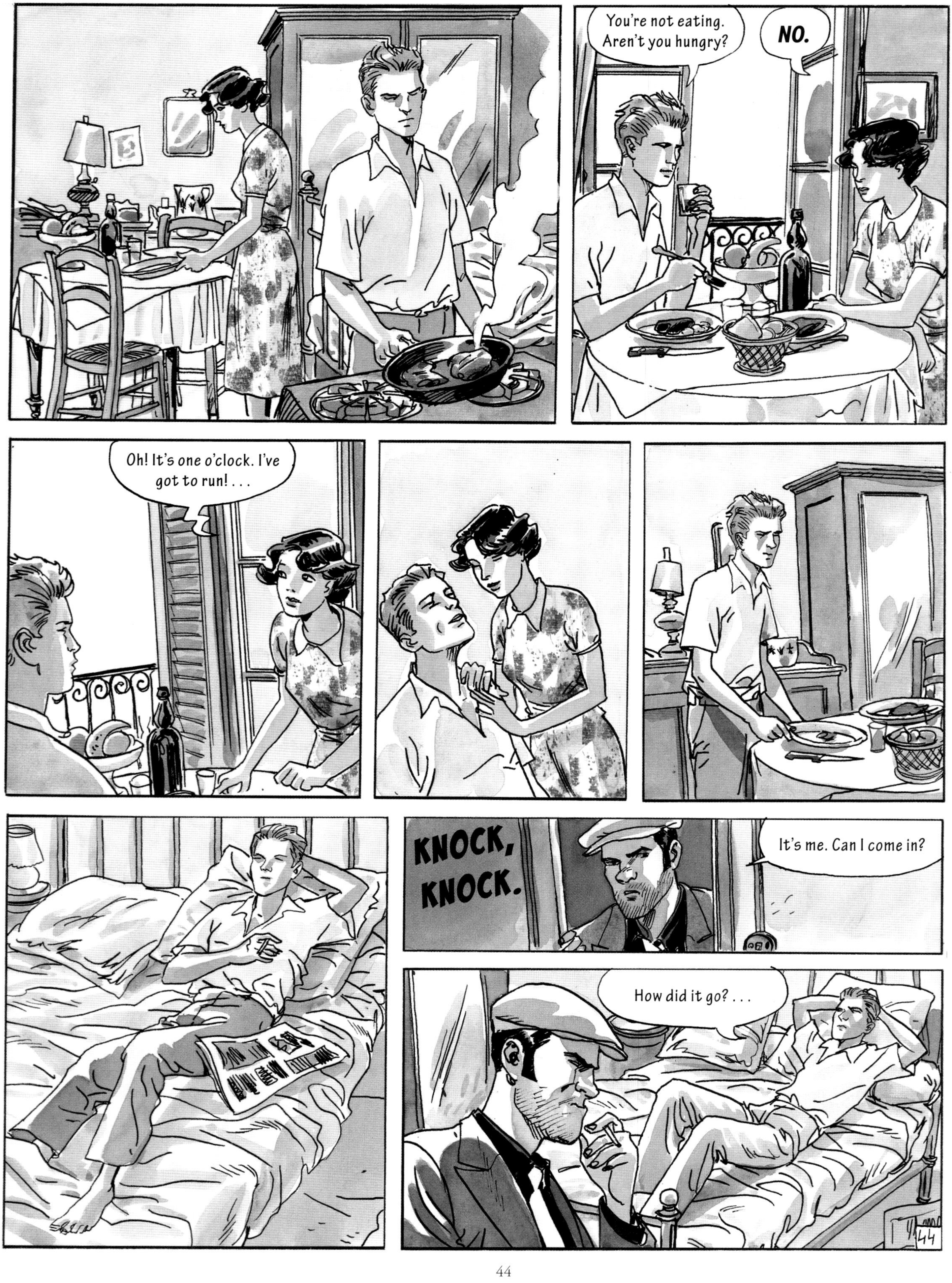
You're not eating. Aren't you hungry?
NO.
Oh! It's one o'clock. I've got to run! . . .
KNOCK, KNOCK.
It's me. Can I come in?
How did it go? . . .
44

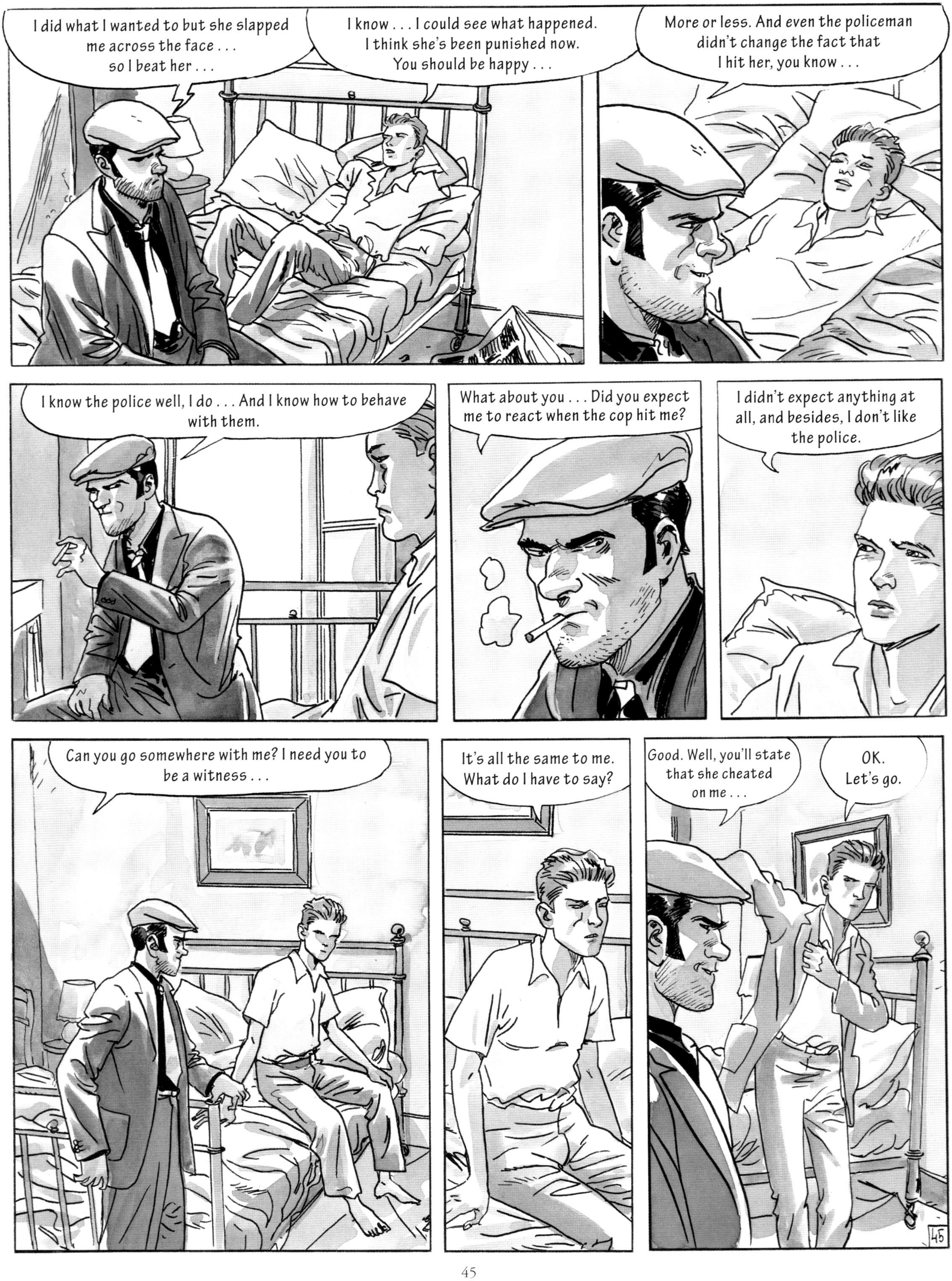
I did what I wanted to but she slapped me across the face . . . so I beat her . . .
I know . . . I could see what happened. I think she's been punished now. You should be happy . . .
More or less. And even the policeman didn't change the fact that I hit her, you know . . .
I know the police well, I do . . . And I know how to behave with them.
What about you . . . Did you expect me to react when the cop hit me?
I didn't expect anything at all, and besides, I don't like the police.
Can you go somewhere with me? I need you to be a witness . . .
It's all the same to me. What do I have to say?
Good. Well, you'll state that she cheated on me . . .
OK. Let's go.

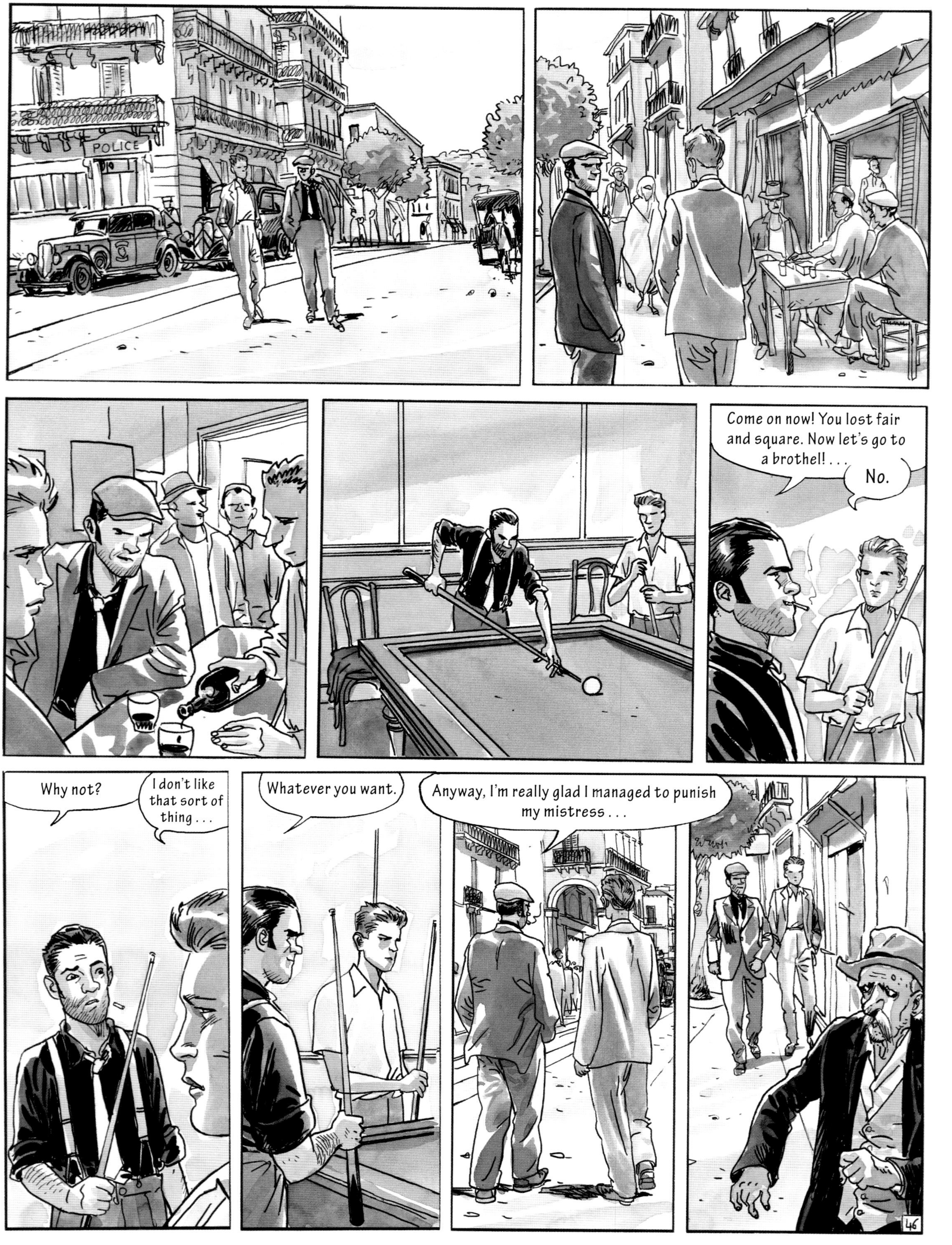
POLICE
Come on now! You lost fair and square. Now let's go to a brothel! . . .
No.
Why not?
I don't like that sort of thing . . .
Whatever you want.
Anyway, I'm really glad I managed to punish my mistress . . .
46

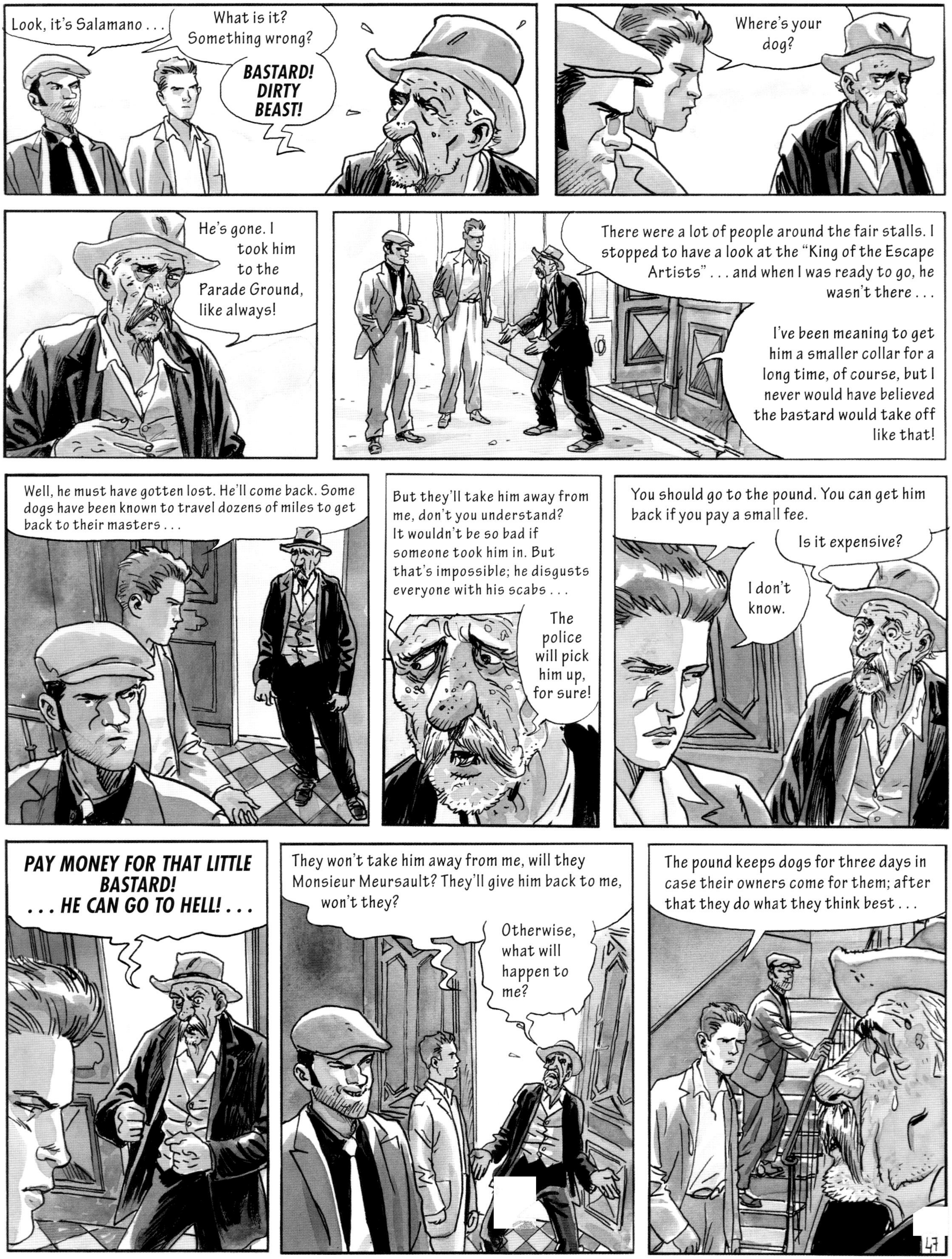
Look, it's Salamano . . .
What is it? Something wrong?
BASTARD! DIRTY BEAST!
Where's your dog?
He's gone. I took him to the Parade Ground, like always!
There were a lot of people around the fair stalls. I stopped to have a look at the "King of the Escape Artists" . . . and when I was ready to go, he wasn't there . . .
I've been meaning to get him a smaller collar for a long time, of course, but I never would have believed the bastard would take off like that!
Well, he must have gotten lost. He'll come back. Some dogs have been known to travel dozens of miles to get back to their masters . . .
But they'll take him away from me, don't you understand? It wouldn't be so bad if someone took him in. But that's impossible; he disgusts everyone with his scabs . . .
The police will pick him up, for sure!
You should go to the pound. You can get him back if you pay a small fee.
Is it expensive?
I don't know.
PAY MONEY FOR THAT LITTLE BASTARD! . . . HE CAN GO TO HELL! . . .
They won't take him away from me, will they Monsieur Meursault? They'll give him back to me, won't they?
Otherwise, what will happen to me?
The pound keeps dogs for three days in case their owners come for them; after that they do what they think best . . .
47

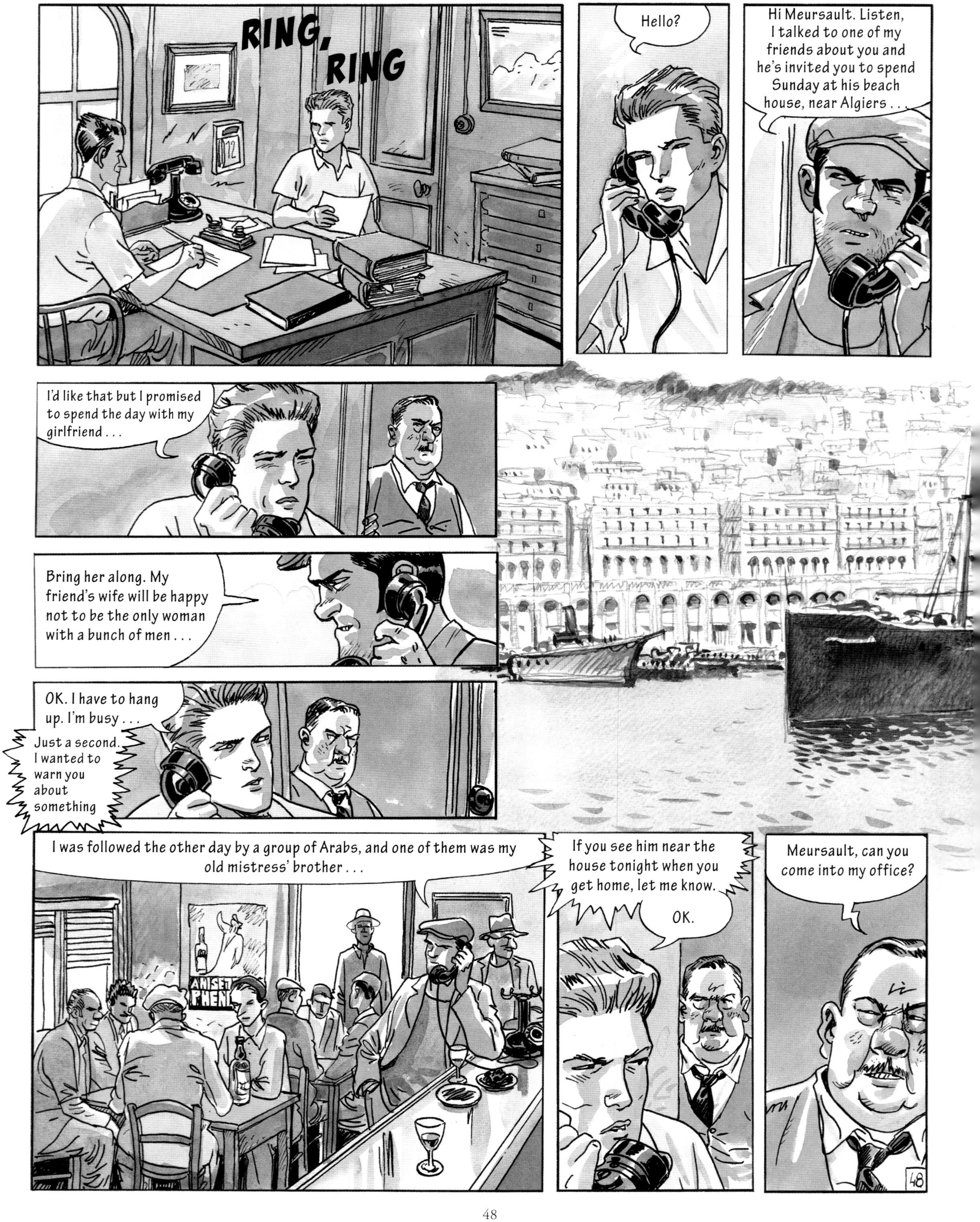
RING, RING
Hello?
Hi Meursault. Listen, I talked to one of my friends about you and he's invited you to spend Sunday at his beach house, near Algiers . . .
I'd like that but I promised to spend the day with my girlfriend . . .
Bring her along. My friend's wife will be happy not to be the only woman with a bunch of men . . .
OK. I have to hang up. I'm busy . . .
Just a second. I wanted to warn you about something
I was followed the other day by a group of Arabs, and one of them was my old mistress' brother . . .
ANISET
If you see him near the house tonight when you get home, let me know.
OK.
Meursault, can you come into my office?
48

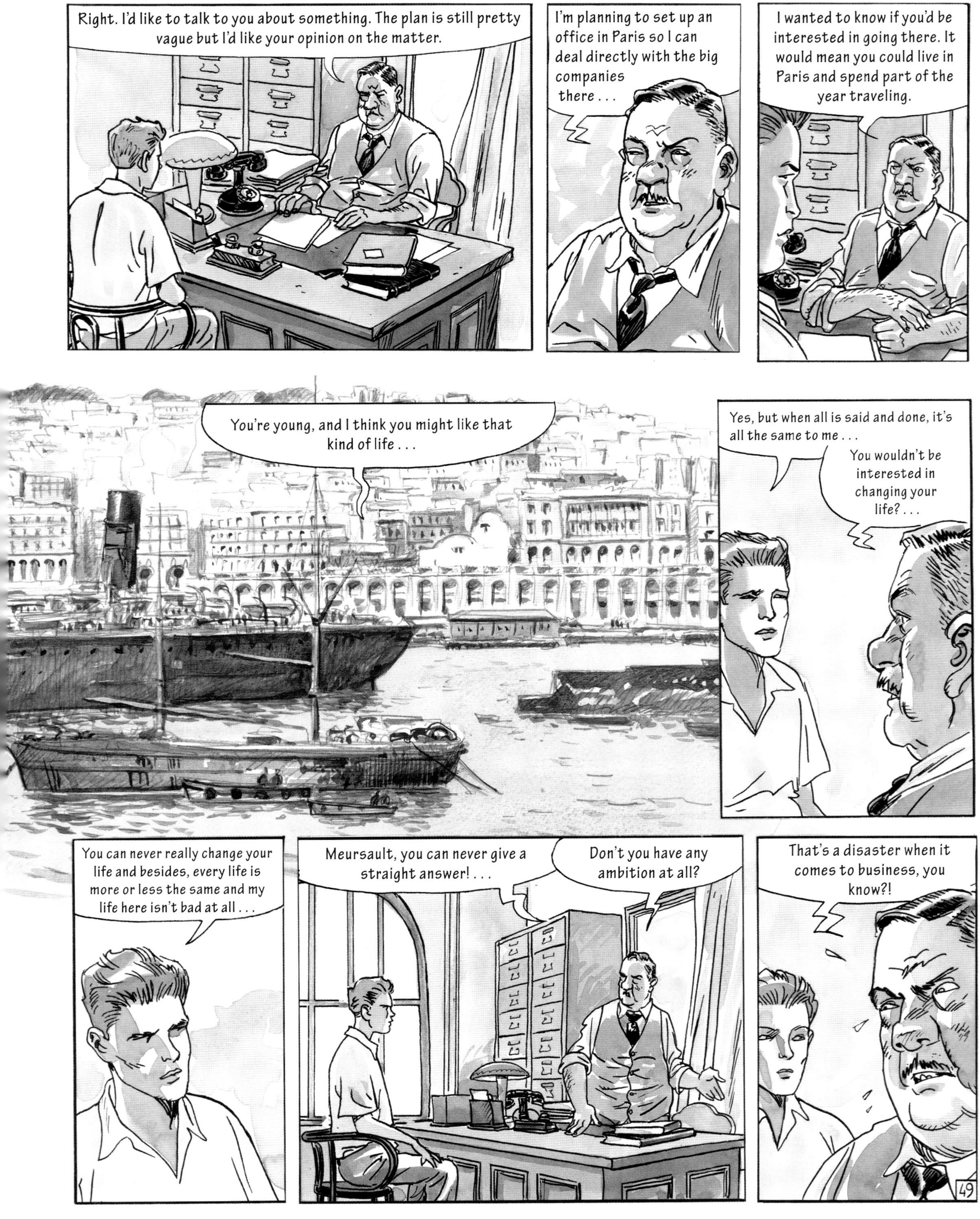
Right. I'd like to talk to you about something. The plan is still pretty vague but I'd like your opinion on the matter.
I'm planning to set up an office in Paris so I can deal directly with the big companies there . . .
I wanted to know if you'd be interested in going there. It would mean you could live in Paris and spend part of the year traveling.
You're young, and I think you might like that kind of life . . .
Yes, but when all is said and done, it's all the same to me . . .
You wouldn't be interested in changing your life? . . .
You can never really change your life and besides, every life is more or less the same and my life here isn't bad at all . . .
Meursault, you can never give a straight answer! . . .
Don't you have any ambition at all?
That's a disaster when it comes to business, you know?!
49

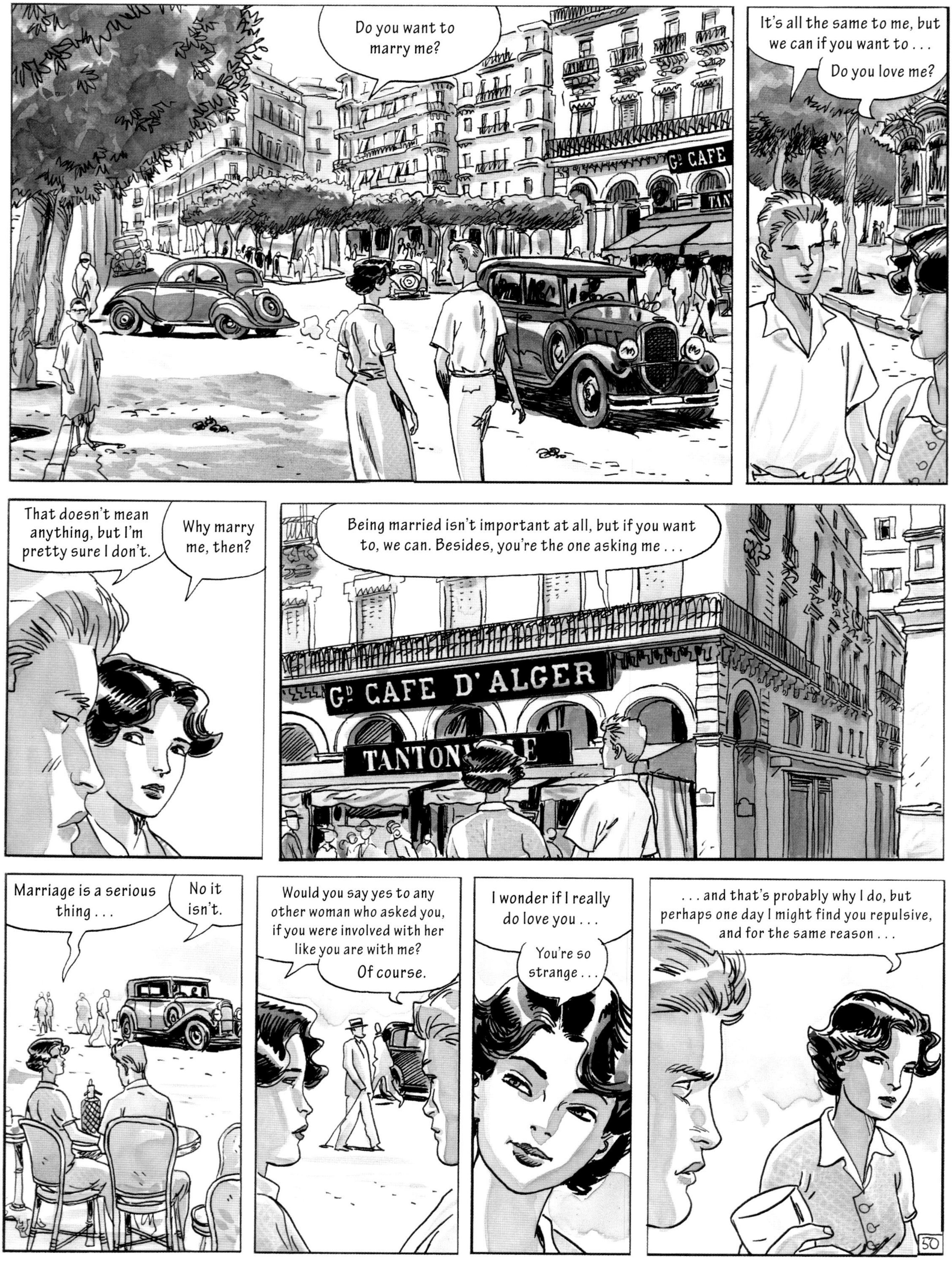
Do you want to marry me?
It's all the same to me, but we can if you want to . . .
Do you love me?
That doesn't mean anything, but I'm pretty sure I don't.
Why marry me, then?
Being married isn't important at all, but if you want to, we can. Besides, you're the one asking me . . .
Gd CAFE D'ALGER
Marriage is a serious thing . . .
No it isn't.
Would you say yes to any other woman who asked you, if you were involved with her like you are with me?
Of course.
I wonder if I really do love you . . .
You're so strange . . .
. . . and that's probably why I do, but perhaps one day I might find you repulsive, and for the same reason . . .

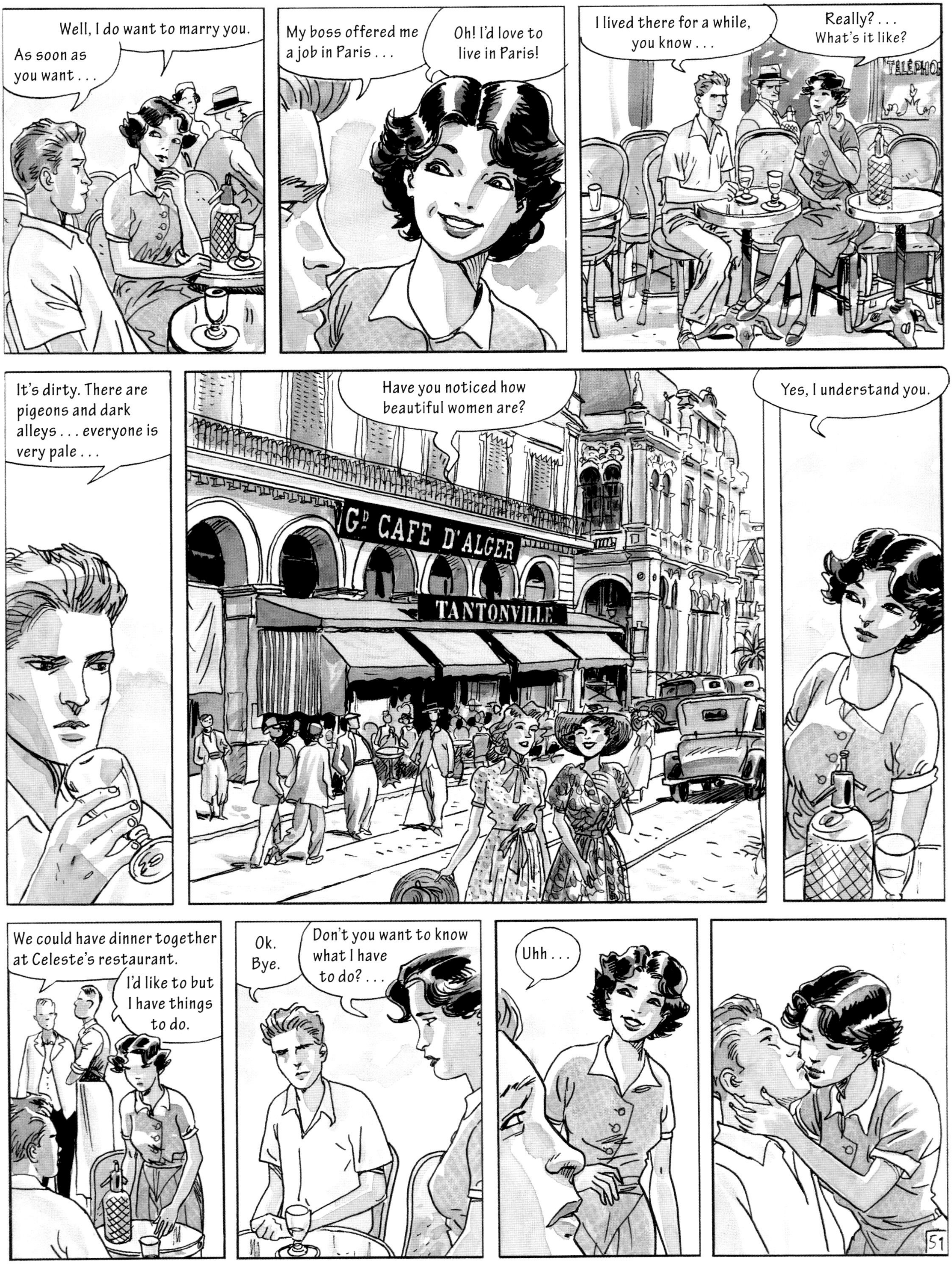
Well, I do want to marry you.
As soon as you want . . .
My boss offered me a job in Paris . . .
Oh! I'd love to live in Paris!
I lived there for a while, you know . . .
Really? . . . What's it like?
TÉLÉPHO
It's dirty. There are pigeons and dark alleys . . . everyone is very pale . . .
Have you noticed how beautiful women are?
Gd CAFE D'ALGER
TANTONVILLE
Yes, I understand you.
We could have dinner together at Celeste's restaurant.
I'd like to but I have things to do.
Ok. Bye.
Don't you want to know what I have to do? . . .
Uhh . . .
51

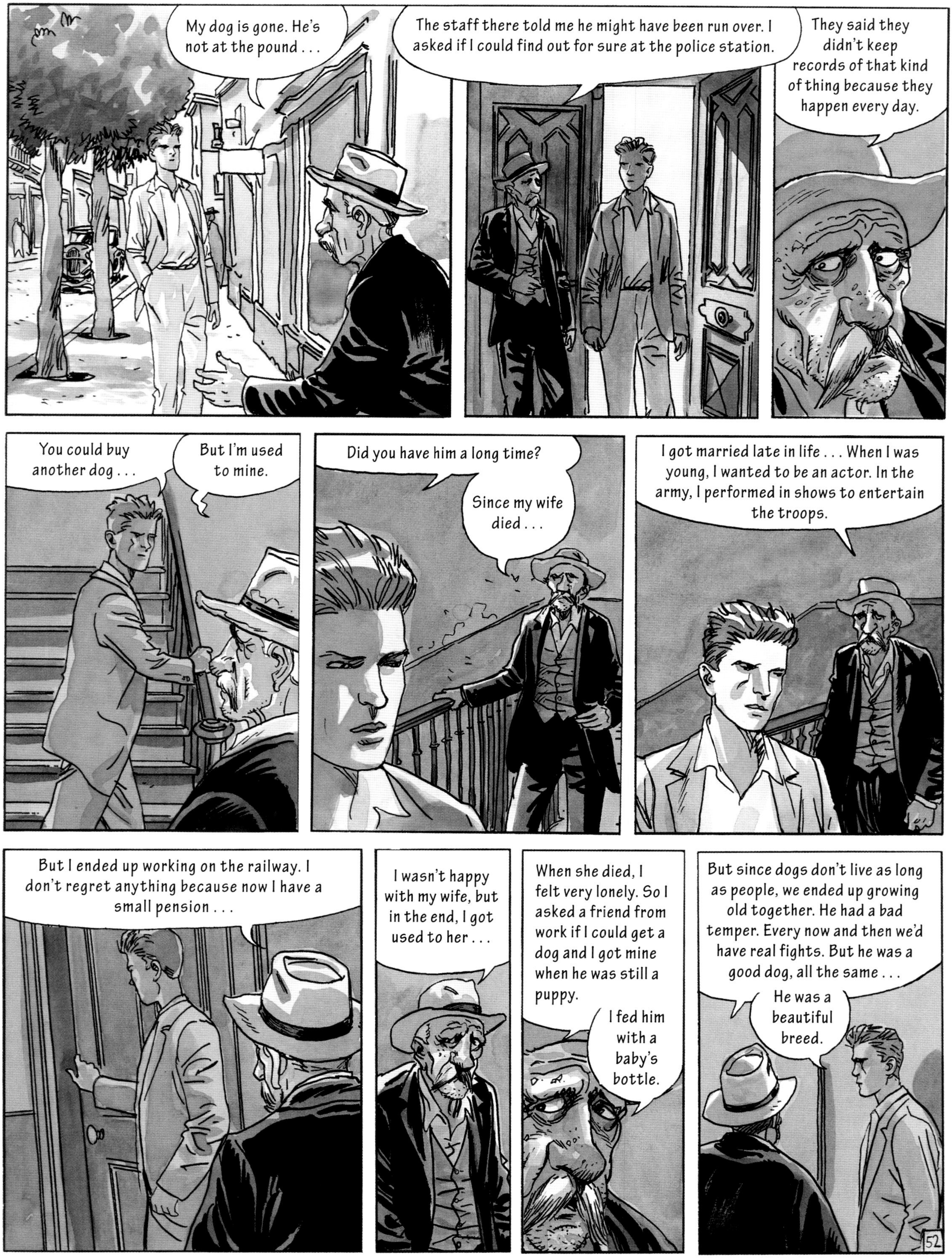
My dog is gone. He's not at the pound . . .
The staff there told me he might have been run over. I asked if I could find out for sure at the police station.
They said they didn't keep records of that kind of thing because they happen every day.
You could buy another dog . . .
But I'm used to mine.
Did you have him a long time?
Since my wife died . . .
I got married late in life . . . When I was young, I wanted to be an actor. In the army, I performed in shows to entertain the troops.
But I ended up working on the railway. I don't regret anything because now I have a small pension . . .
I wasn't happy with my wife, but in the end, I got used to her . . .
When she died, I felt very lonely. So I asked a friend from work if I could get a dog and I got mine when he was still a puppy.
I fed him with a baby's bottle.
But since dogs don't live as long as people, we ended up growing old together. He had a bad temper. Every now and then we'd have real fights. But he was a good dog, all the same . . .
He was a beautiful breed.
52

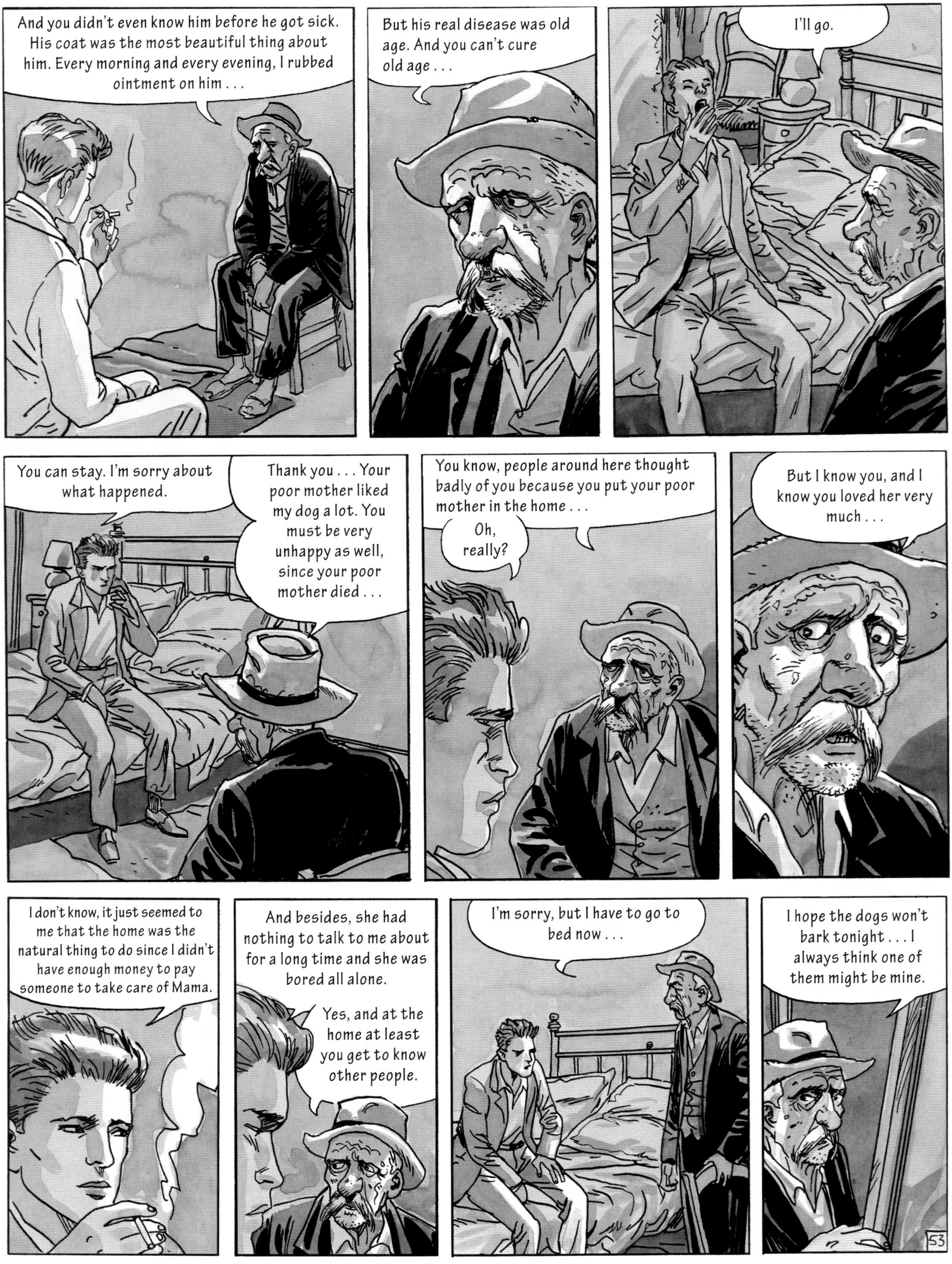
And you didn't even know him before he got sick. His coat was the most beautiful thing about him. Every morning and every evening, I rubbed ointment on him . . .
But his real disease was old age. And you can't cure old age . . .
I'll go.
You can stay. I'm sorry about what happened.
Thank you . . . Your poor mother liked my dog a lot. You must be very unhappy as well, since your poor mother died . . .
You know, people around here thought badly of you because you put your poor mother in the home . . .
Oh, really?
But I know you, and I know you loved her very much . . .
I don't know, it just seemed to me that the home was the natural thing to do since I didn't have enough money to pay someone to take care of Mama.
And besides, she had nothing to talk to me about for a long time and she was bored all alone.
Yes, and at the home at least you get to know other people.
I'm sorry, but I have to go to bed now . . .
I hope the dogs won't bark tonight . . . I always think one of them might be mine.
53

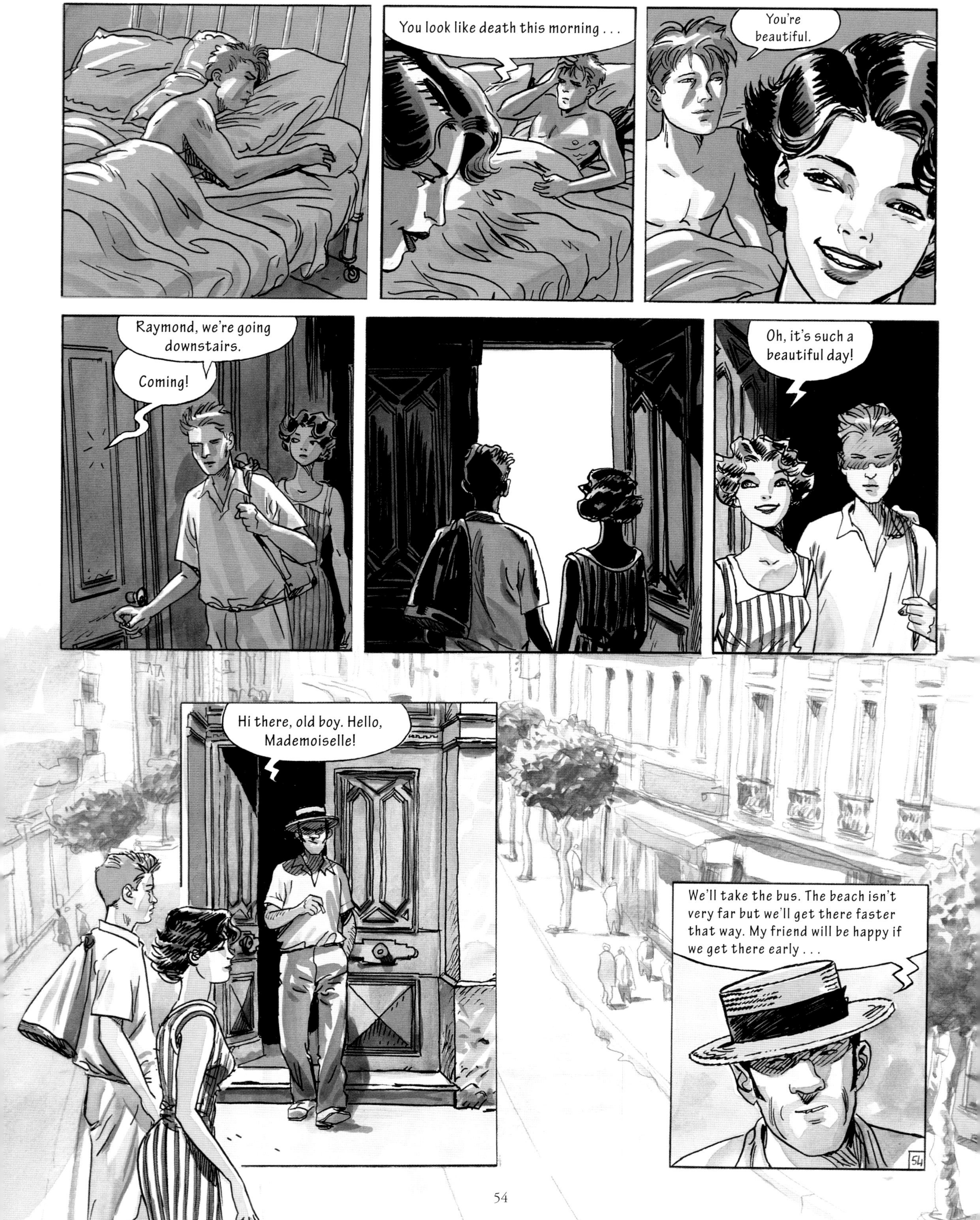
You look like death this morning . . .
You're beautiful.
Raymond, we're going downstairs.
Coming!
Oh, it's such a beautiful day!
Hi there, old boy. Hello, Mademoiselle!
We'll take the bus. The beach isn't very far but we'll get there faster that way. My friend will be happy if we get there early . . .
54

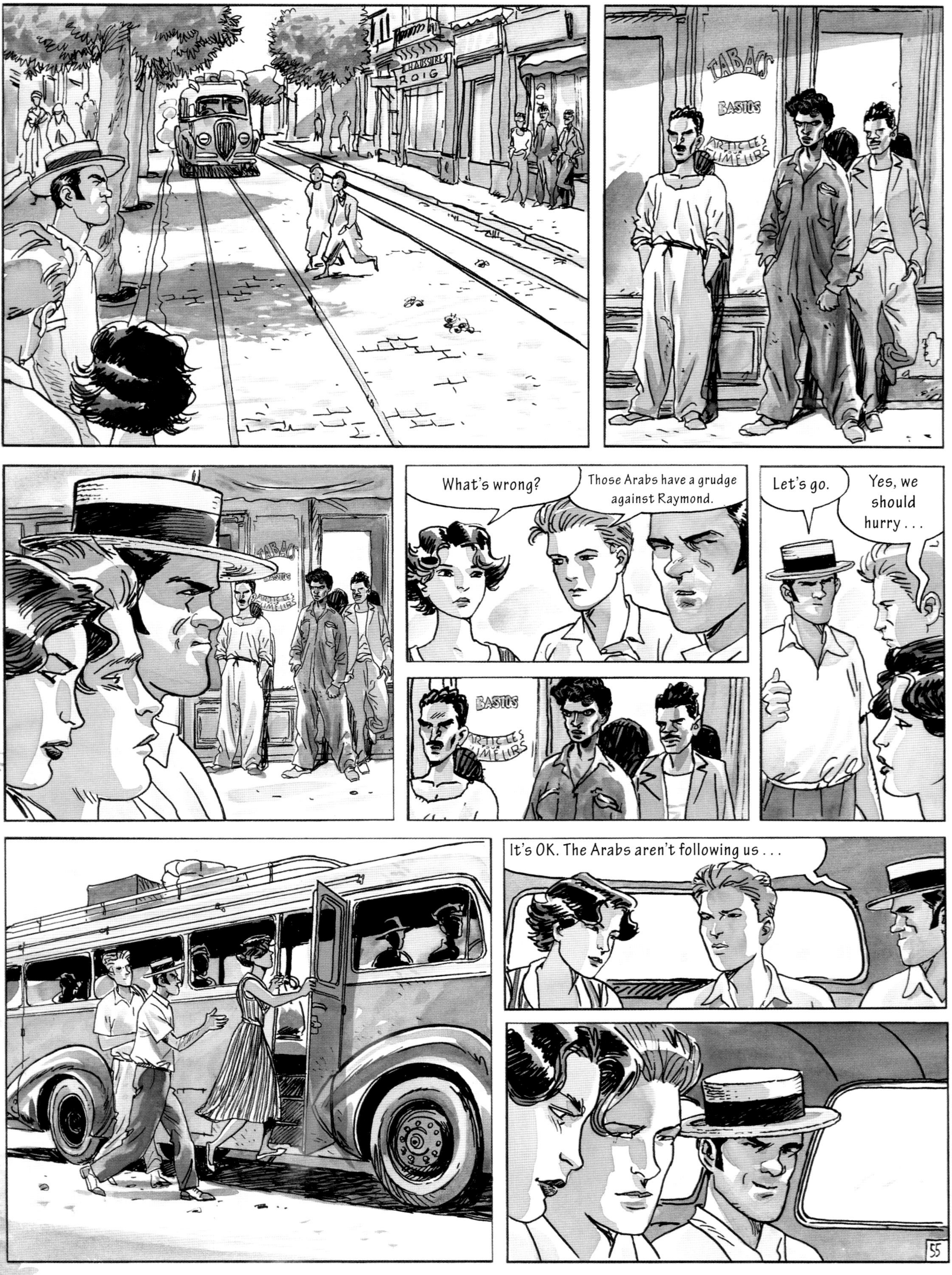
CHAUSSURES
ROIG
TABACS
BASTOS
ARTICLES POUR FUMEURS
What's wrong?
Those Arabs have a grudge against Raymond.
Let's go.
Yes, we should hurry . . .
It's OK. The Arabs aren't following us . . .
55

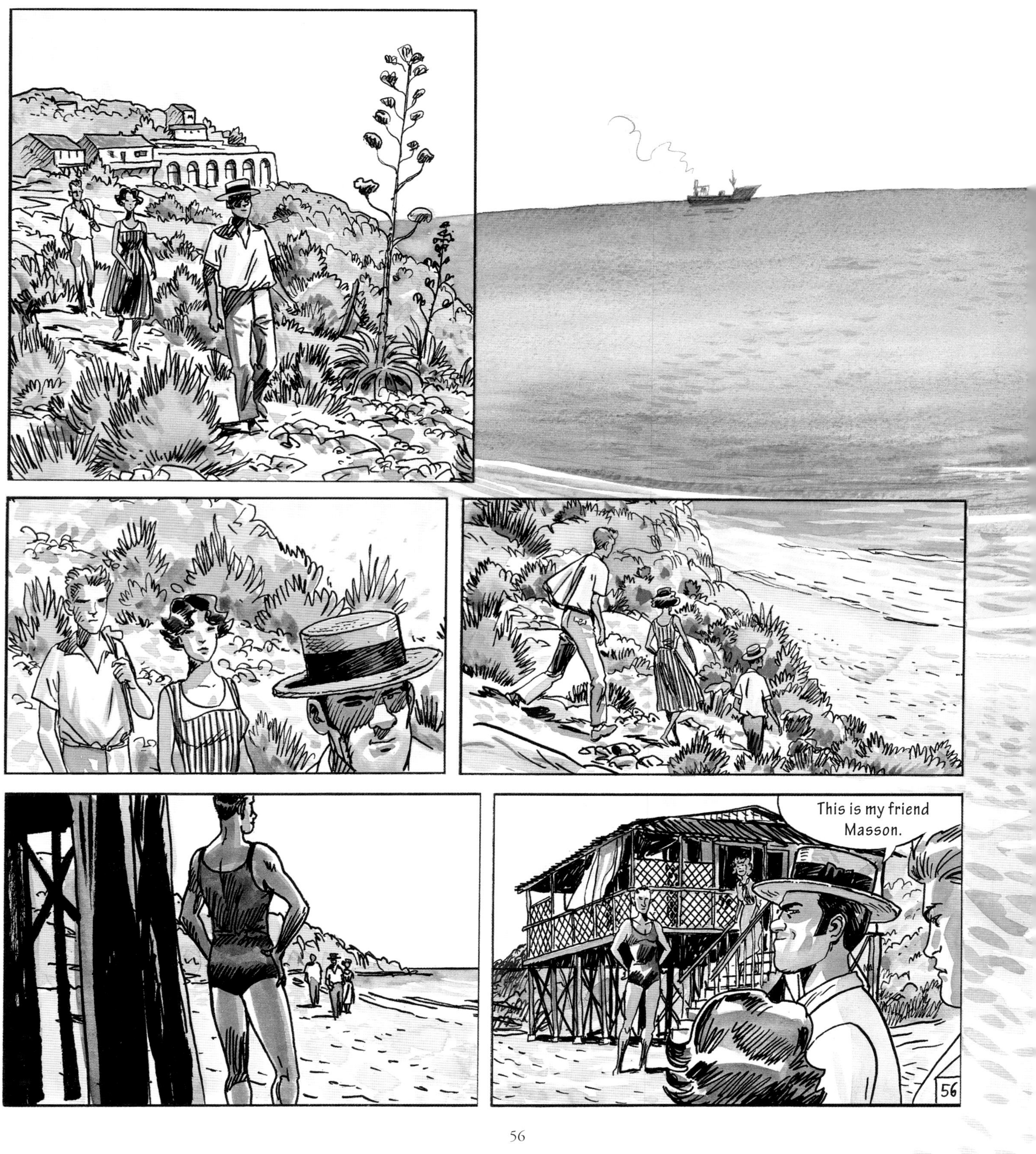
This is my friend
Masson.
56

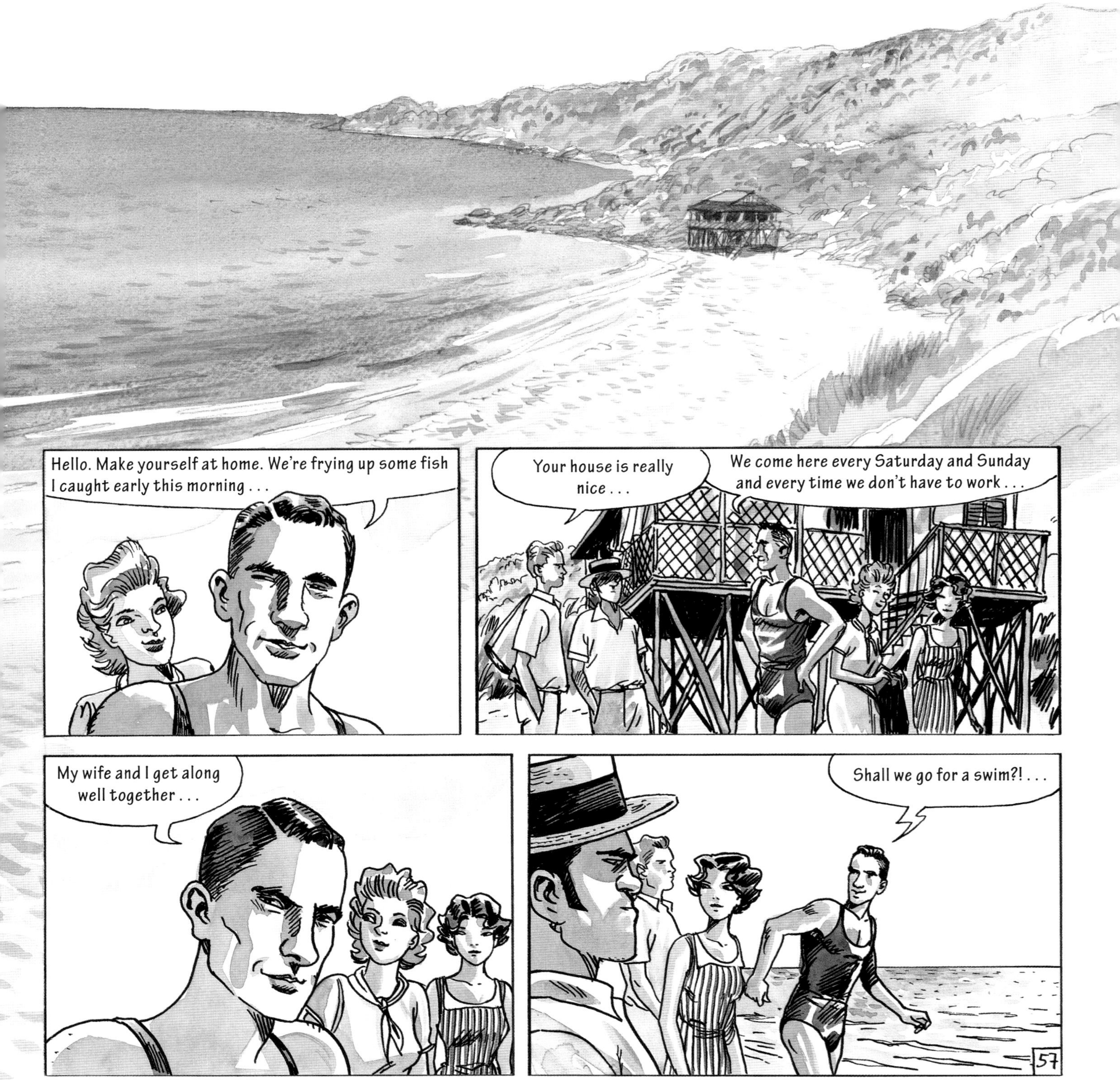
Hello. Make yourself at home. We're frying up some fish I caught early this morning . . .
Your house is really nice . . .
We come here every Saturday and Sunday and every time we don't have to work . . .
My wife and I get along well together . . .
Shall we go for a swim?! . . .
57

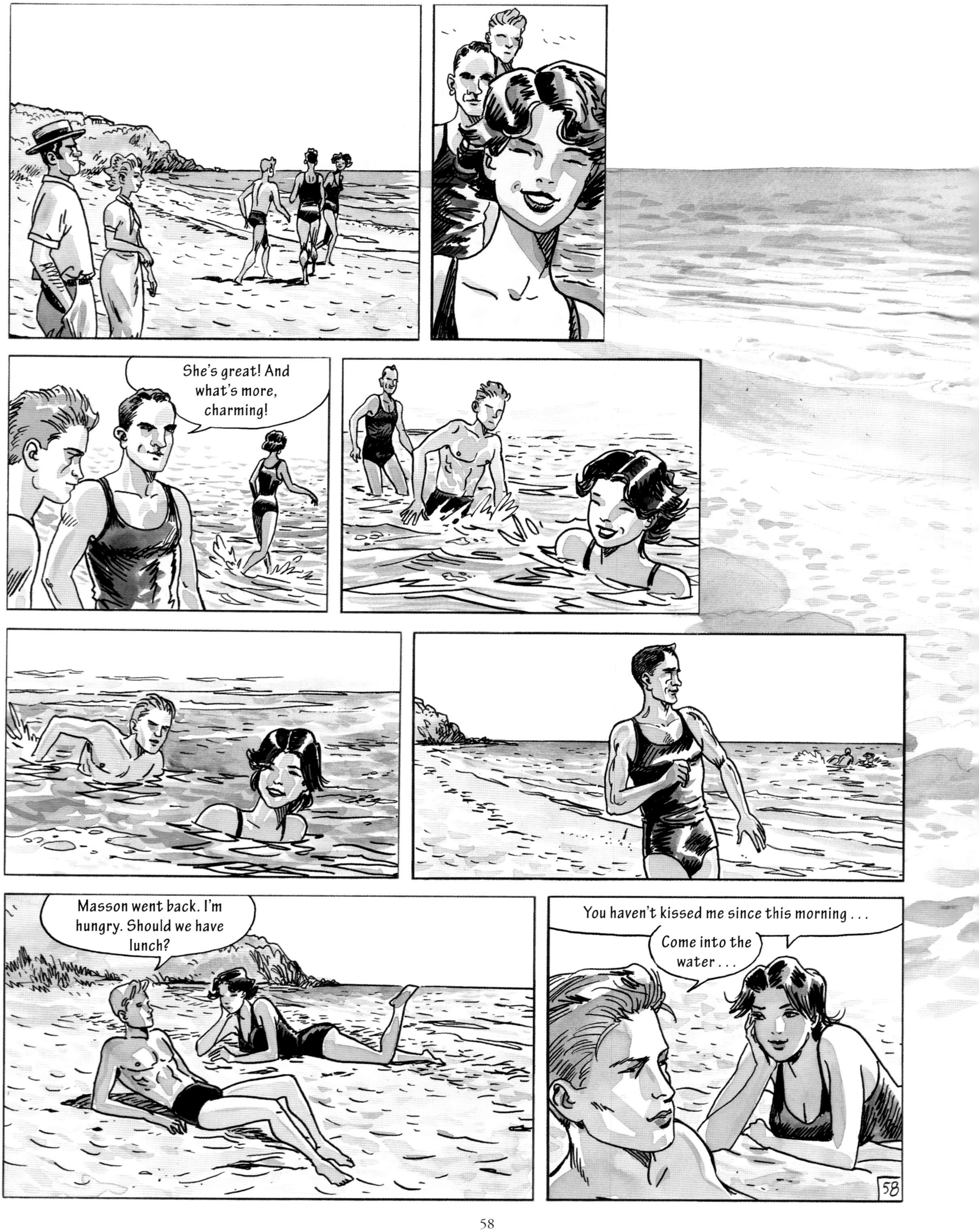
She's great! And what's more, charming!
Masson went back. I'm hungry. Should we have lunch?
You haven't kissed me since this morning . . .
Come into the water . . .
58

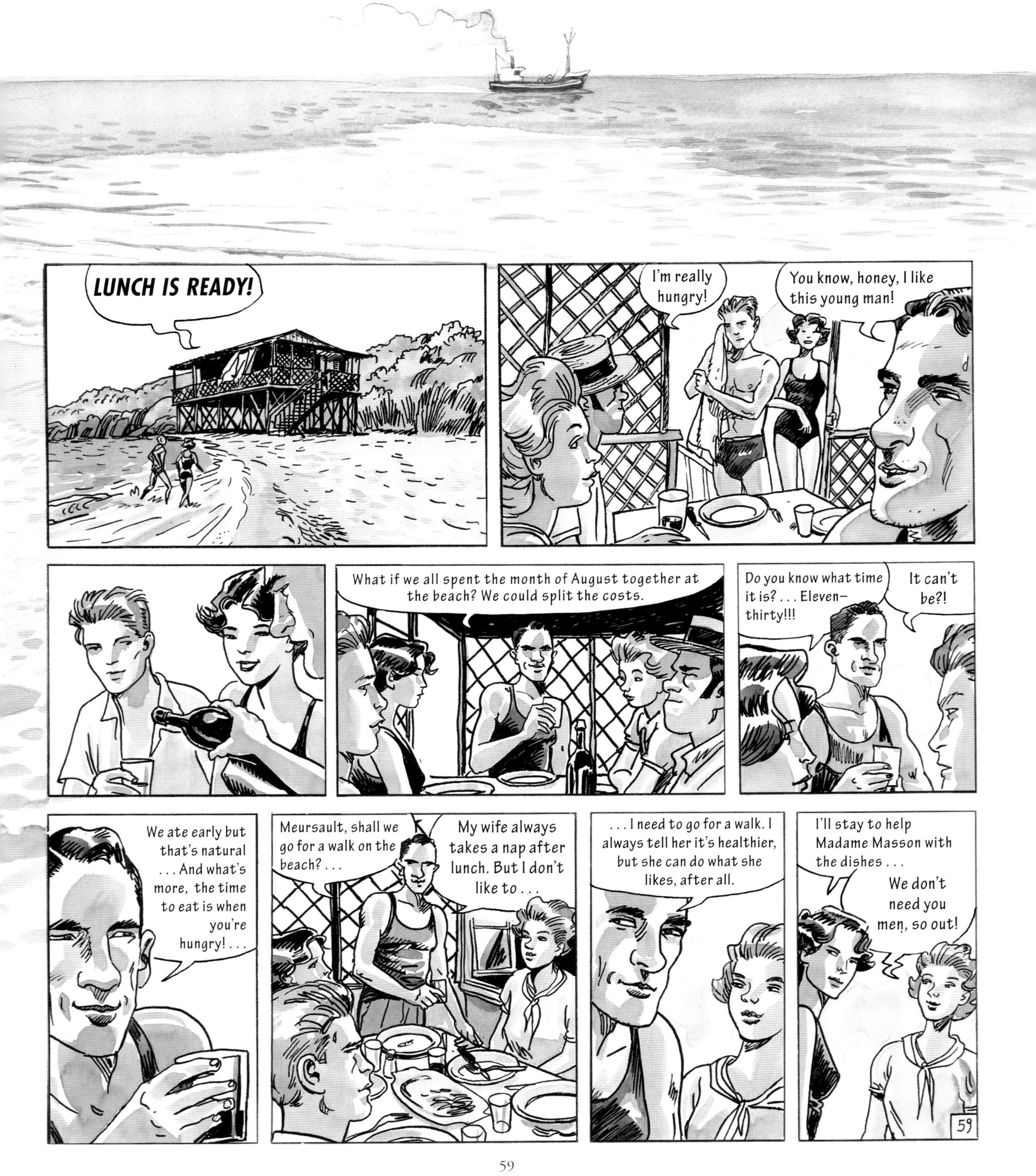
LUNCH IS READY!
I'm really hungry!
You know, honey, I like this young man!
What if we all spent the month of August together at the beach? We could split the costs.
Do you know what time it is? . . . Eleven-thirty!!!
It can't be?!
We ate early but that's natural . . . And what's more, the time to eat is when you're hungry! . . .
Meursault, shall we go for a walk on the beach? . . .
My wife always takes a nap after lunch. But I don't like to . . .
. . . I need to go for a walk. I always tell her it's healthier, but she can do what she likes, after all.
I'll stay to help Madame Masson with the dishes . . .
We don't need you men, so out!
59

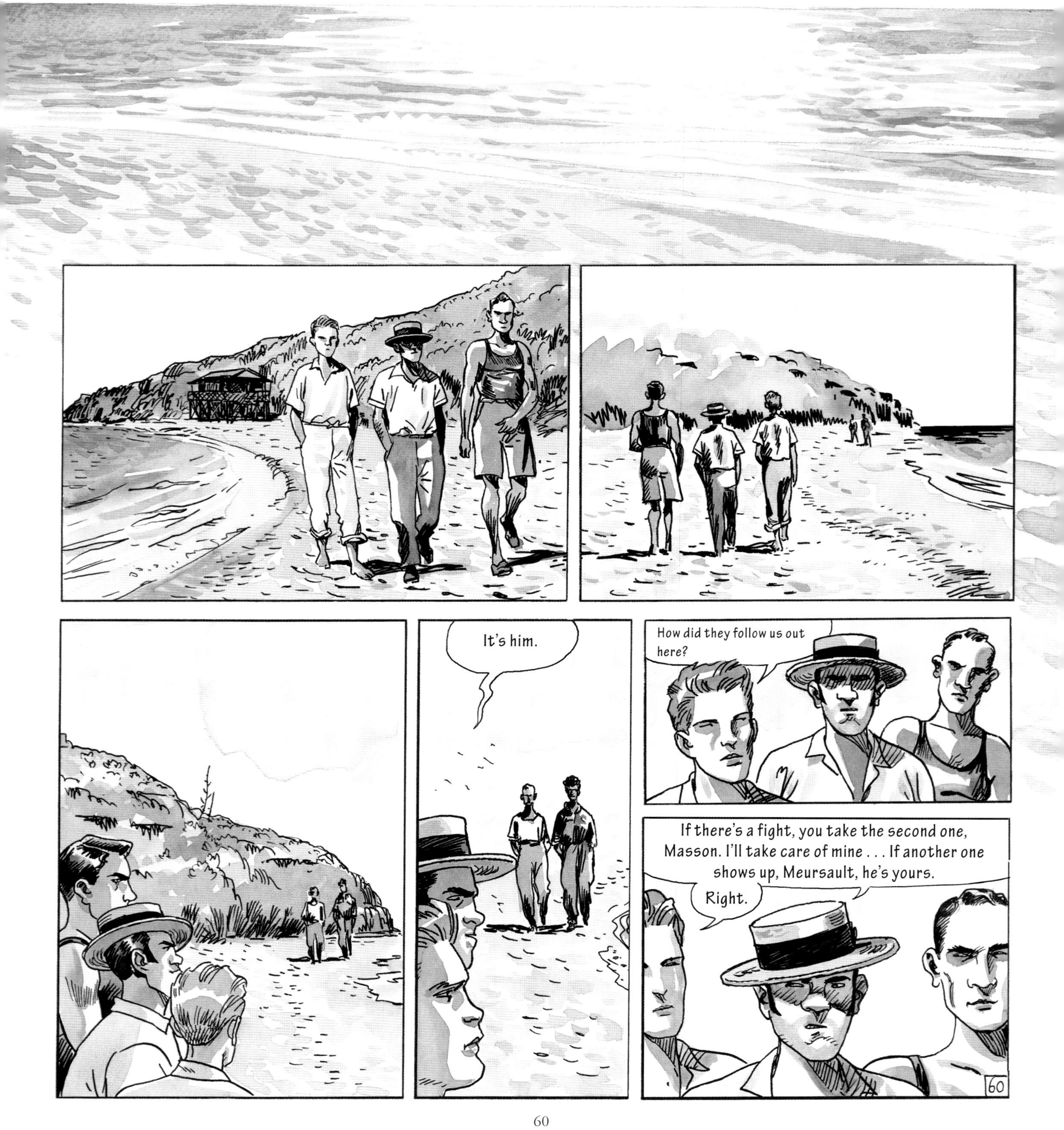
It's him.
How did they follow us out here?
If there's a fight, you take the second one, Masson. I'll take care of mine . . . If another one shows up, Meursault, he's yours.
Right.
60

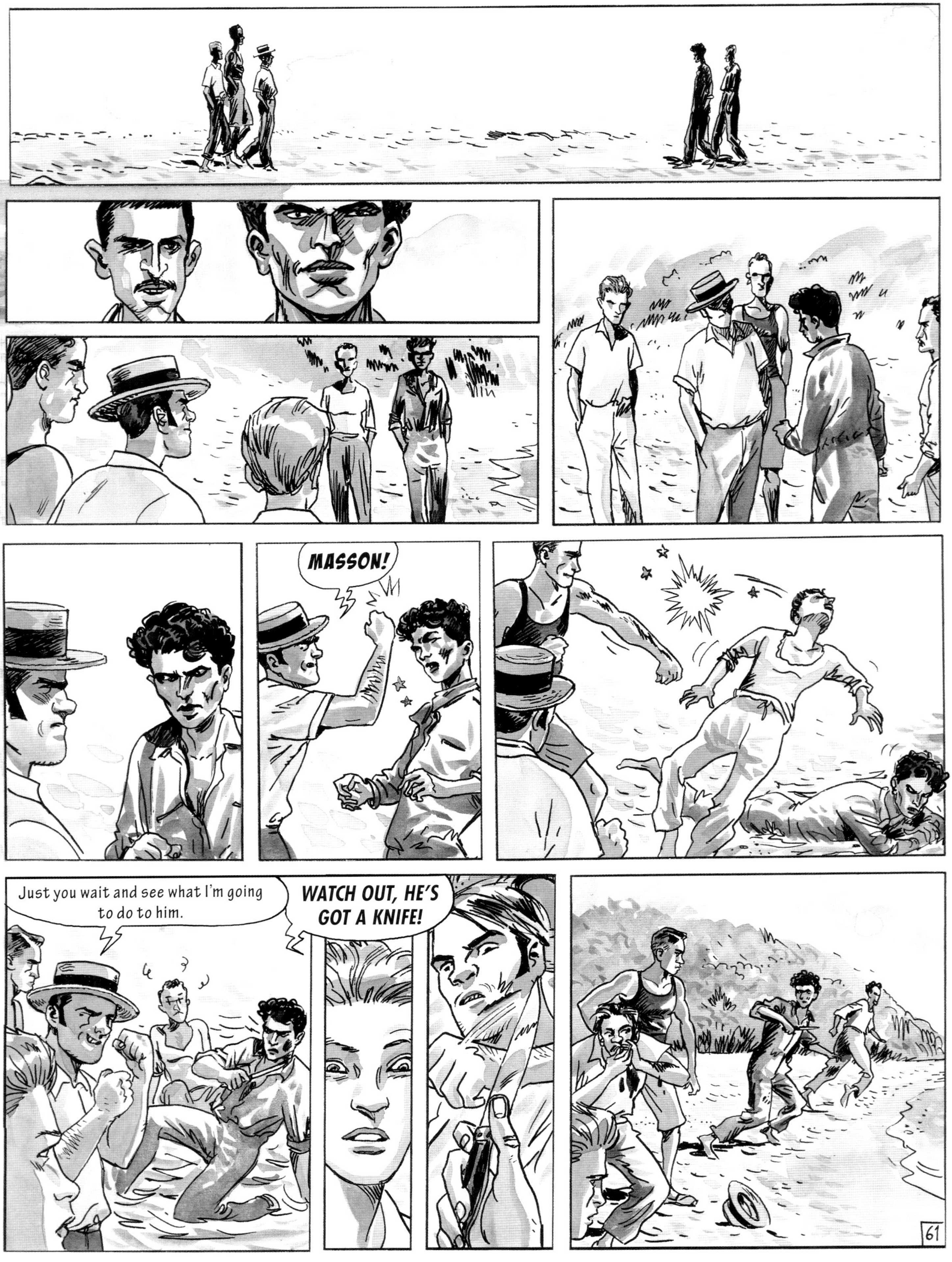
MASSON!
Just you wait and see what I'm going to do to him.
WATCH OUT, HE'S GOT A KNIFE!
61

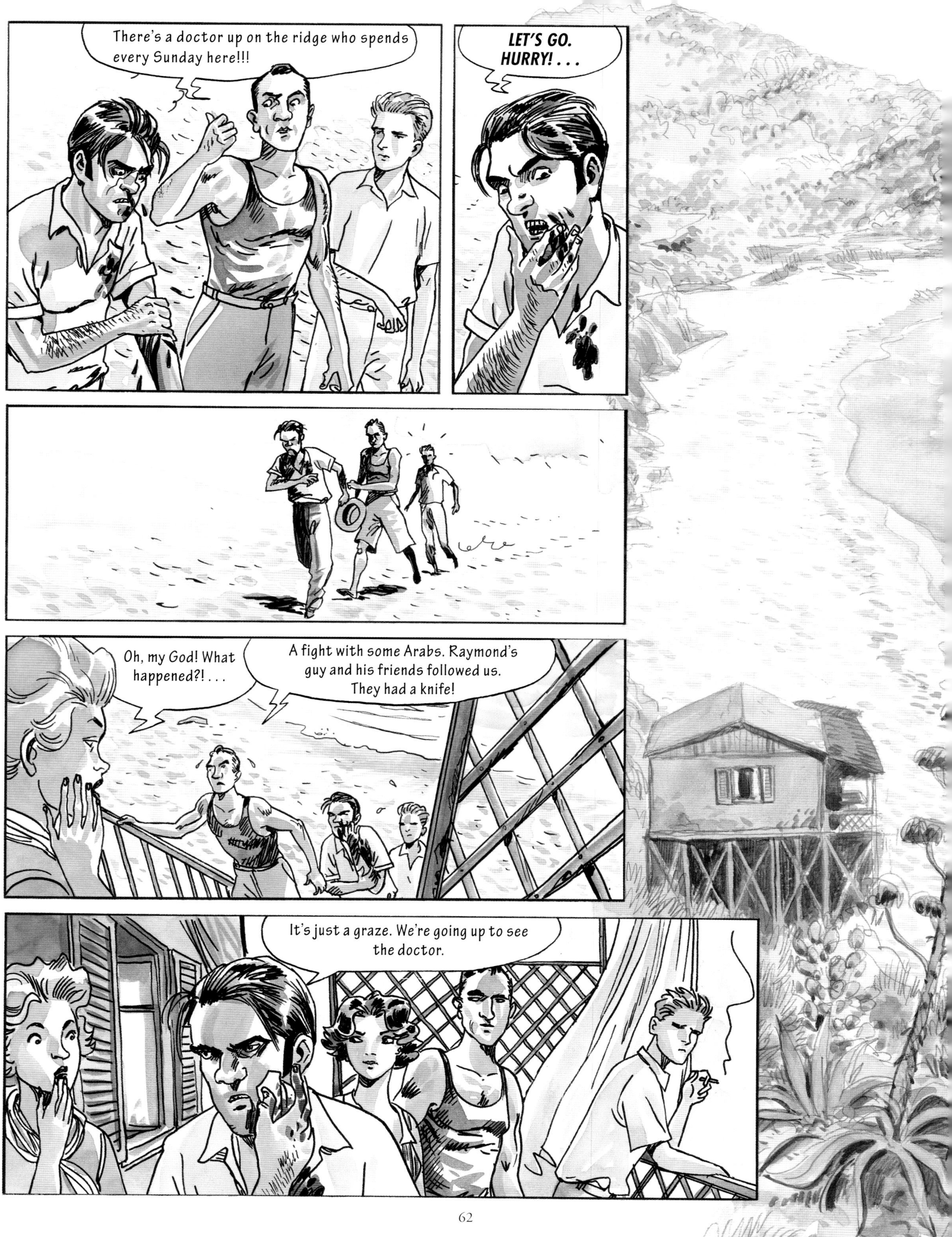
There's a doctor up on the ridge who spends every Sunday here!!!
LET'S GO. HURRY! . . .
Oh, my God! What happened?! . . .
A fight with some Arabs. Raymond's guy and his friends followed us. They had a knife!
It's just a graze. We're going up to see the doctor.

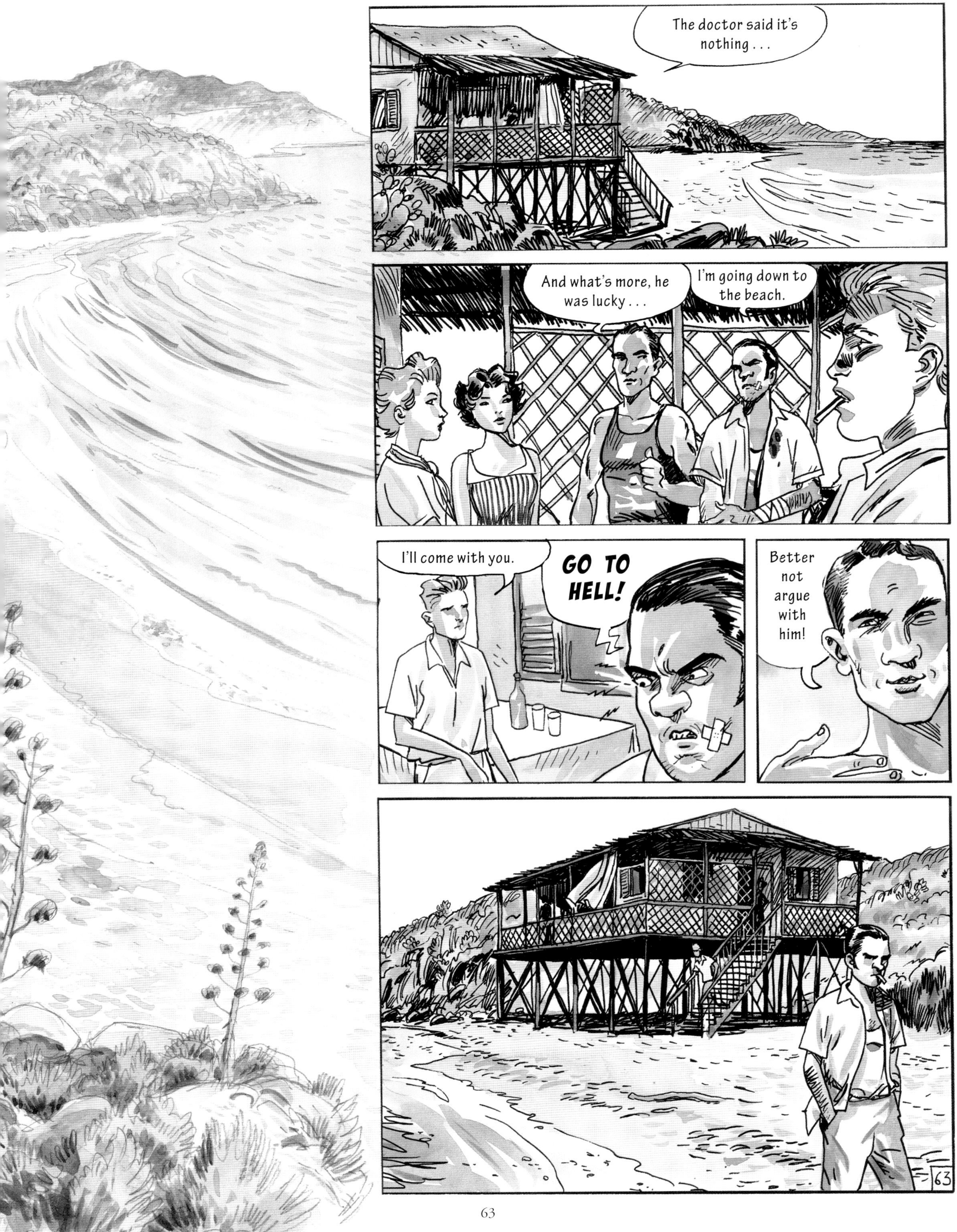
The doctor said it's nothing . . .
And what's more, he was lucky . . .
I'm going down to the beach.
I'll come with you.
GO TO HELL!
Better not argue with him!
63

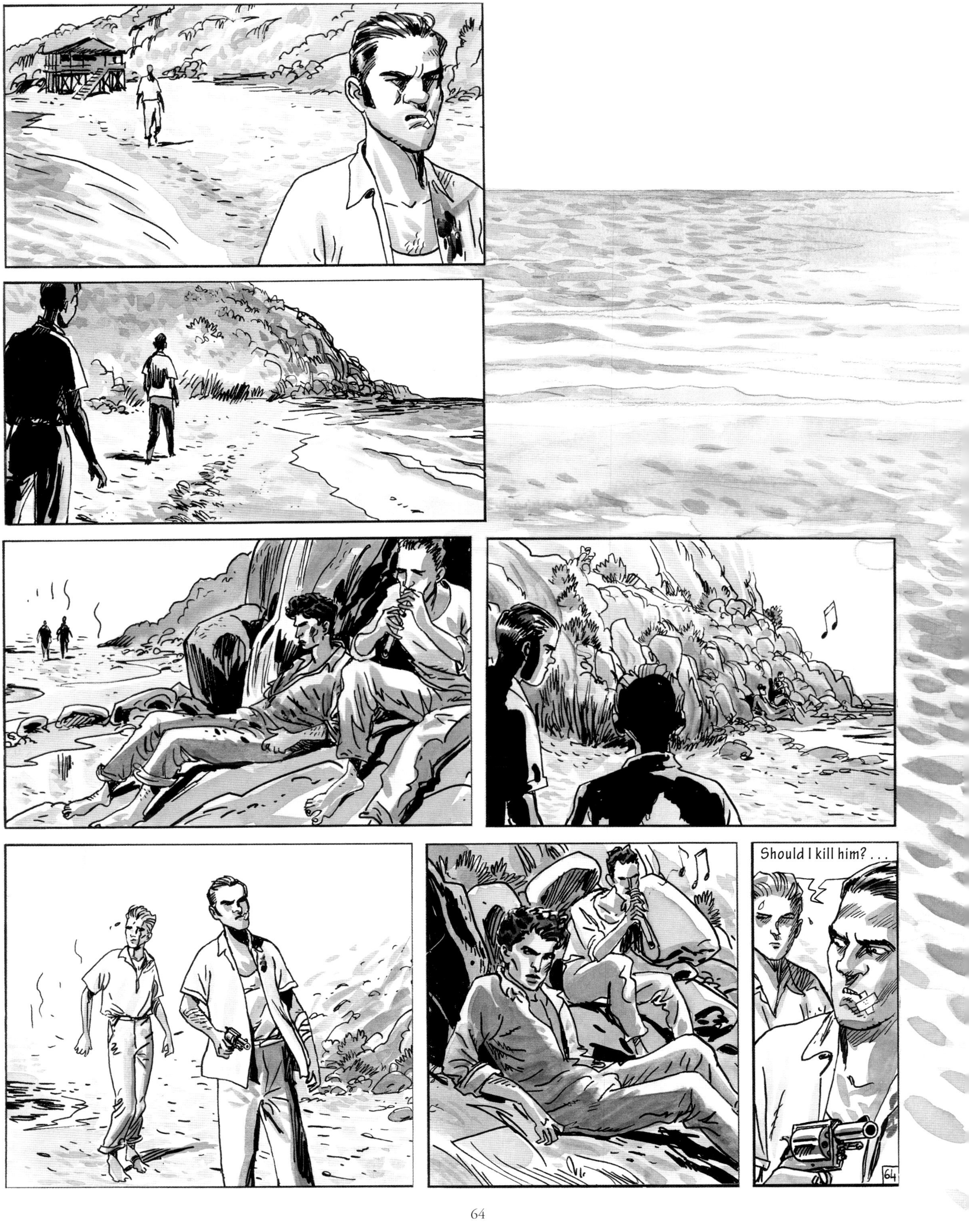
Should I kill him? . . .
64

He hasn't said anything to you yet. It wouldn't be right to just shoot him like that.

Then I'll curse at him and when he answers, I'll shoot him . . .

OK, but you can't shoot him unless he takes out his knife.

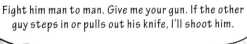

Fight him man to man. Give me your gun. If the other guy steps in or pulls out his knife, I'll shoot him.

You see how we scared the pants off them?!

65

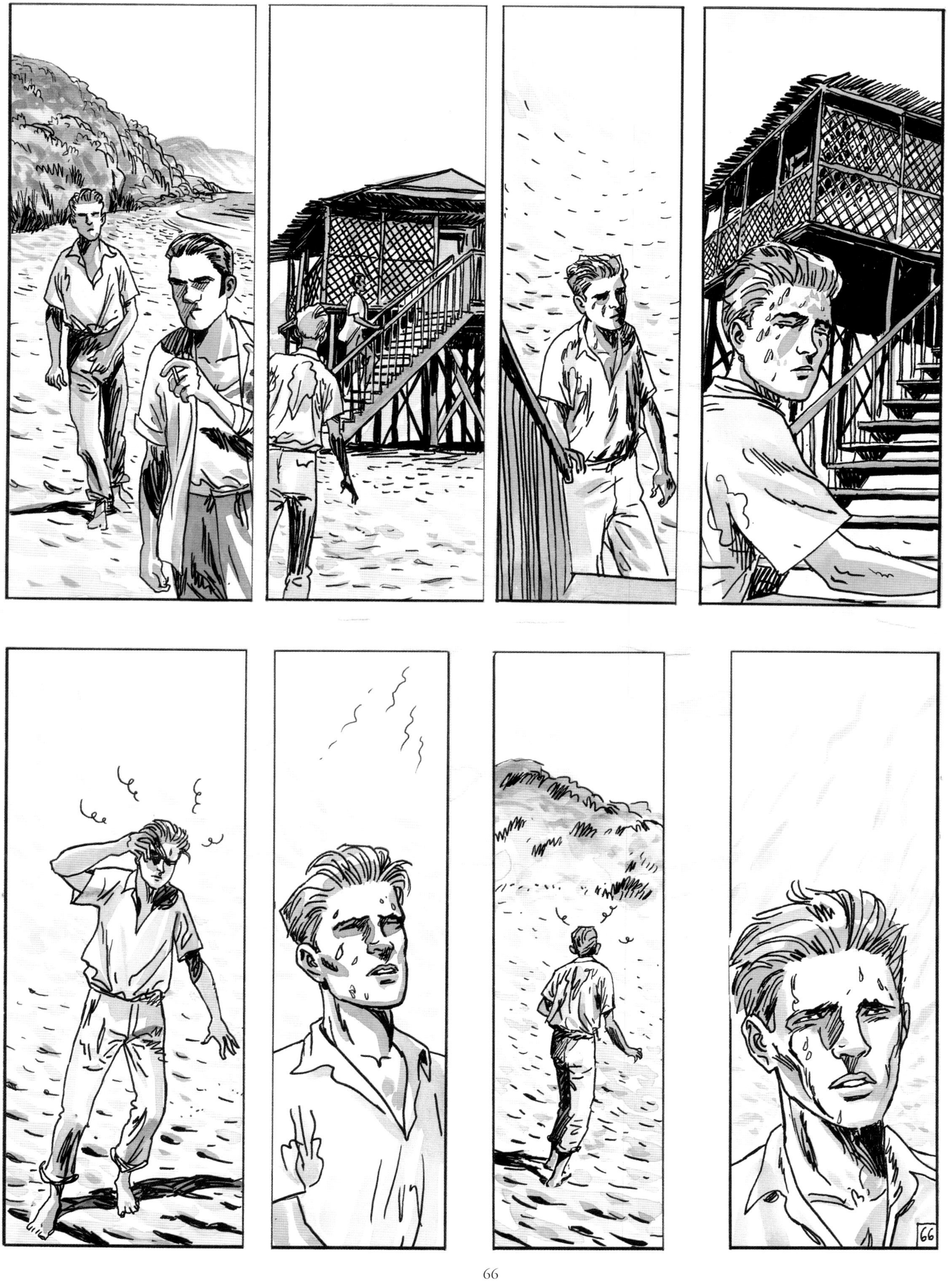
66

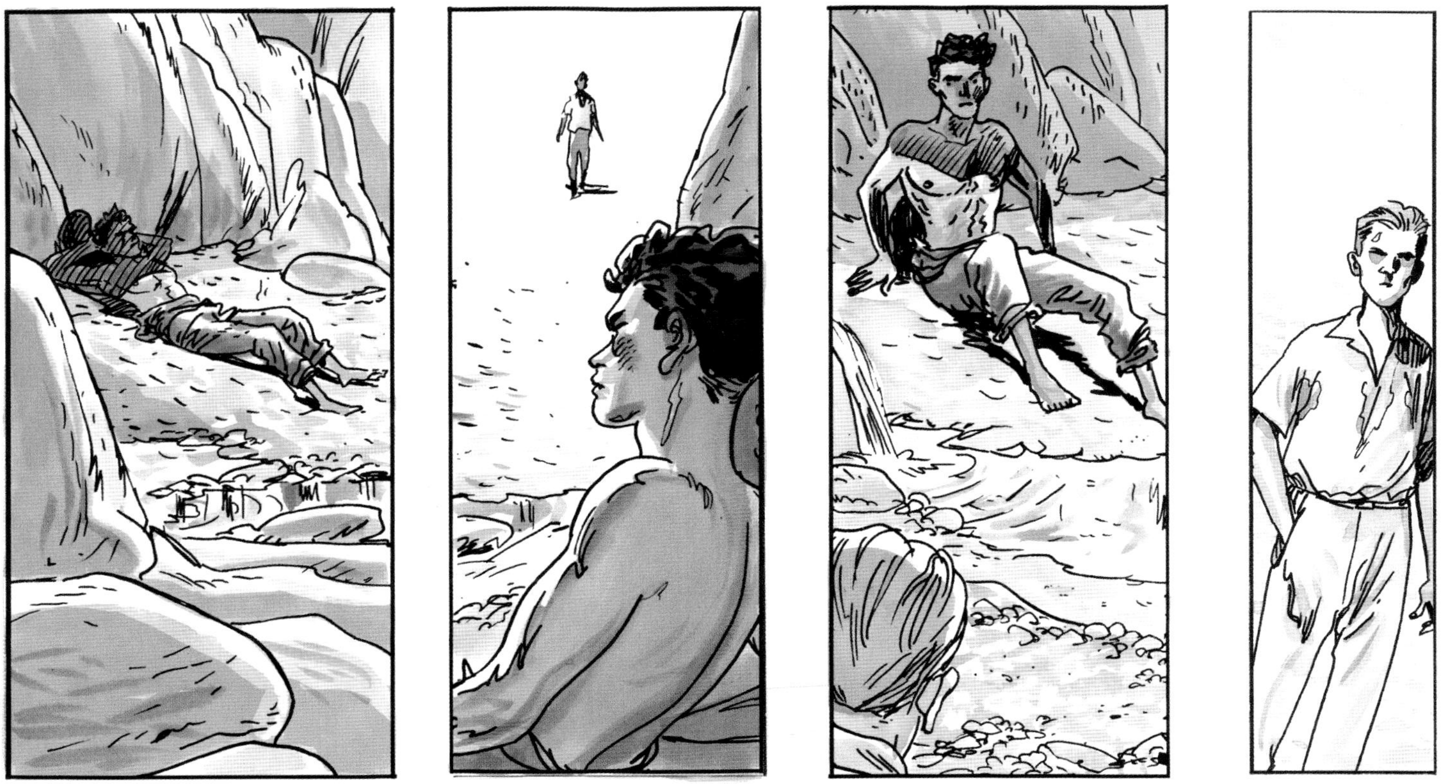

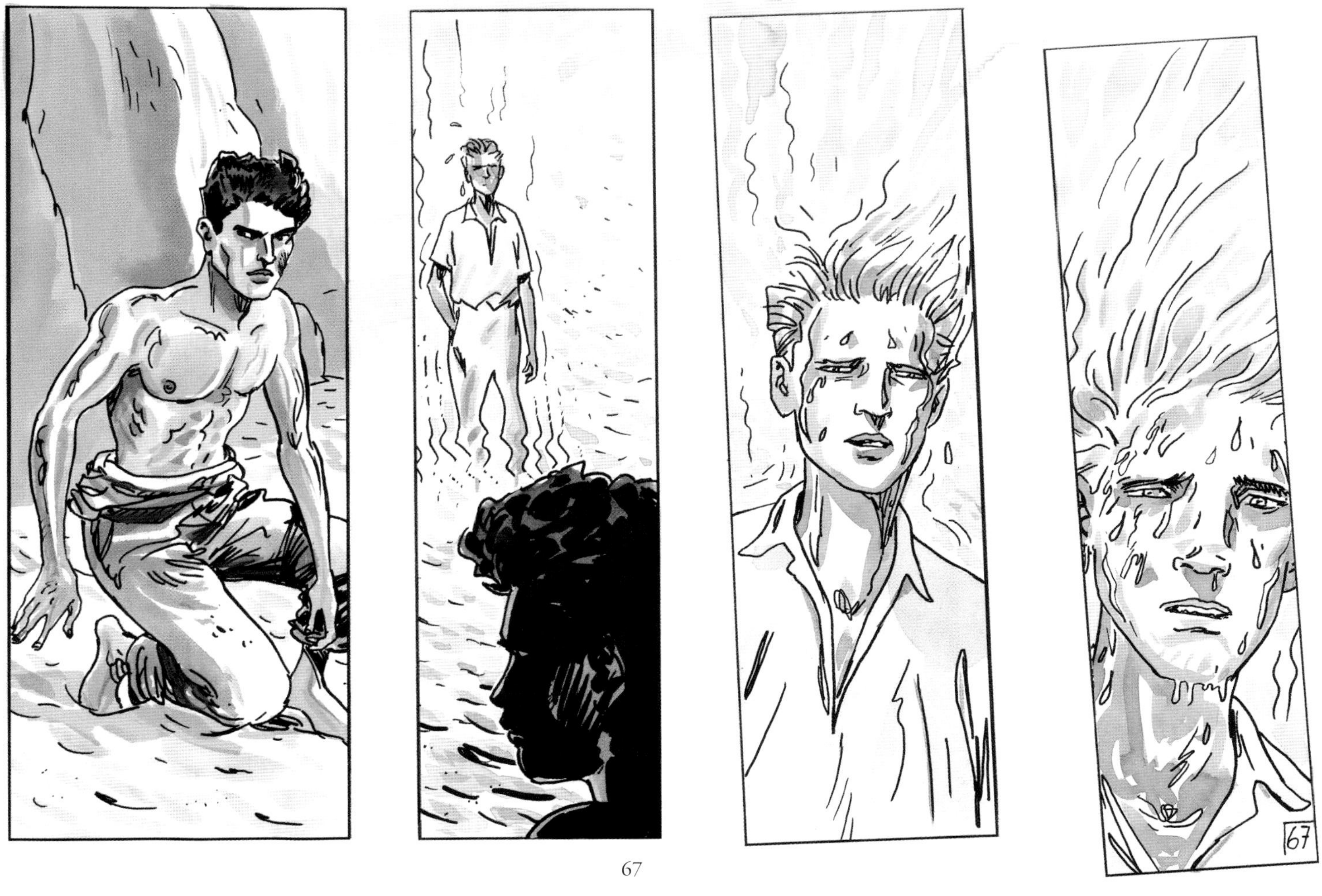
67

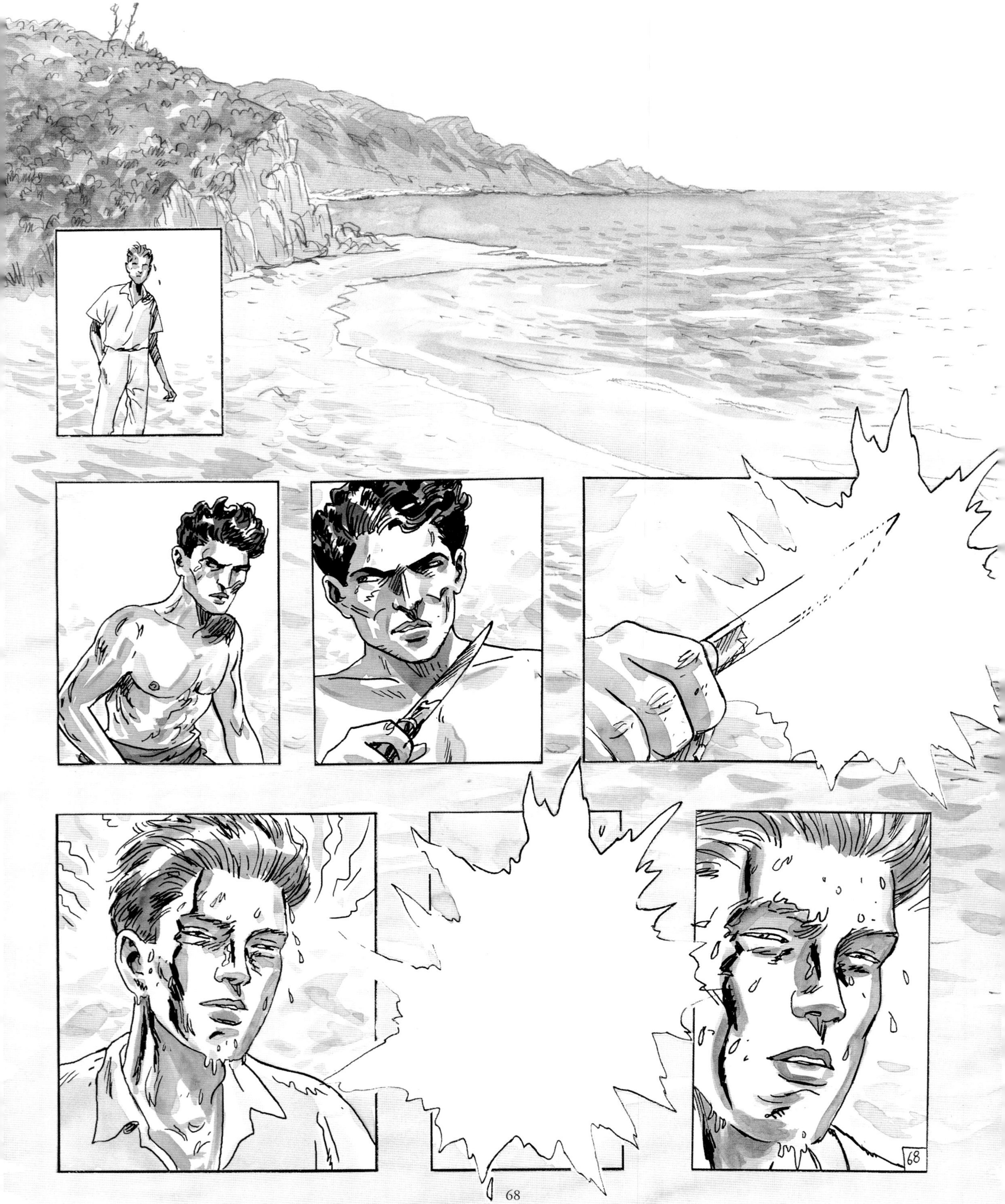

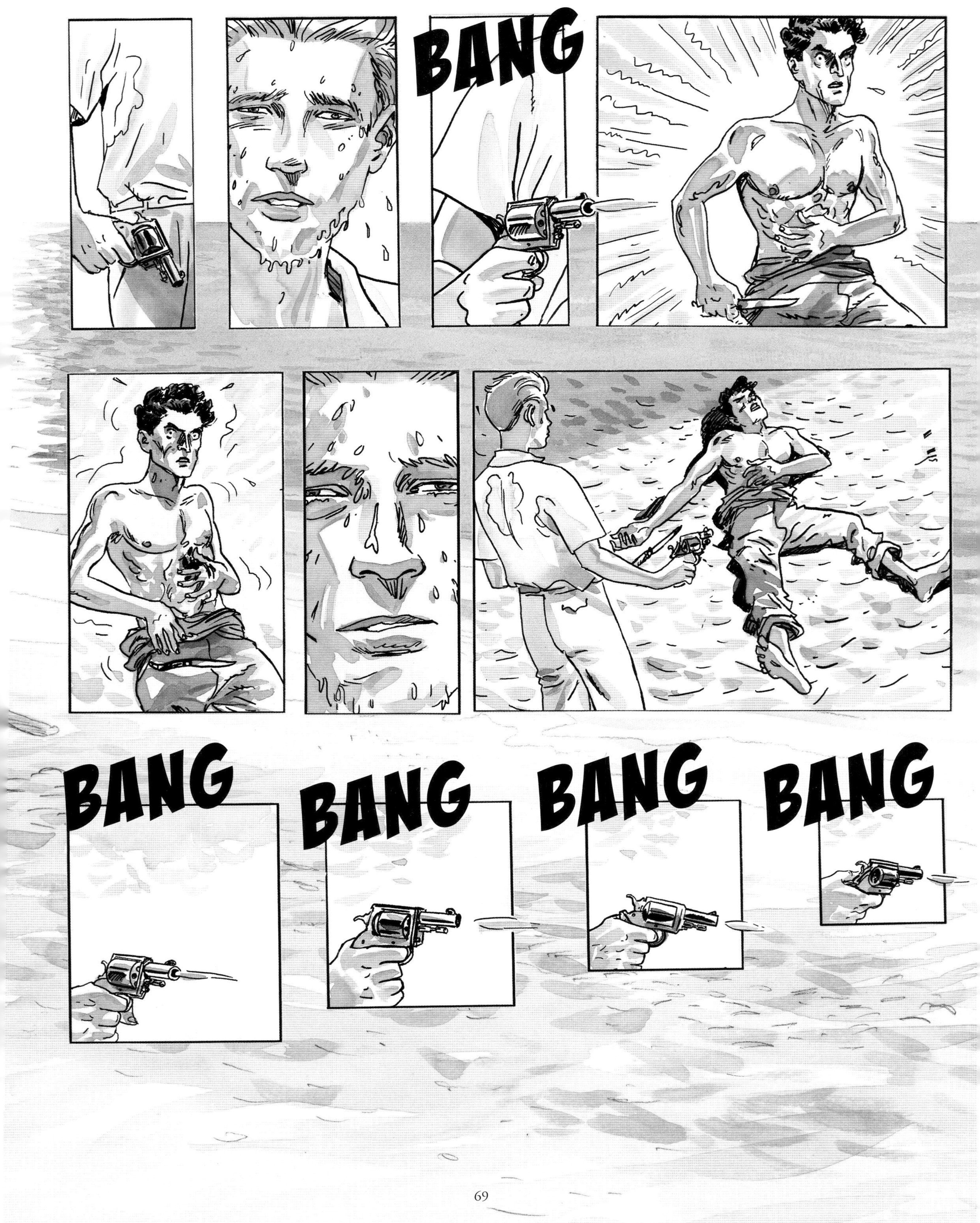
BANG
BANG
BANG
BANG
BANG

PART TWO

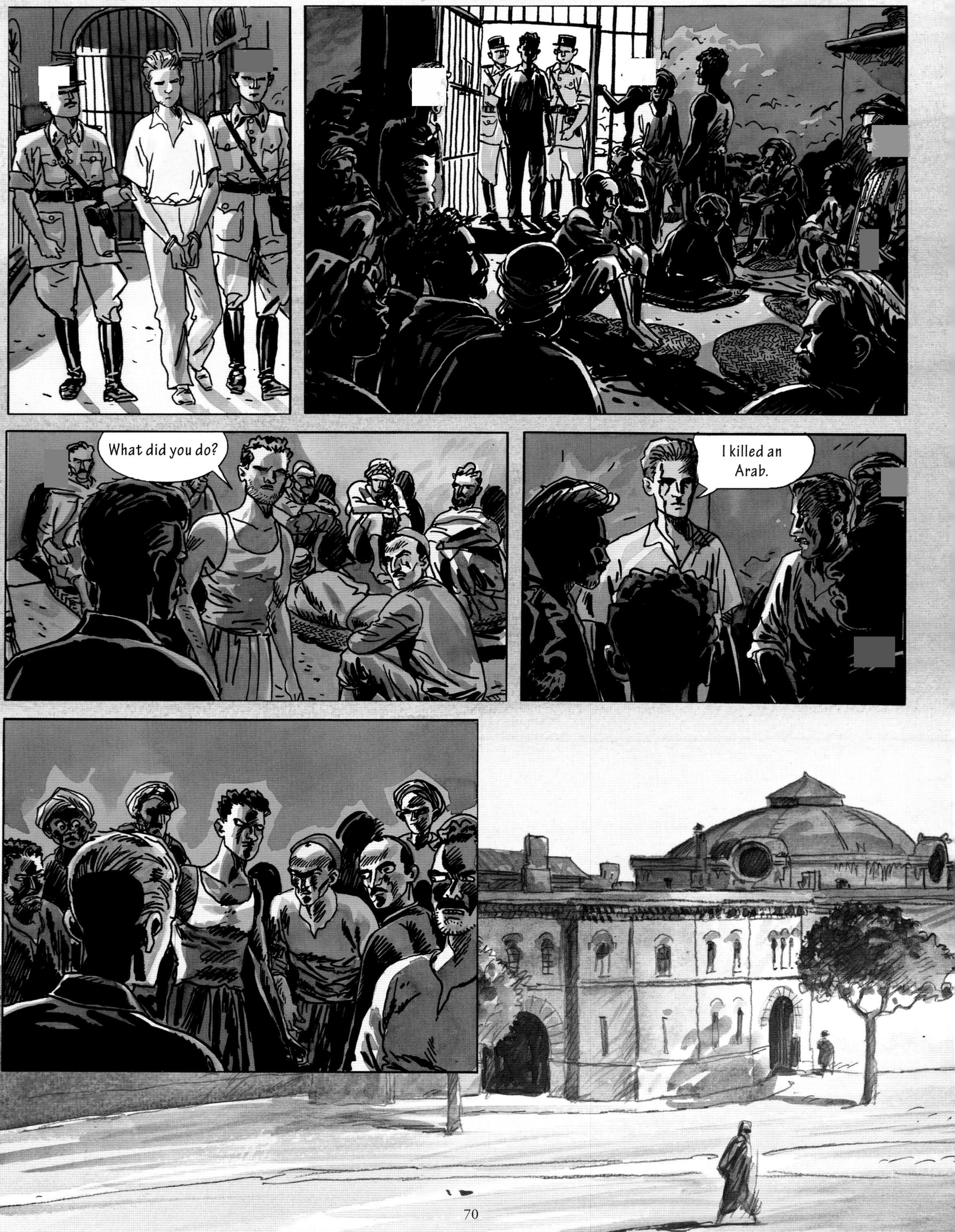
What did you do?
I killed an Arab.

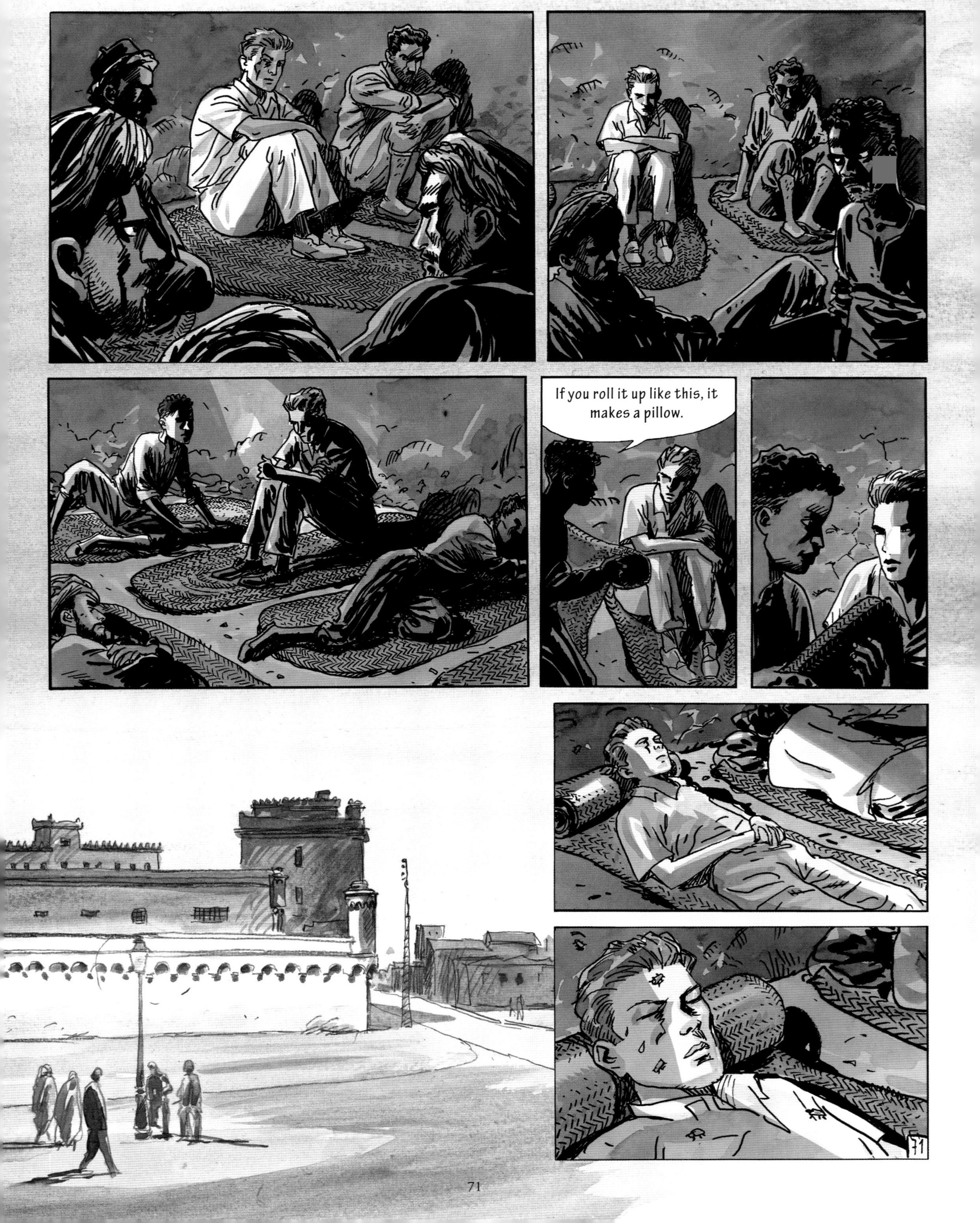
If you roll it up like this, it makes a pillow.

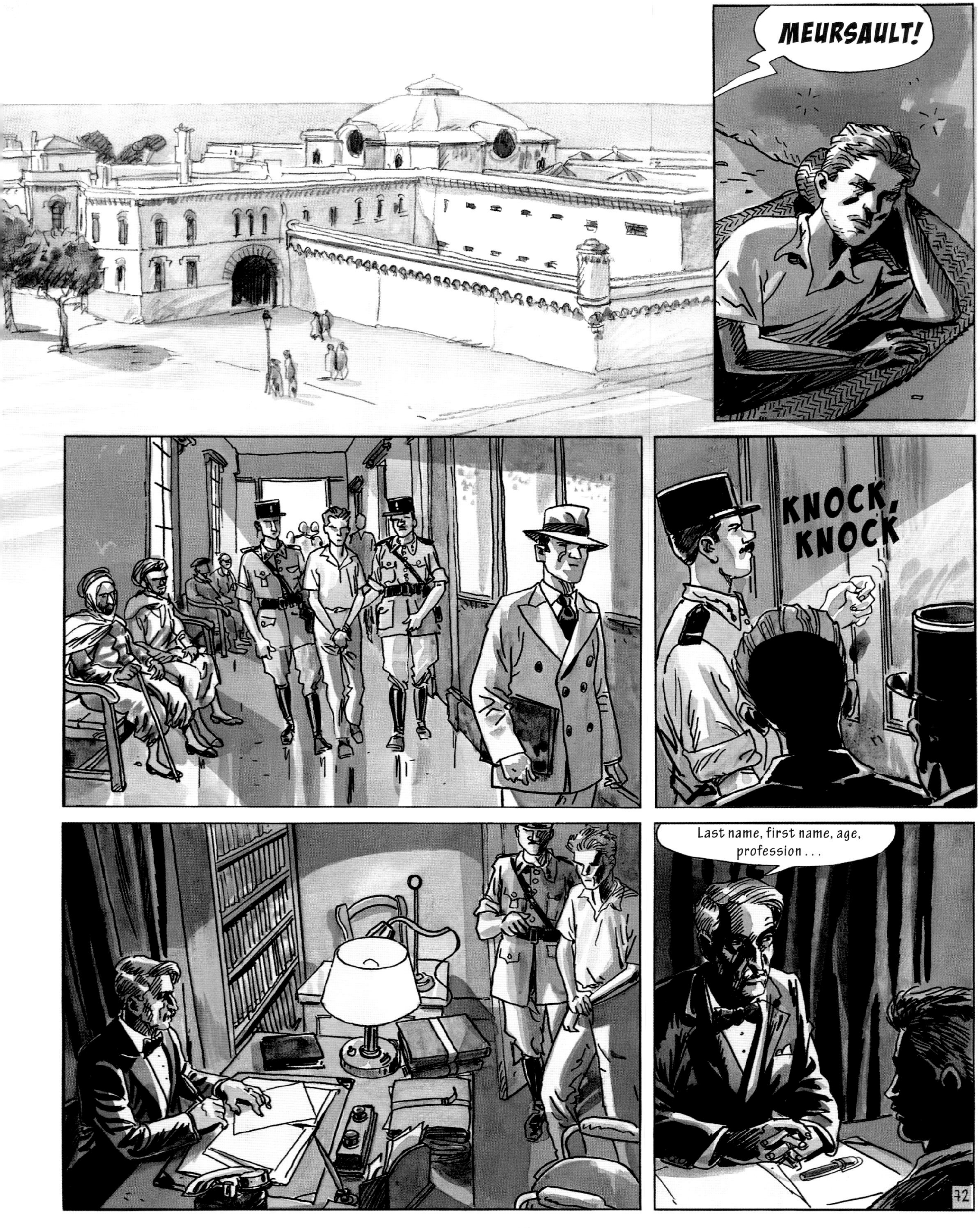
MEURSAULT!
KNOCK, KNOCK
Last name, first name, age, profession . . .
72

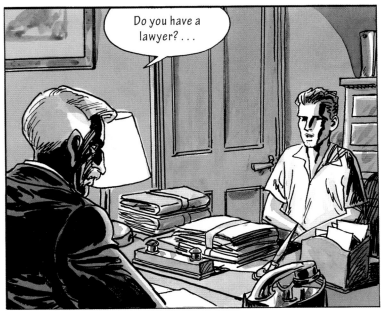

Do you have a lawyer? . . .

No. Do I really have to?

My case is very simple . . .

That's one way to look at it . . .

But it's the law. If you don't choose a lawyer, we'll assign you one . . .

It's very convenient that the legal system takes care of such details . . .

Yes, the law is well thought out . . .

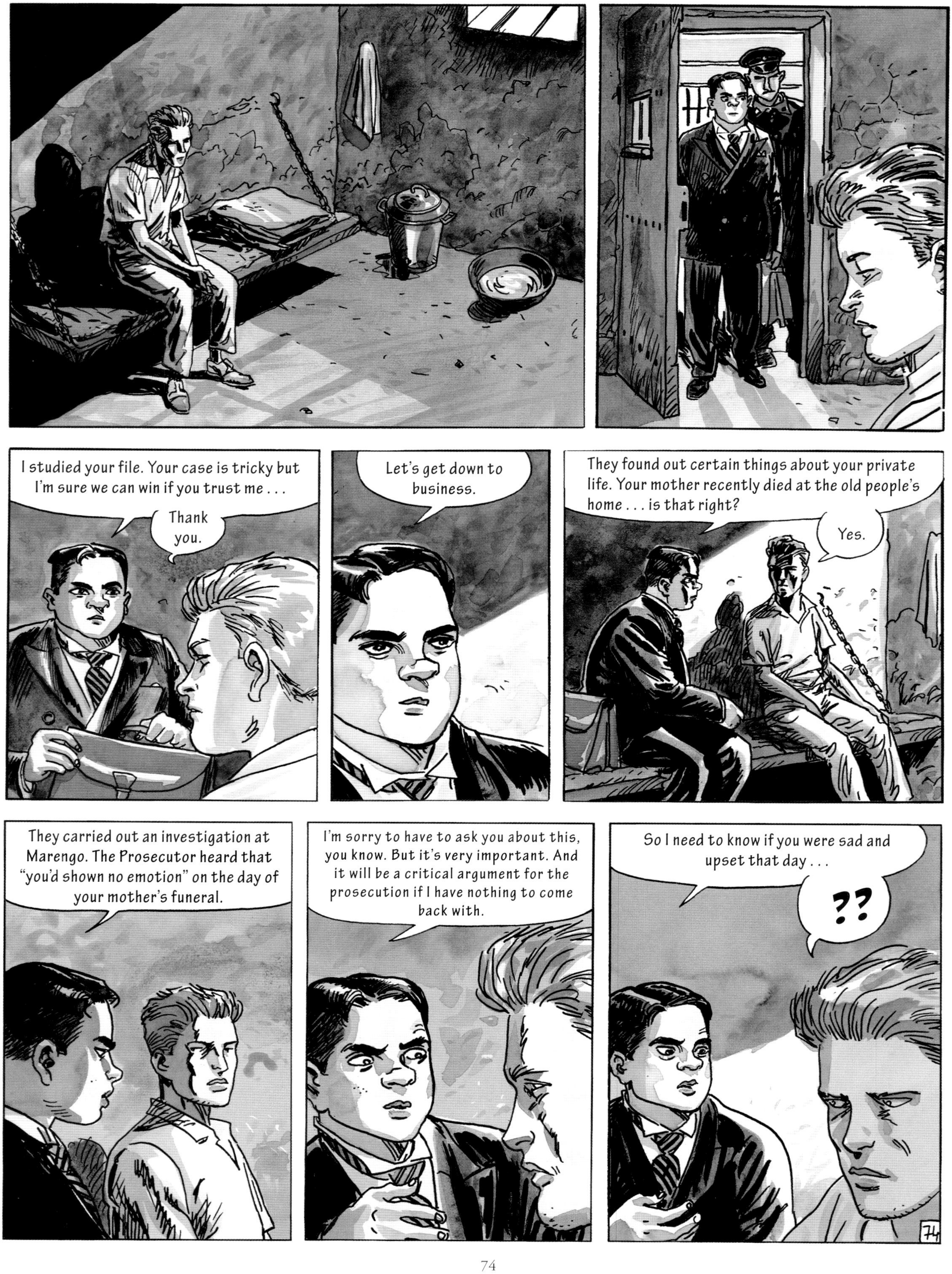
I studied your file. Your case is tricky but I'm sure we can win if you trust me . . .
Thank you.
Let's get down to business.
They found out certain things about your private life. Your mother recently died at the old people's home . . . is that right?
Yes.
They carried out an investigation at Marengo. The Prosecutor heard that "you'd shown no emotion" on the day of your mother's funeral.
I'm sorry to have to ask you about this, you know. But it's very important. And it will be a critical argument for the prosecution if I have nothing to come back with.
So I need to know if you were sad and upset that day . . .
??
74

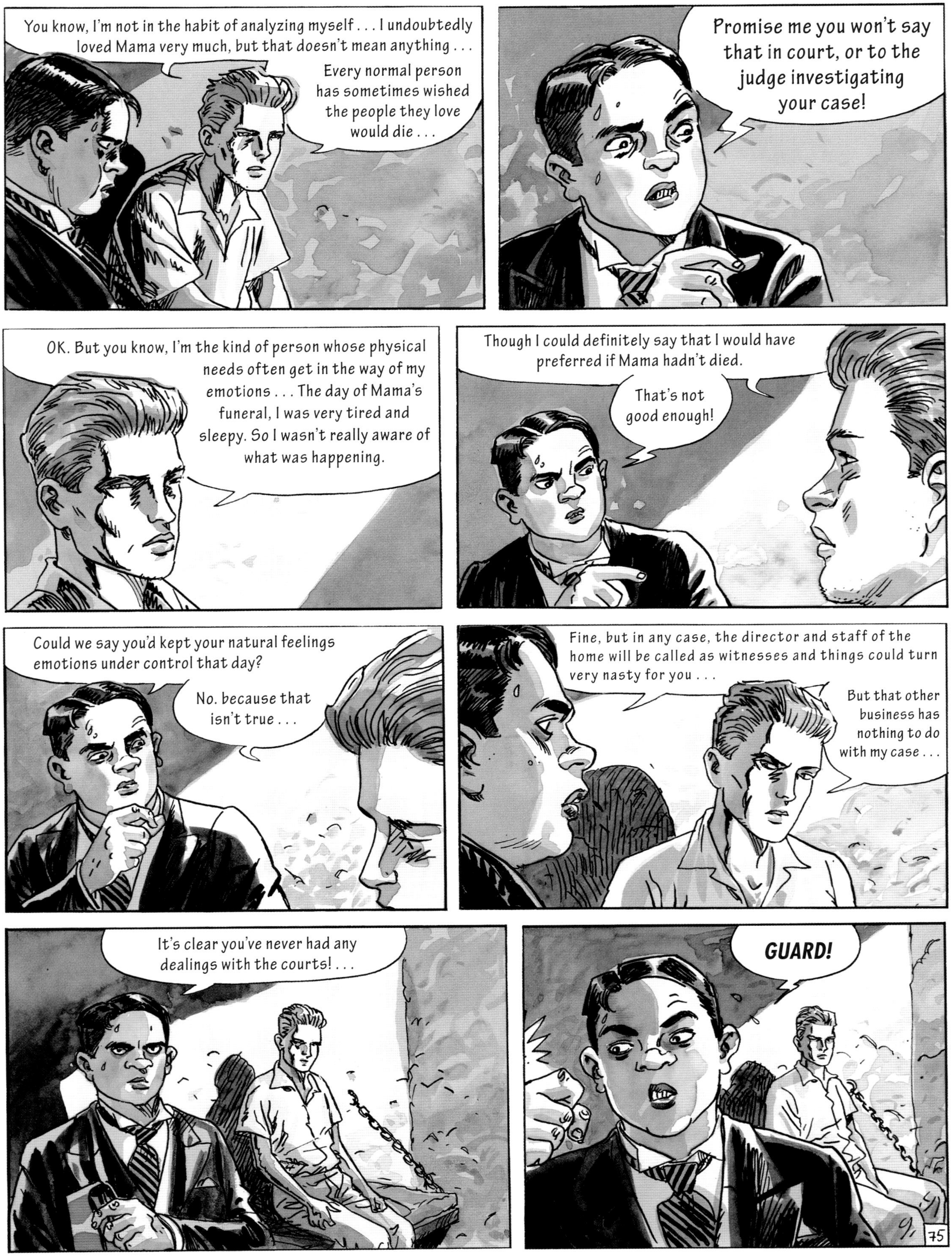
You know, I'm not in the habit of analyzing myself . . . I undoubtedly loved Mama very much, but that doesn't mean anything . . .
Every normal person has sometimes wished the people they love would die . . .
Promise me you won't say that in court, or to the judge investigating your case!
OK. But you know, I'm the kind of person whose physical needs often get in the way of my emotions . . . The day of Mama's funeral, I was very tired and sleepy. So I wasn't really aware of what was happening.
Though I could definitely say that I would have preferred if Mama hadn't died.
That's not good enough!
Could we say you'd kept your natural feelings emotions under control that day?
No. because that isn't true . . .
Fine, but in any case, the director and staff of the home will be called as witnesses and things could turn very nasty for you . . .
But that other business has nothing to do with my case . . .
It's clear you've never had any dealings with the courts! . . .
GUARD!
75

Your lawyer can't be here due to unforeseen circumstances . . .

You have the right to refuse to answer my questions and to wait to have your lawyer to help you. I can answer by myself.

Good, you've been described as taciturn and uncommunicative. What do you think about that?

Well, I don't have much to say, so I keep quiet.

That's the best reason . . .

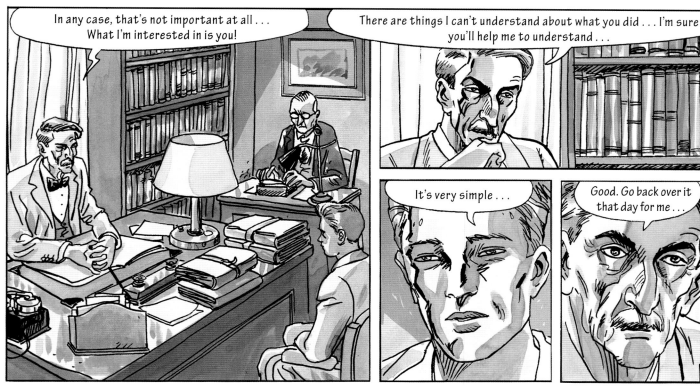

In any case, that's not important at all . . . What I'm interested in is you!

There are things I can't understand about what you did . . . I'm sure you'll help me to understand . . .

It's very simple . . .

Good. Go back over it that day for me . . .

76

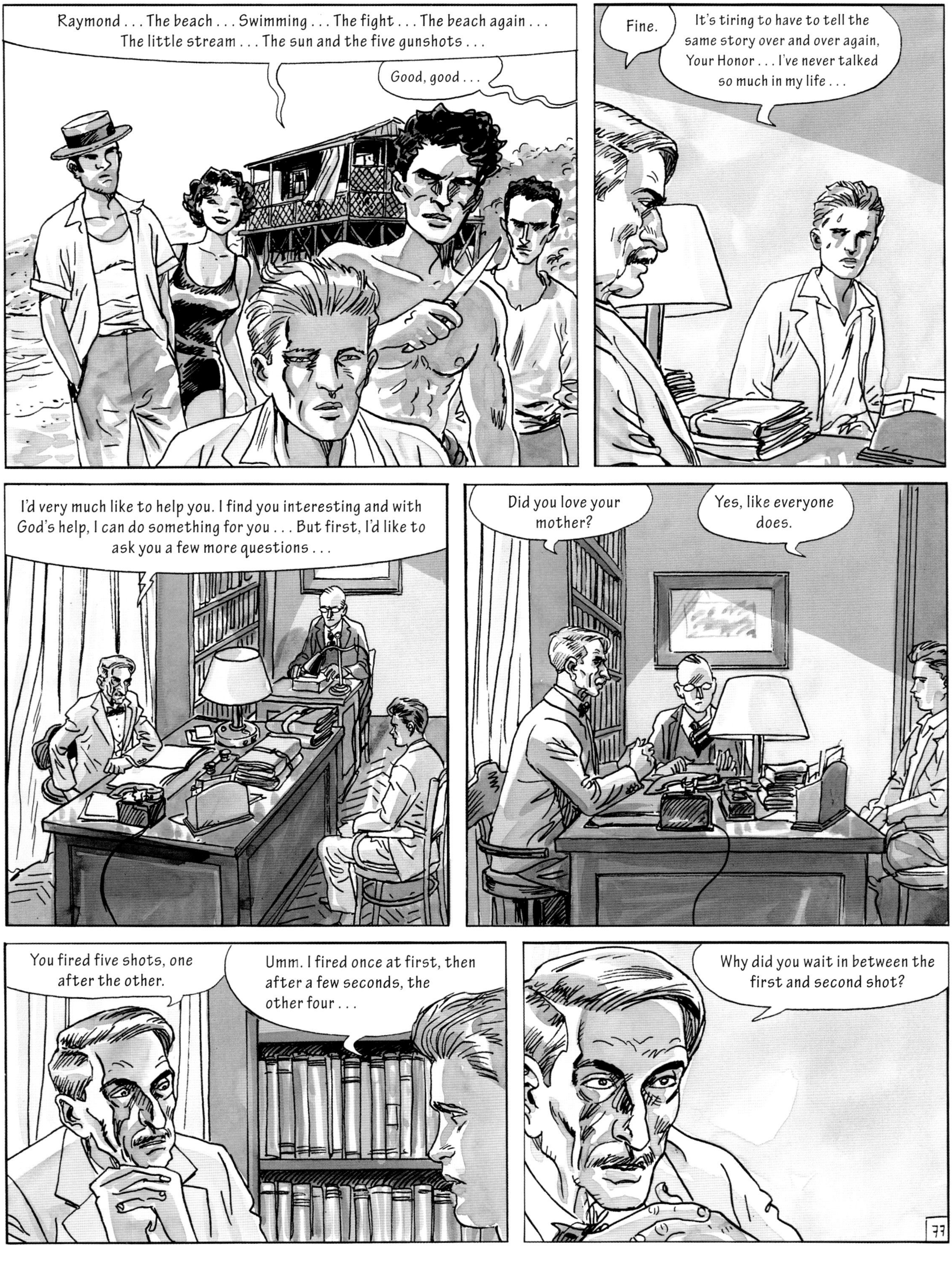
Raymond . . . The beach . . . Swimming . . . The fight . . . The beach again . . . The little stream . . . The sun and the five gunshots . . .
Good, good . . .
Fine.
It's tiring to have to tell the same story over and over again, Your Honor . . . I've never talked so much in my life . . .
I'd very much like to help you. I find you interesting and with God's help, I can do something for you . . . But first, I'd like to ask you a few more questions . . .
Did you love your mother?
Yes, like everyone does.
You fired five shots, one after the other.
Umm. I fired once at first, then after a few seconds, the other four . . .
Why did you wait in between the first and second shot?
77

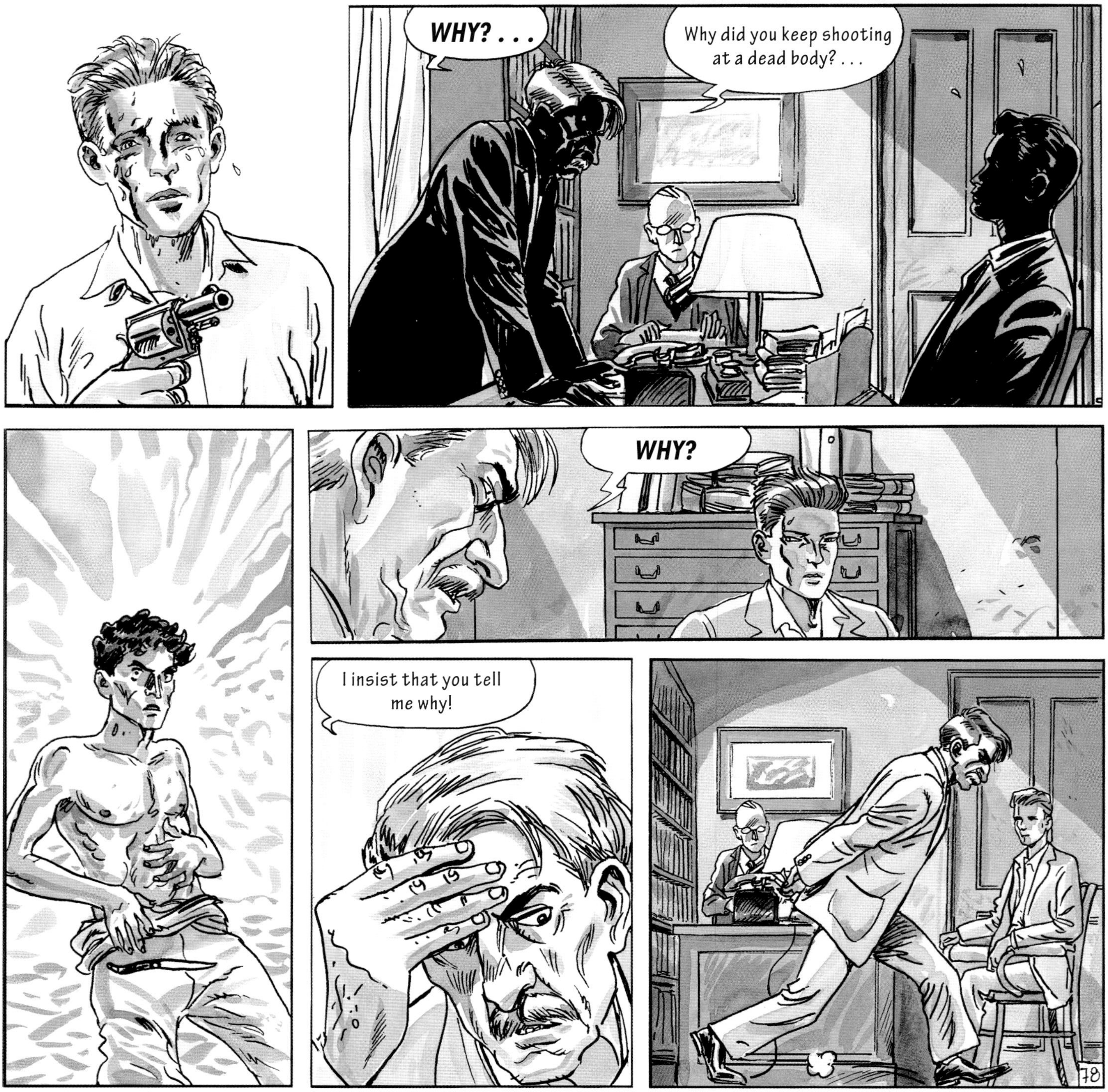
WHY? . . .
Why did you keep shooting at a dead body? . . .
WHY?
I insist that you tell me why!
78

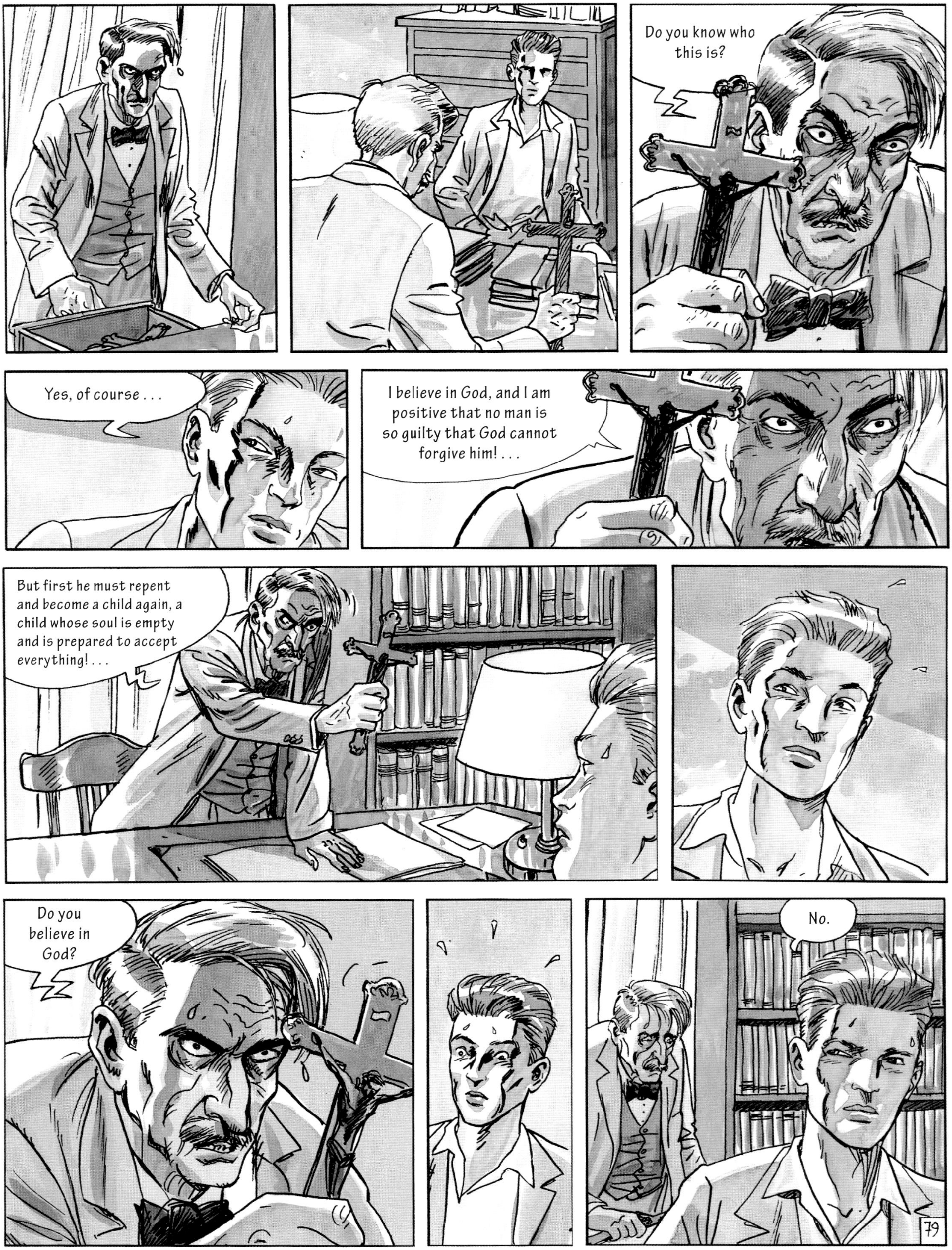
Do you know who this is?
Yes, of course . . .
I believe in God, and I am positive that no man is so guilty that God cannot forgive him! . . .
But first he must repent and become a child again, a child whose soul is empty and is prepared to accept everything! . . .
Do you believe in God?
No.
79

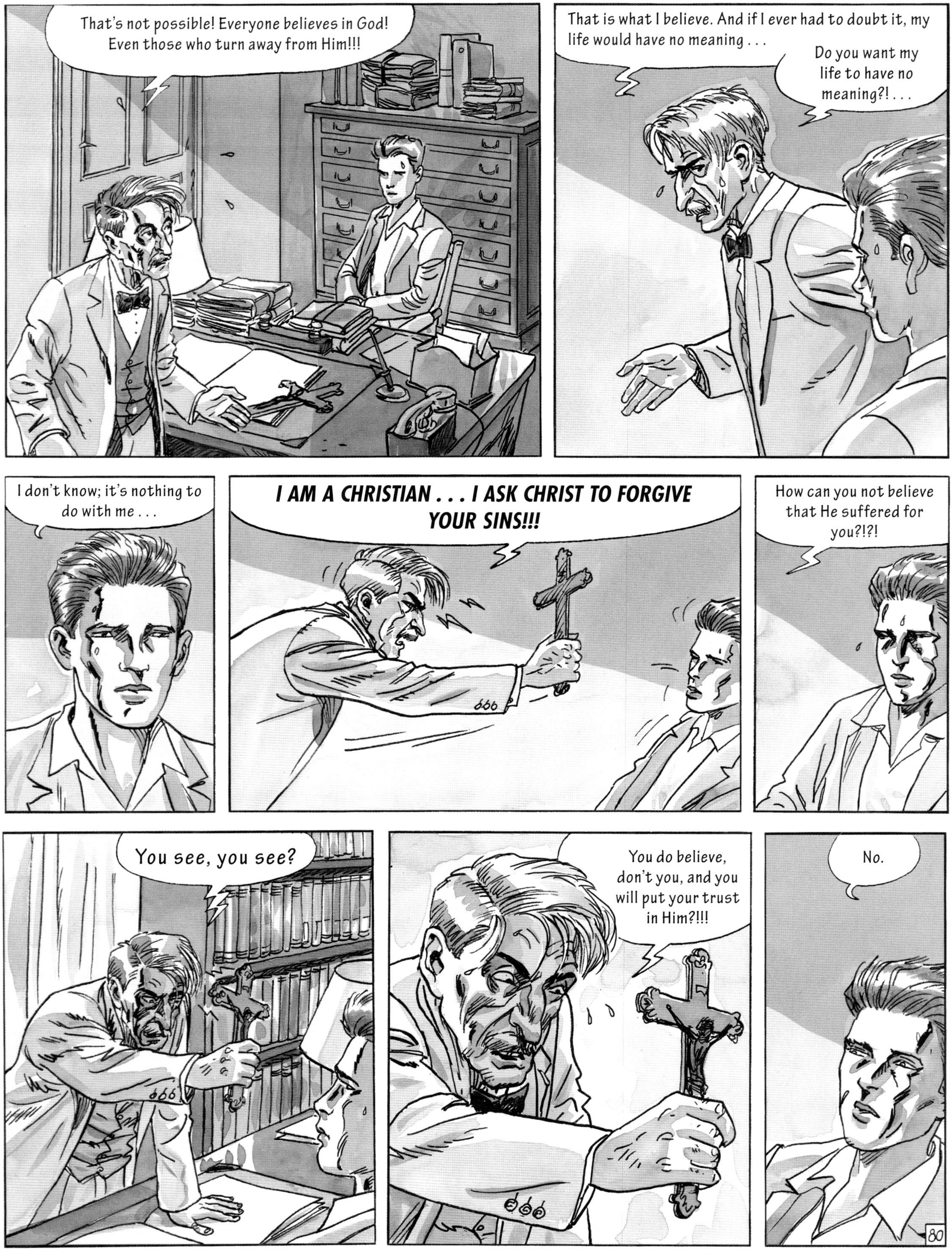
That's not possible! Everyone believes in God! Even those who turn away from Him!!!
That is what I believe. And if I ever had to doubt it, my life would have no meaning . . .
Do you want my life to have no meaning?! . . .
I don't know; it's nothing to do with me . . .
I AM A CHRISTIAN . . . I ASK CHRIST TO FORGIVE YOUR SINS!!!
How can you not believe that He suffered for you?!?!
You see, you see?
You do believe, don't you, and you will put your trust in Him?!!!
No.
80

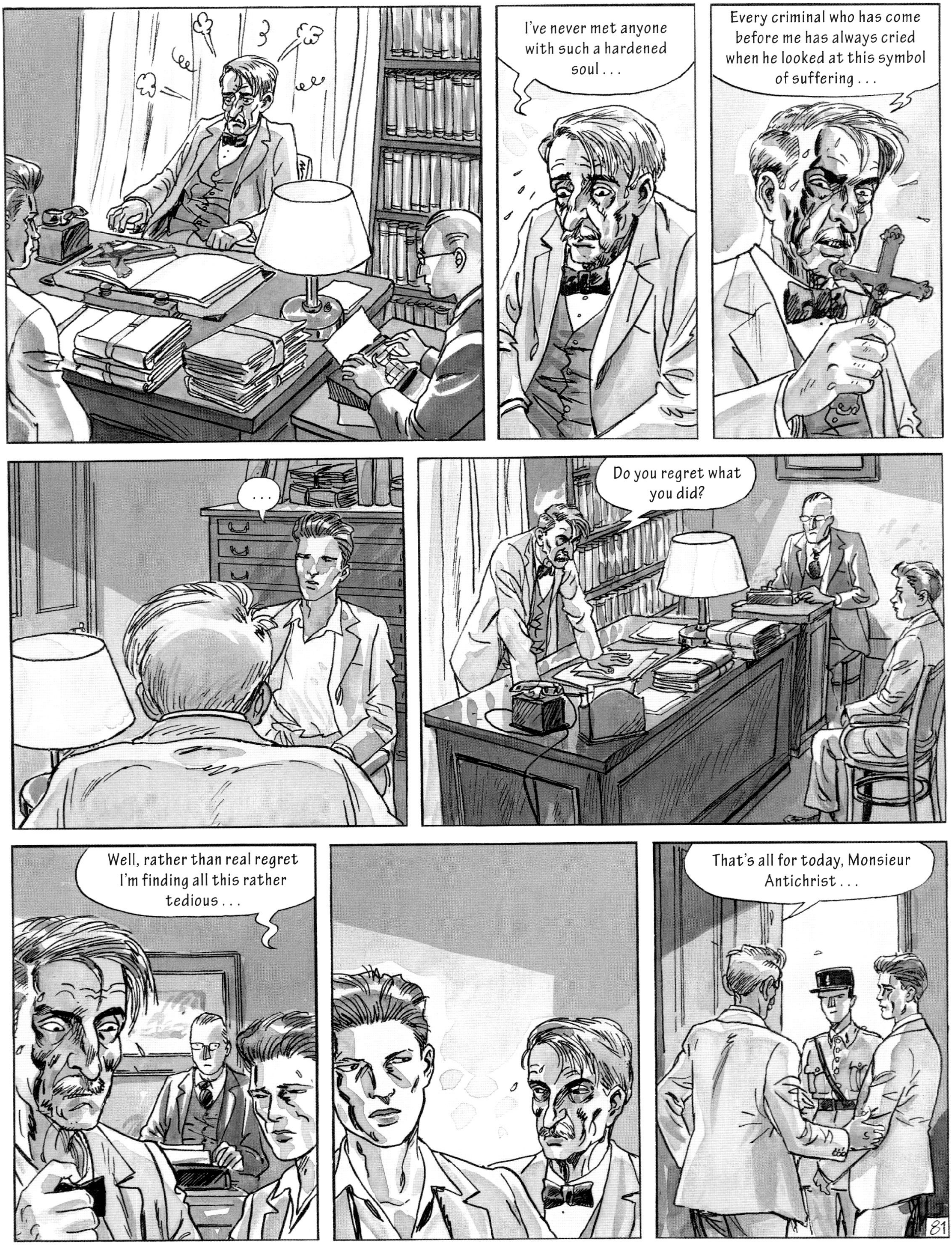

I've never met anyone with such a hardened soul . . .
Every criminal who has come before me has always cried when he looked at this symbol of suffering . . .
. . .
Do you regret what you did?
Well, rather than real regret I'm finding all this rather tedious . . .
That's all for today, Monsieur Antichrist . . .
81

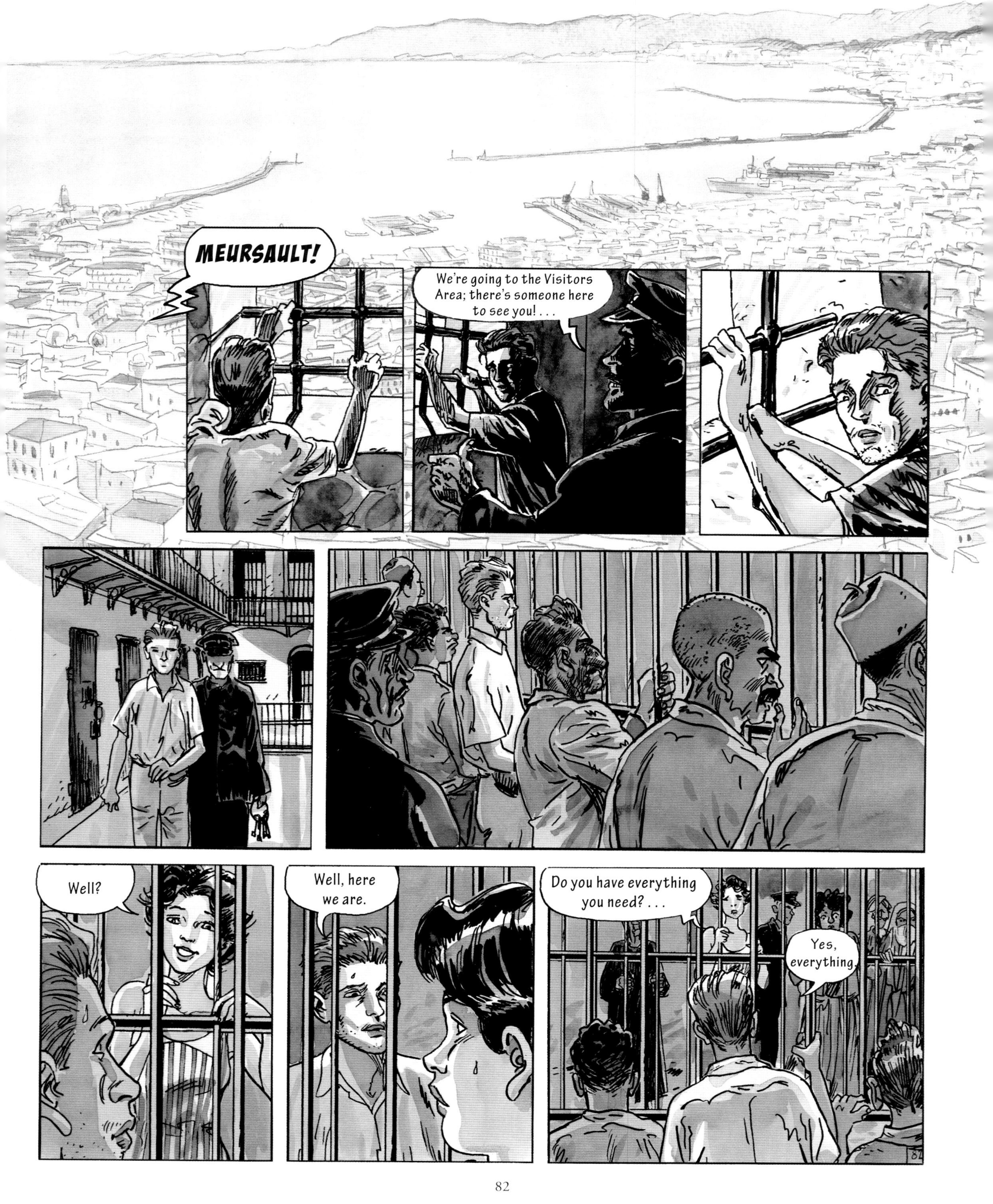
MEURSAULT!
We're going to the Visitors Area; there's someone here to see you! . . .
Well?
Well, here we are.
Do you have everything you need? . . .
Yes, everything.

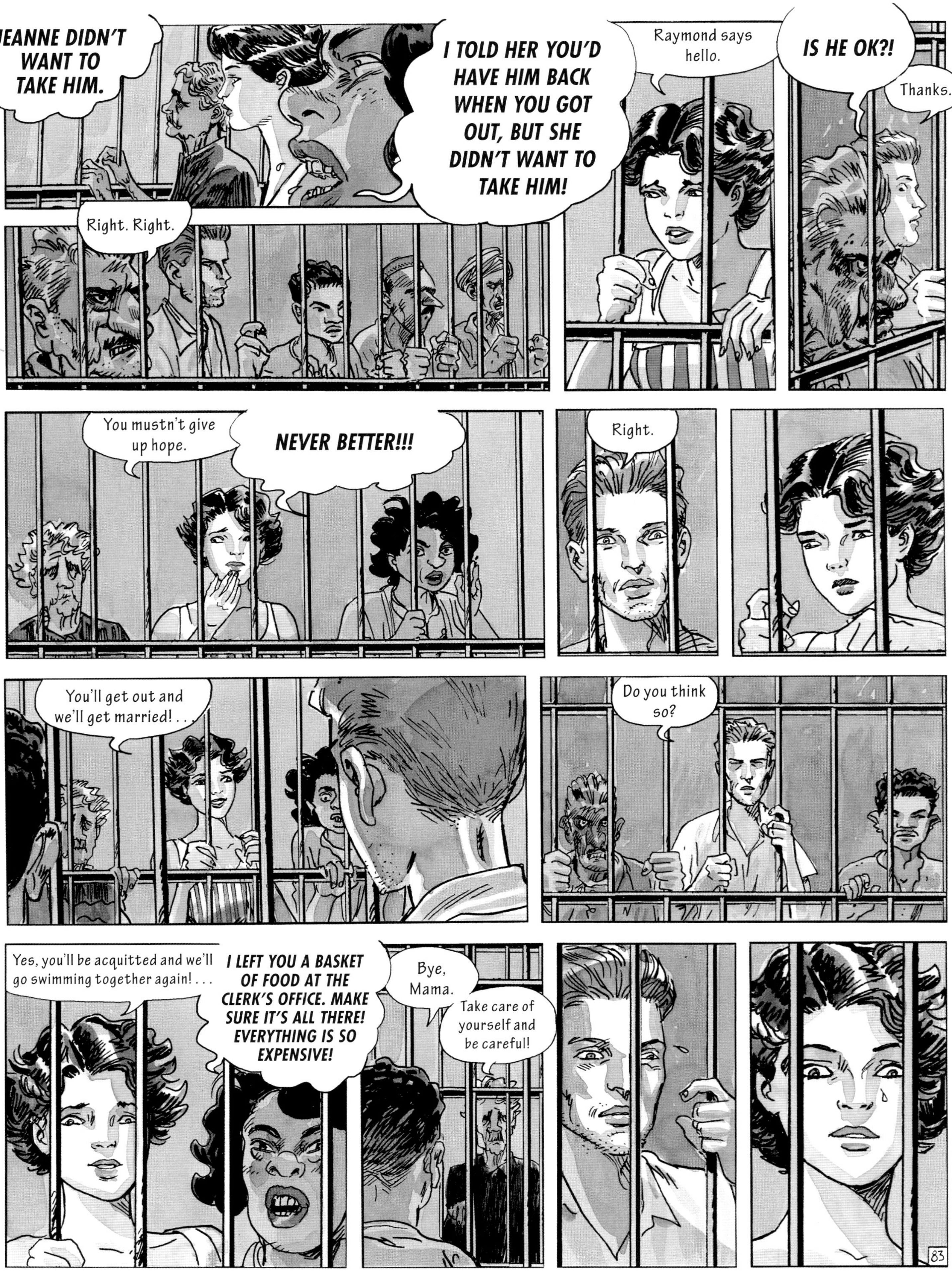
JEANNE DIDN'T WANT TO TAKE HIM.
I TOLD HER YOU'D HAVE HIM BACK WHEN YOU GOT OUT, BUT SHE DIDN'T WANT TO TAKE HIM!
Raymond says hello.
IS HE OK?!
Thanks.
Right. Right.
You mustn't give up hope.
NEVER BETTER!!!
Right.
You'll get out and we'll get married! . . .
Do you think so?
Yes, you'll be acquitted and we'll go swimming together again! . . .
I LEFT YOU A BASKET OF FOOD AT THE CLERK'S OFFICE. MAKE SURE IT'S ALL THERE! EVERYTHING IS SO EXPENSIVE!
Bye, Mama.
Take care of yourself and be careful!
83

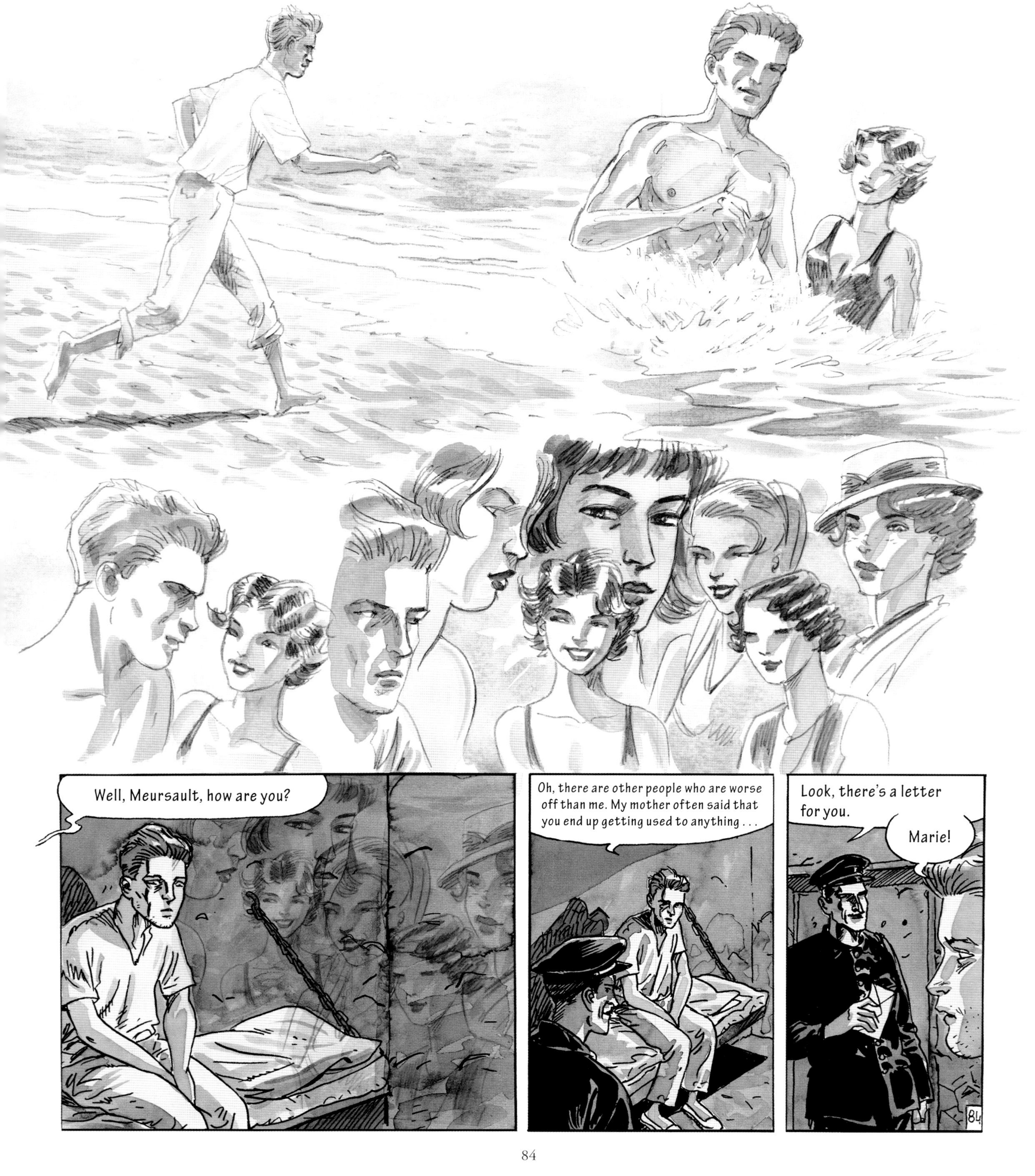
Well, Meursault, how are you?
Oh, there are other people who are worse off than me. My mother often said that you end up getting used to anything . . .
Look, there's a letter for you.
Marie!
84

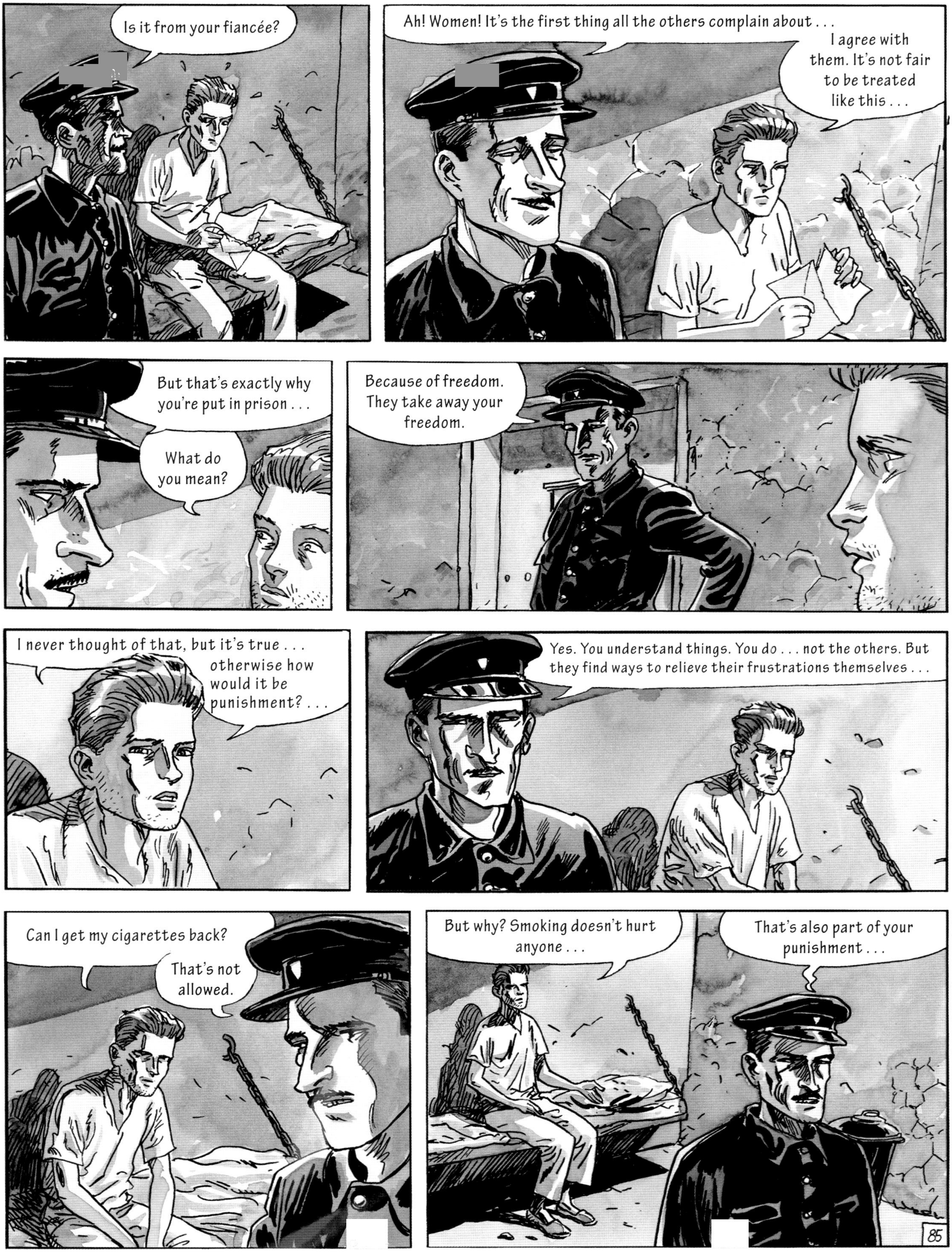
Is it from your fiancée?
Ah! Women! It's the first thing all the others complain about . . .
I agree with them. It's not fair to be treated like this . . .
But that's exactly why you're put in prison . . .
What do you mean?
Because of freedom. They take away your freedom.
I never thought of that, but it's true . . . otherwise how would it be punishment? . . .
Yes. You understand things. You do . . . not the others. But they find ways to relieve their frustrations themselves . . .
Can I get my cigarettes back?
That's not allowed.
But why? Smoking doesn't hurt anyone . . .
That's also part of your punishment . . .
85

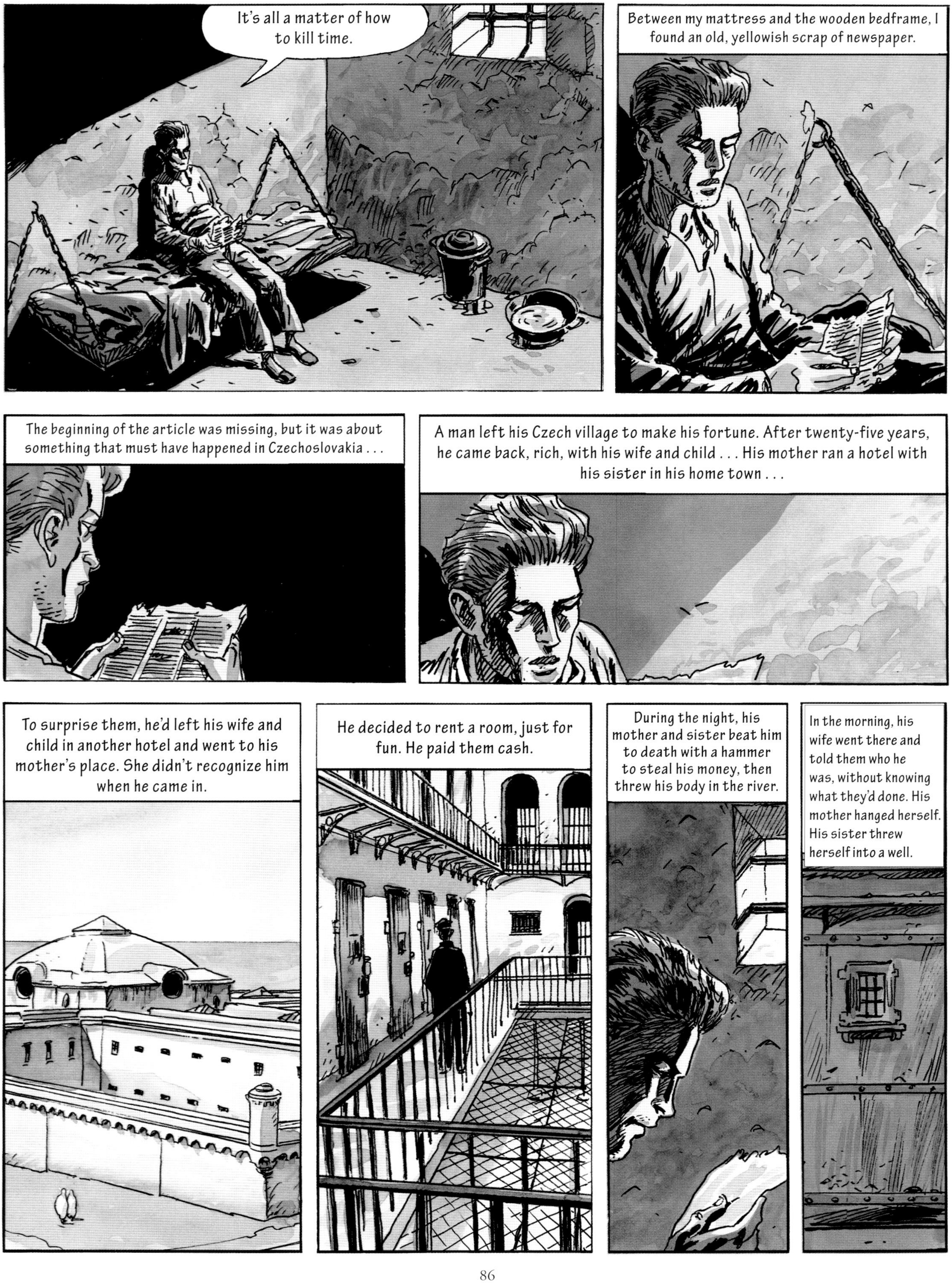
It's all a matter of how to kill time.
Between my mattress and the wooden bedframe, I found an old, yellowish scrap of newspaper.
The beginning of the article was missing, but it was about something that must have happened in Czechoslovakia . . .
A man left his Czech village to make his fortune. After twenty-five years, he came back, rich, with his wife and child . . . His mother ran a hotel with his sister in his home town . . .
To surprise them, he'd left his wife and child in another hotel and went to his mother's place. She didn't recognize him when he came in.
He decided to rent a room, just for fun. He paid them cash.
During the night, his mother and sister beat him to death with a hammer to steal his money, then threw his body in the river.
In the morning, his wife went there and told them who he was, without knowing what they'd done. His mother hanged herself. His sister threw herself into a well.

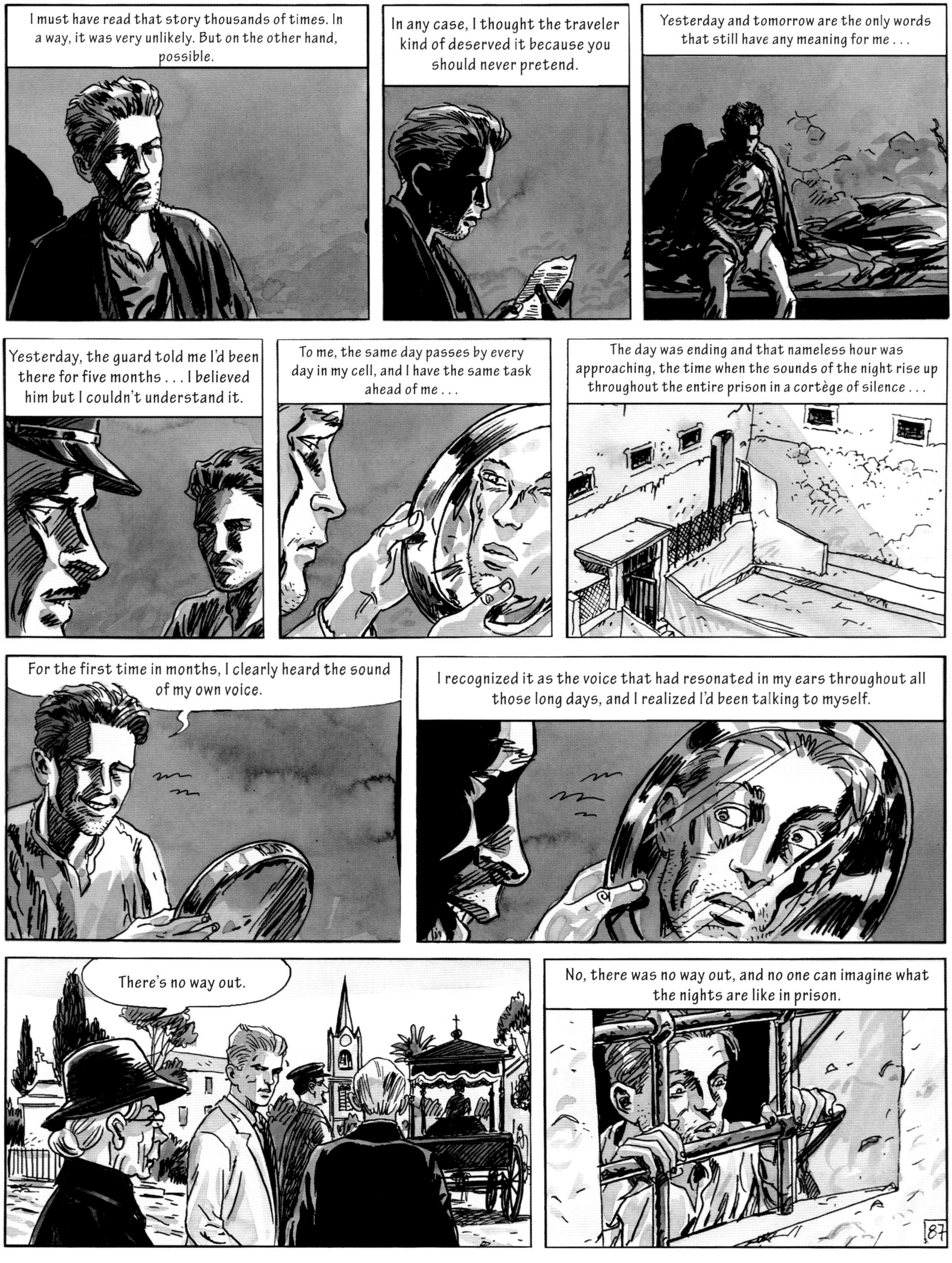
I must have read that story thousands of times. In a way, it was very unlikely. But on the other hand, possible.
In any case, I thought the traveler kind of deserved it because you should never pretend.
Yesterday and tomorrow are the only words that still have any meaning for me . . .
Yesterday, the guard told me I'd been there for five months . . . I believed him but I couldn't understand it.
To me, the same day passes by every day in my cell, and I have the same task ahead of me . . .
The day was ending and that nameless hour was approaching, the time when the sounds of the night rise up throughout the entire prison in a cortège of silence . . .
For the first time in months, I clearly heard the sound of my own voice.
I recognized it as the voice that had resonated in my ears throughout all those long days, and I realized I'd been talking to myself.
There's no way out.
No, there was no way out, and no one can imagine what the nights are like in prison.
87

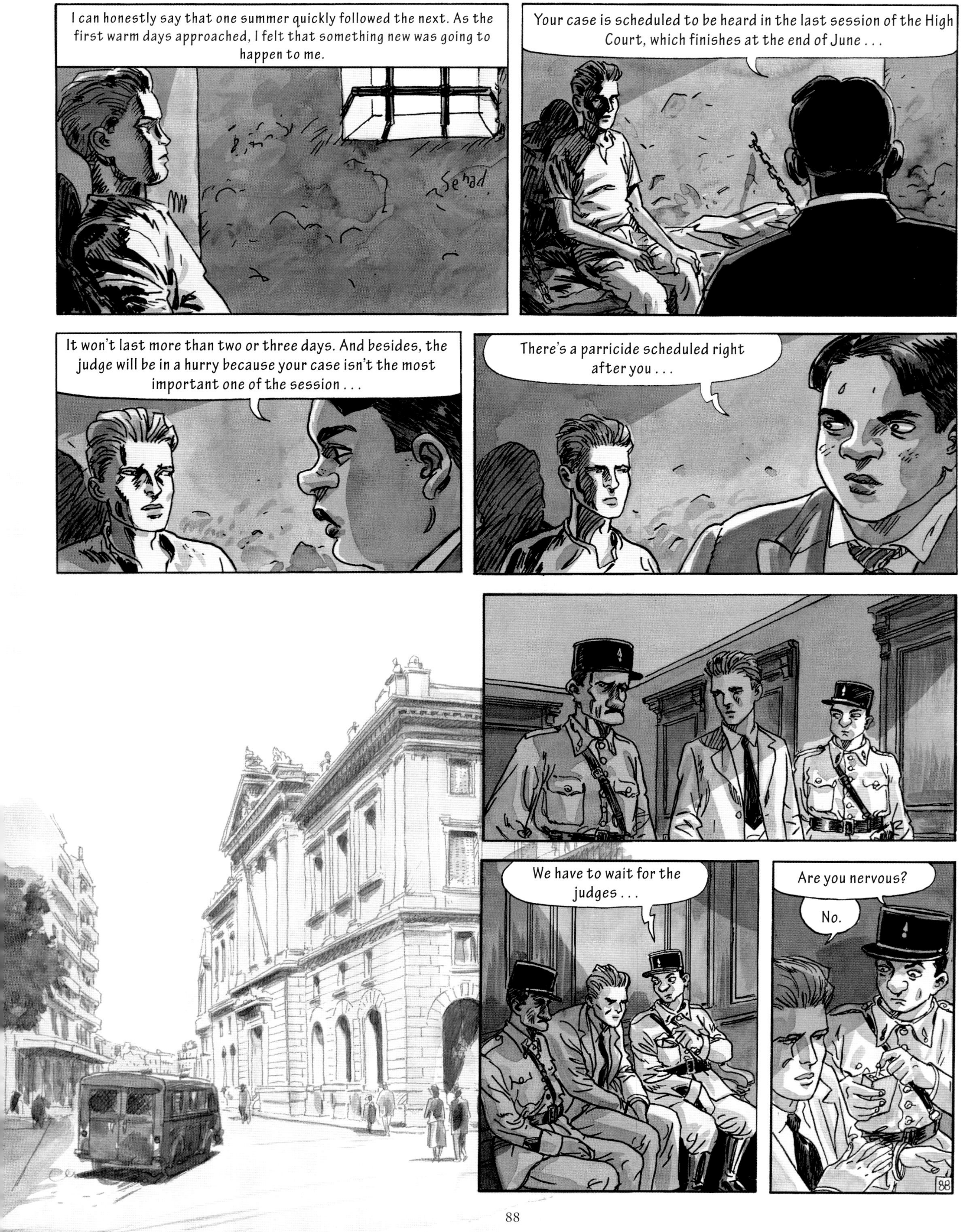
I can honestly say that one summer quickly followed the next. As the first warm days approached, I felt that something new was going to happen to me.
Your case is scheduled to be heard in the last session of the High Court, which finishes at the end of June . . .
It won't last more than two or three days. And besides, the judge will be in a hurry because your case isn't the most important one of the session . . .
There's a parricide scheduled right after you . . .
We have to wait for the judges . . .
Are you nervous?
No.

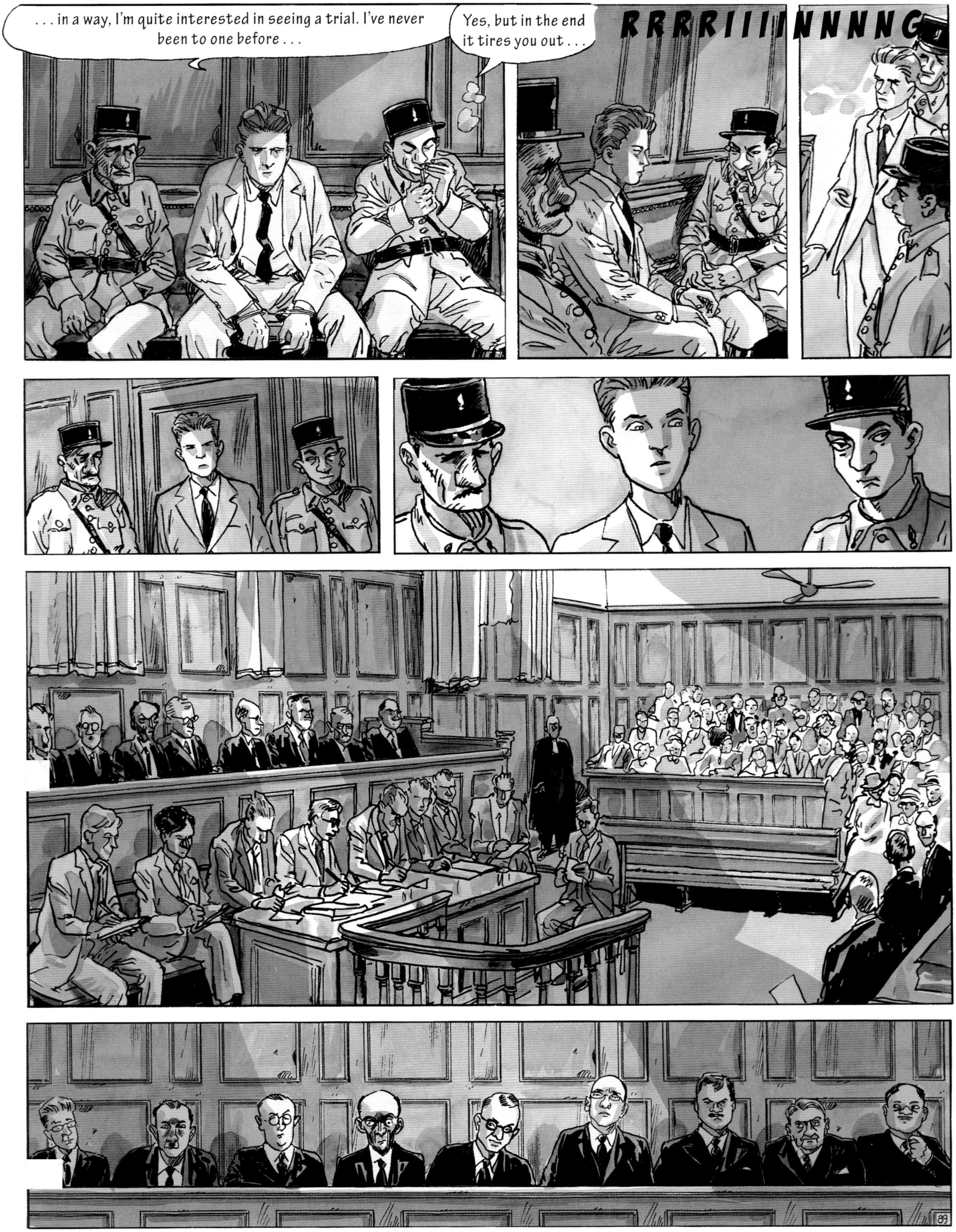
. . . in a way, I'm quite interested in seeing a trial. I've never been to one before . . .
Yes, but in the end it tires you out . . .
RRRRIIIINNNNG

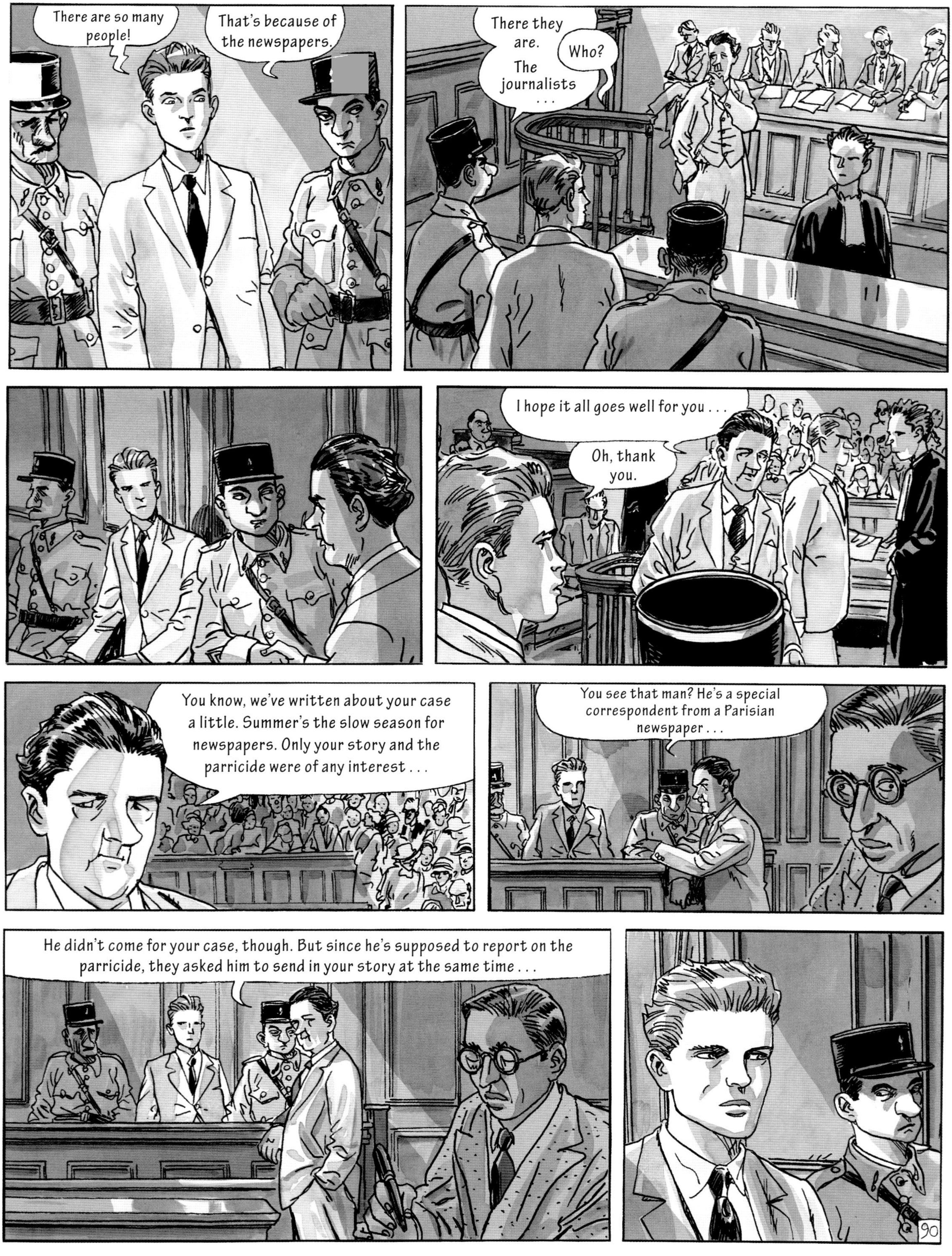
There are so many people!
That's because of the newspapers.
There they are.
Who?
The journalists . . .
I hope it all goes well for you . . .
Oh, thank you.
You know, we've written about your case a little. Summer's the slow season for newspapers. Only your story and the parricide were of any interest . . .
You see that man? He's a special correspondent from a Parisian newspaper . . .
He didn't come for your case, though. But since he's supposed to report on the parricide, they asked him to send in your story at the same time . . .
90

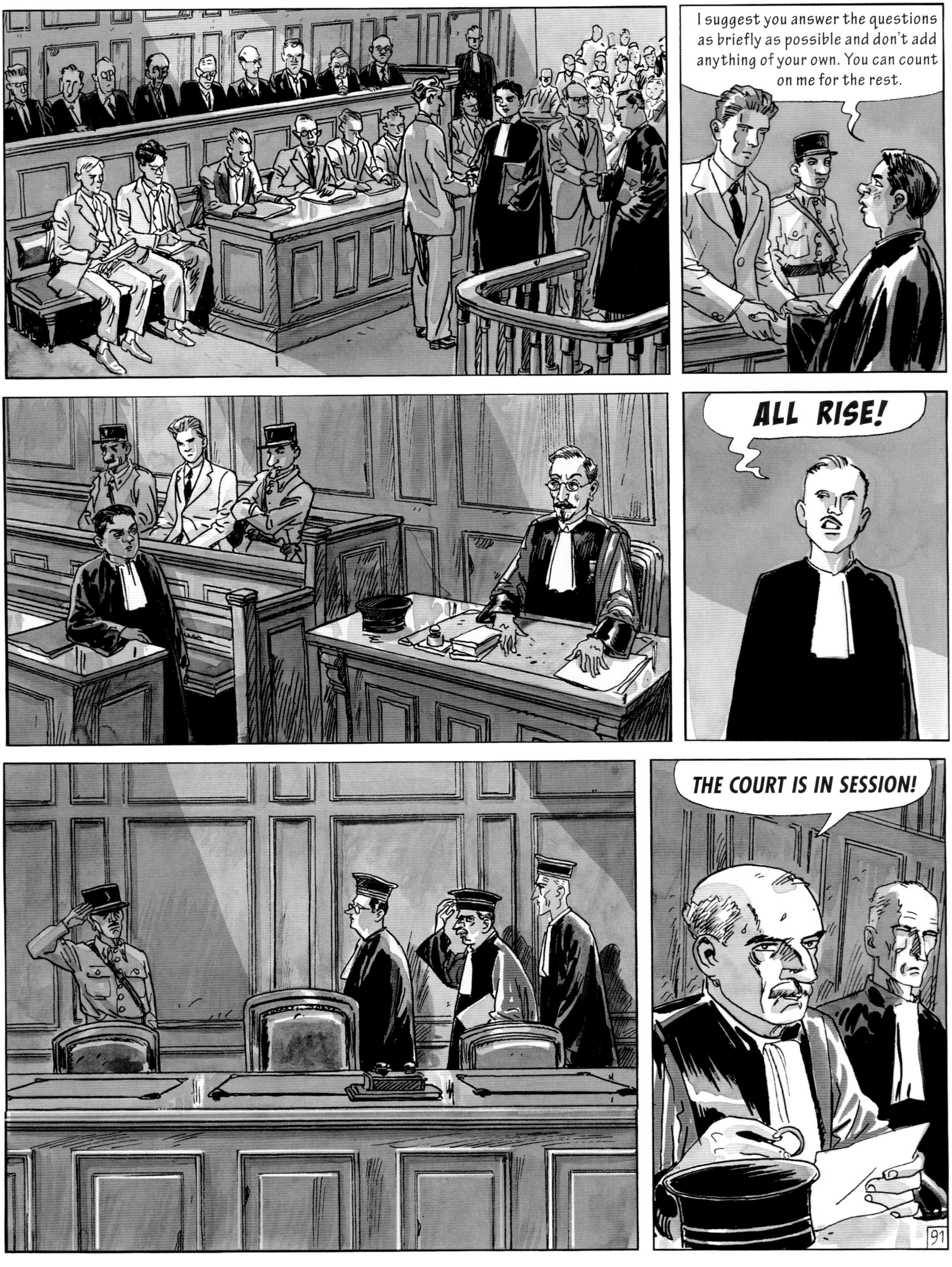
I suggest you answer the questions as briefly as possible and don't add anything of your own. You can count on me for the rest.
ALL RISE!
THE COURT IS IN SESSION!
91

Thomas Pérez  Raymond Sintès  Georges Masson  Albert Salamano  Marie Cardona  Monsieur Céleste

We will begin by calling the witnesses . . .

Thomas Pérez  Raymond Sintès  Georges Masson  Albert Salamano  Marie Cardona  Monsieur Céleste

The official proceedings are about to begin.

I wish to remind the members of the public to remain calm . . .

We are here to conduct an impartial trial which we will consider objectively.

The Jury's sentence will be made in the spirit of justice and, in any case, I will clear the courtroom for the slightest reason.

The Defendant will rise.

Full name, age and profession.

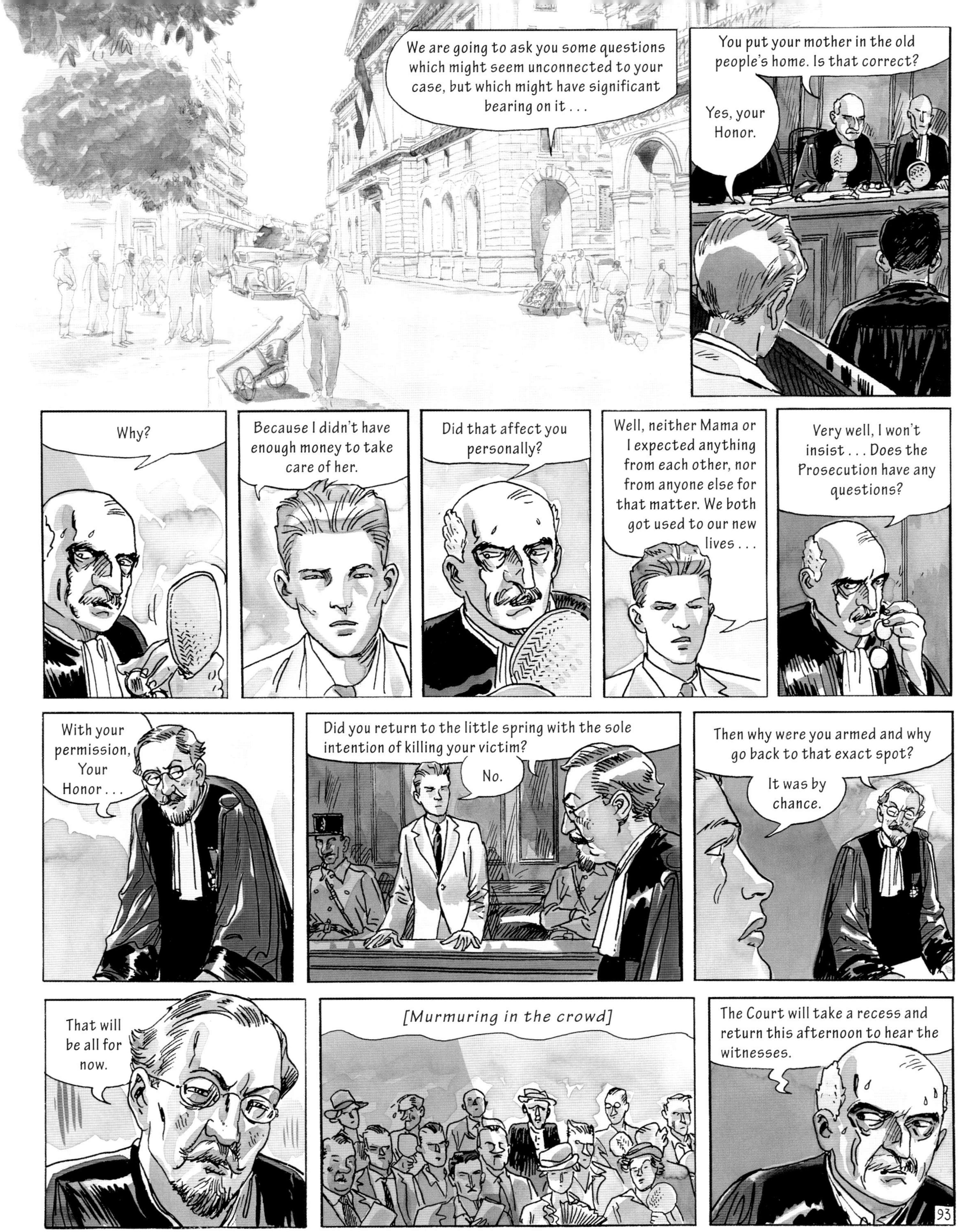
We are going to ask you some questions which might seem unconnected to your case, but which might have significant bearing on it . . .
You put your mother in the old people's home. Is that correct?
Yes, your Honor.
Why?
Because I didn't have enough money to take care of her.
Did that affect you personally?
Well, neither Mama or I expected anything from each other, nor from anyone else for that matter. We both got used to our new lives . . .
Very well, I won't insist . . . Does the Prosecution have any questions?
With your permission, Your Honor . . .
Did you return to the little spring with the sole intention of killing your victim?
No.
Then why were you armed and why go back to that exact spot?
It was by chance.
That will be all for now.
[Murmuring in the crowd]
The Court will take a recess and return this afternoon to hear the witnesses.
93

As Director of the home, can you tell us if Madame Meursault ever complained about her son?

. . . Yes, but it was a bit of an obsession for the residents to complain about their relatives . . .

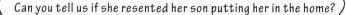

Can you tell us if she resented her son putting her in the home?

Yes.

Can you please describe Monsieur Meursault's conduct on the day of the funeral?

I was surprised at how calm he was . . .

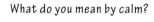

What do you mean by calm?

He didn't want to see his mother. He didn't cry once and he left immediately after the funeral without spending time by himself at the graveside . . . And another thing surprised me: one of the staff told me he didn't know how old his mother was . . .

Does the Prosecution have any questions?

No, Your Honor, I think that will do!

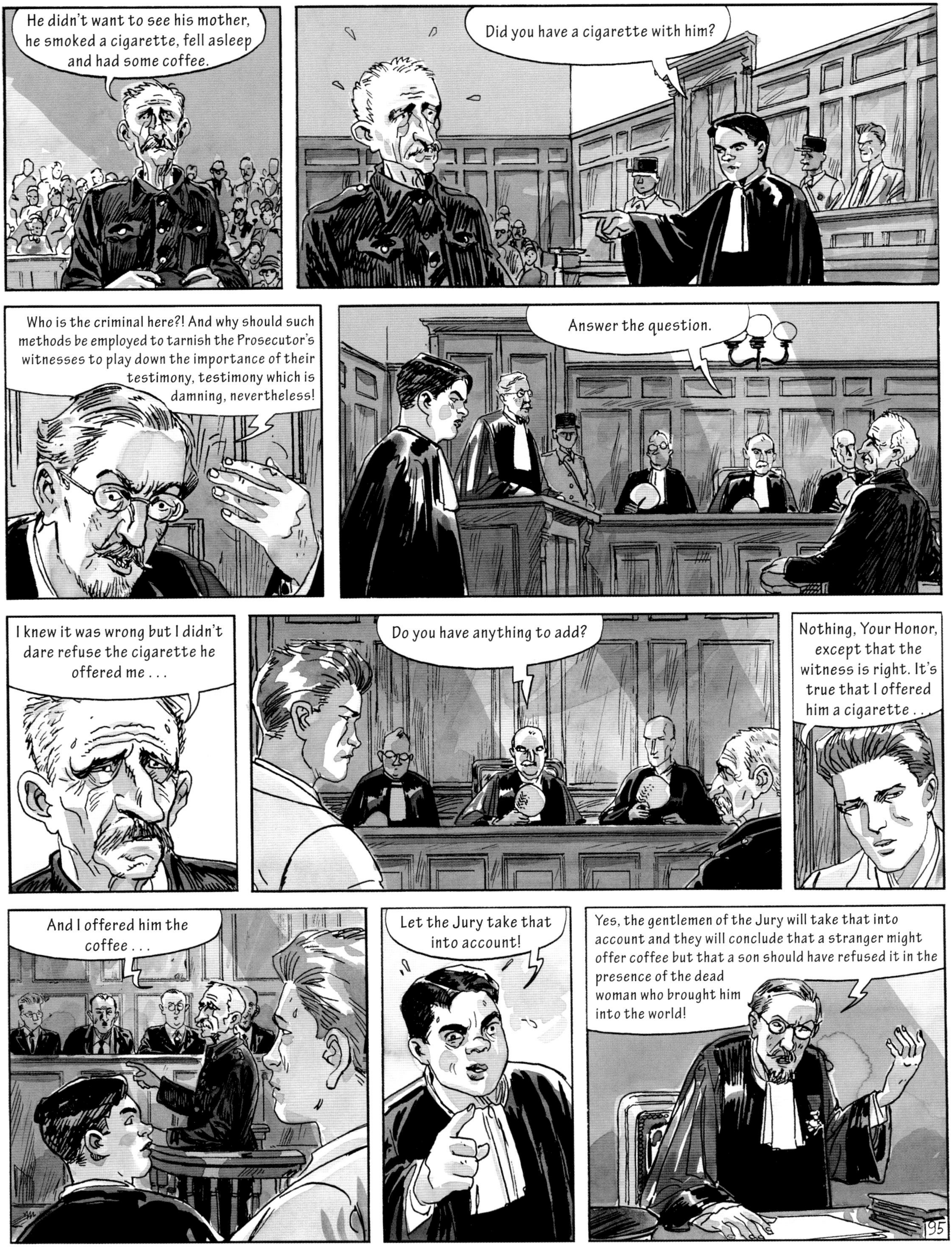
He didn't want to see his mother, he smoked a cigarette, fell asleep and had some coffee.
Did you have a cigarette with him?
Who is the criminal here?! And why should such methods be employed to tarnish the Prosecutor's witnesses to play down the importance of their testimony, testimony which is damning, nevertheless!
Answer the question.
I knew it was wrong but I didn't dare refuse the cigarette he offered me . . .
Do you have anything to add?
Nothing, Your Honor, except that the witness is right. It's true that I offered him a cigarette . . .
And I offered him the coffee . . .
Let the Jury take that into account!
Yes, the gentlemen of the Jury will take that into account and they will conclude that a stranger might offer coffee but that a son should have refused it in the presence of the dead woman who brought him into the world!
95

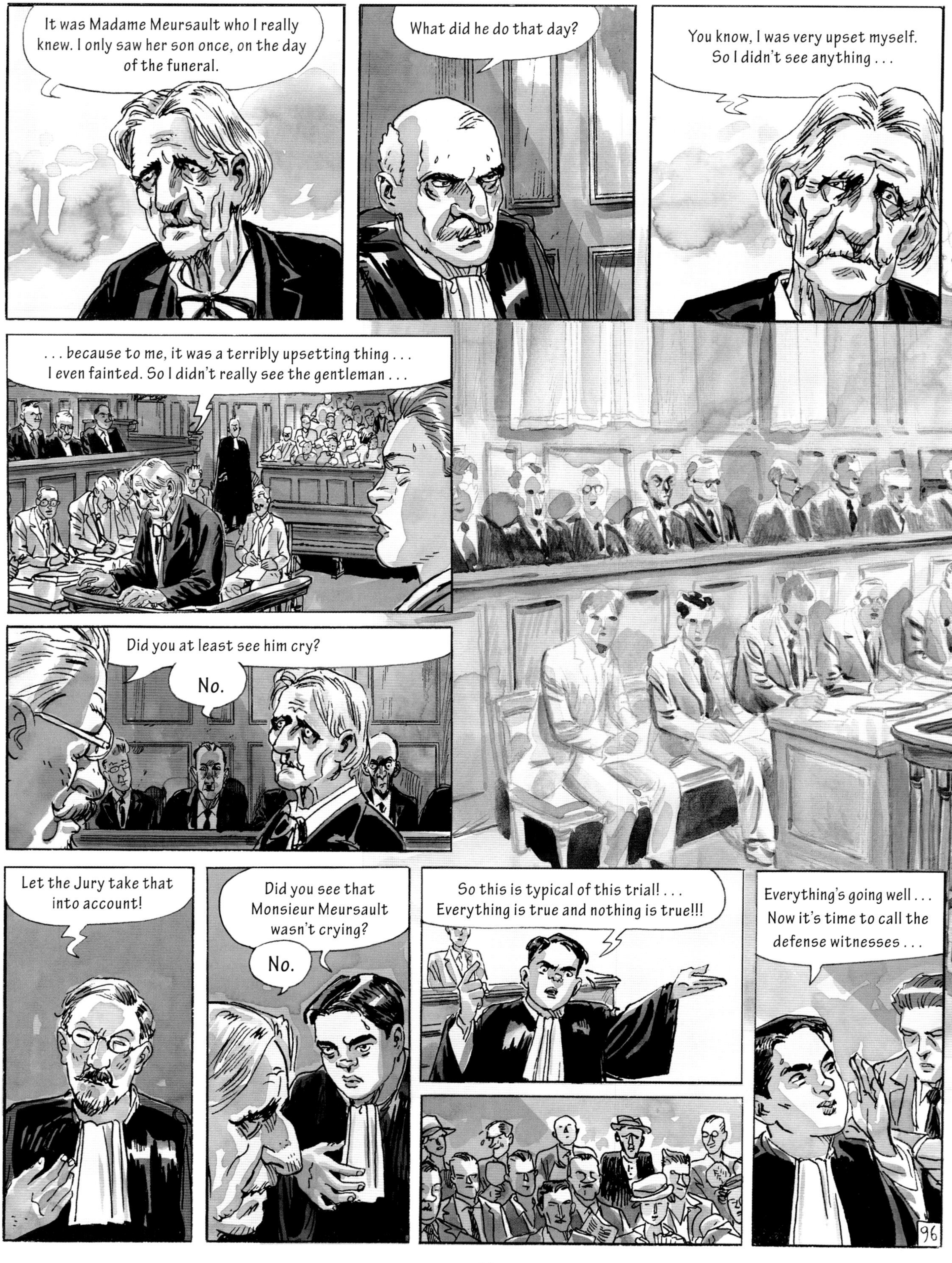

It was Madame Meursault who I really knew. I only saw her son once, on the day of the funeral.
What did he do that day?
You know, I was very upset myself. So I didn't see anything . . .
. . . because to me, it was a terribly upsetting thing . . . I even fainted. So I didn't really see the gentleman . . .
Did you at least see him cry?
No.
Let the Jury take that into account!
Did you see that Monsieur Meursault wasn't crying?
No.
So this is typical of this trial! . . . Everything is true and nothing is true!!!
Everything's going well . . . Now it's time to call the defense witnesses . . .
96

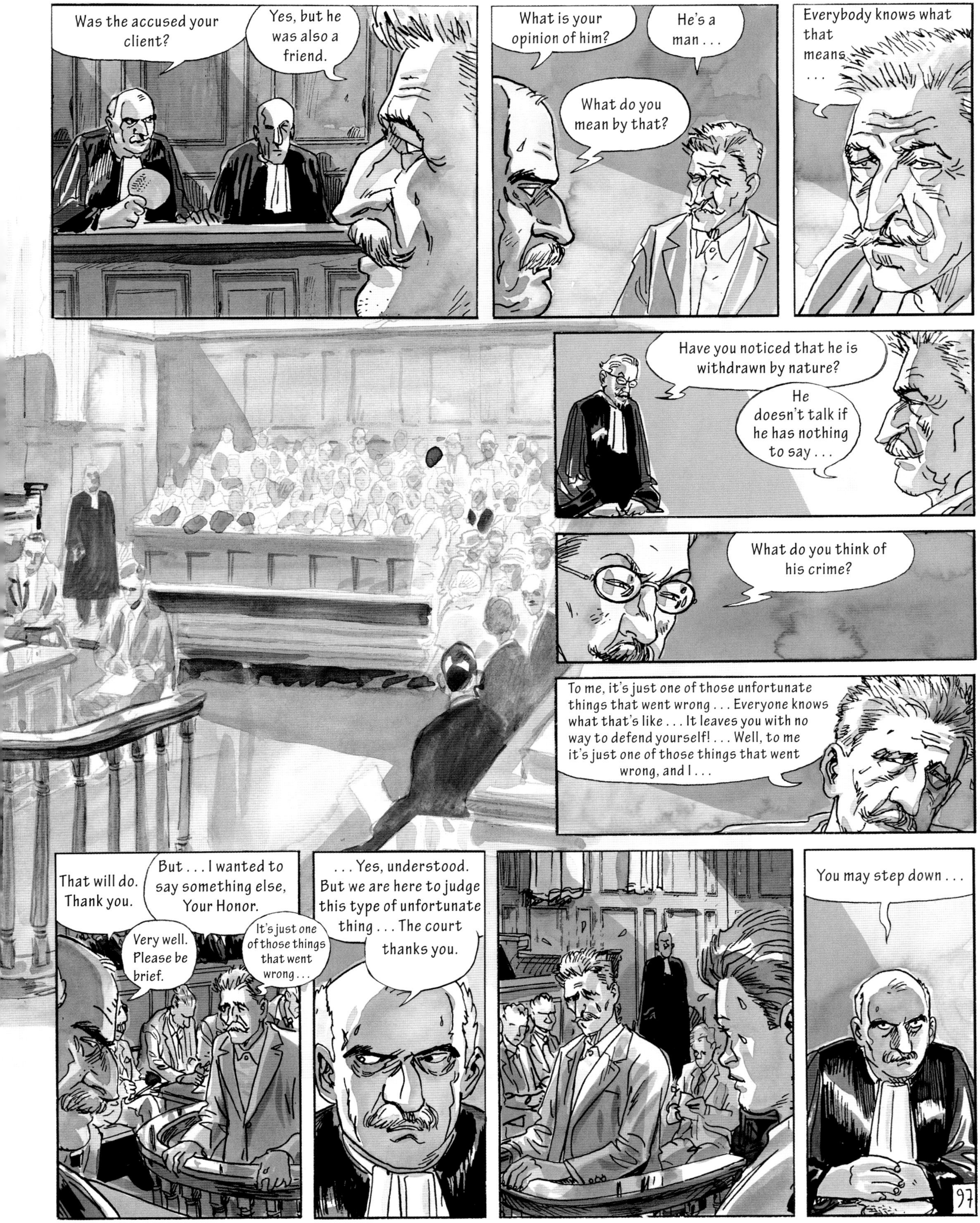
Was the accused your client?
Yes, but he was also a friend.
What is your opinion of him?
He's a man . . .
What do you mean by that?
Everybody knows what that means . . .
Have you noticed that he is withdrawn by nature?
He doesn't talk if he has nothing to say . . .
What do you think of his crime?
To me, it's just one of those unfortunate things that went wrong . . . Everyone knows what that's like . . . It leaves you with no way to defend yourself! . . . Well, to me it's just one of those things that went wrong, and I . . .
That will do. Thank you.
But . . . I wanted to say something else, Your Honor.
Very well. Please be brief.
It's just one of those things that went wrong . . .
. . . Yes, understood. But we are here to judge this type of unfortunate thing . . . The court thanks you.
You may step down . . .
97

What is your relationship with the defendant?

I'm his girlfriend . . .

Is it true that you intended to get married?

Yes, Your Honor, it's true . . .

How long have you been in a relationship with the defendant?

I . . . well, I mean . . . we already knew each other from work before I got another job and . . . we saw each other again by chance one day . . .

I believe that was the day after the defendant's mother died. Isn't that right?

I . . .

I do not wish to dwell on such a delicate matter . . . I understand your scruples very well, Mademoiselle, but it is my duty to rise above such social conventions . . . Can you please tell us what you did on the day you met the defendant again?

I . . . I mean . . .

In your statement, you told the investigator that you went swimming with the defendant . . . then you went to the movies together.

Then you went back to his apartment where you spent the night . . . Is that correct?

Yes . . .

I've consulted the movie listings for that date. Can you tell the court what movie you saw that day?

It was . . . a comedy . . . starring Fernandel . . .

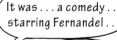

[Murmuring]

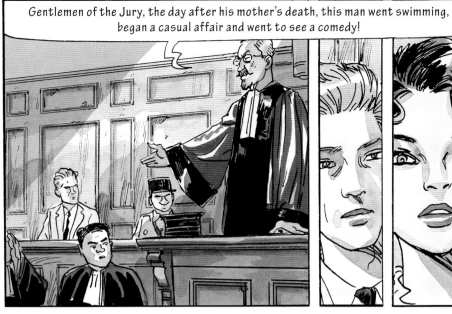

Gentlemen of the Jury, the day after his mother's death, this man went swimming, began a casual affair and went to see a comedy!

I have nothing more to say...

No, it wasn't like that!... It's not that simple!

I'm being forced to say the opposite of what I think!... I know him really well!... He didn't do anything wrong!!!

He didn't do anything wrong!

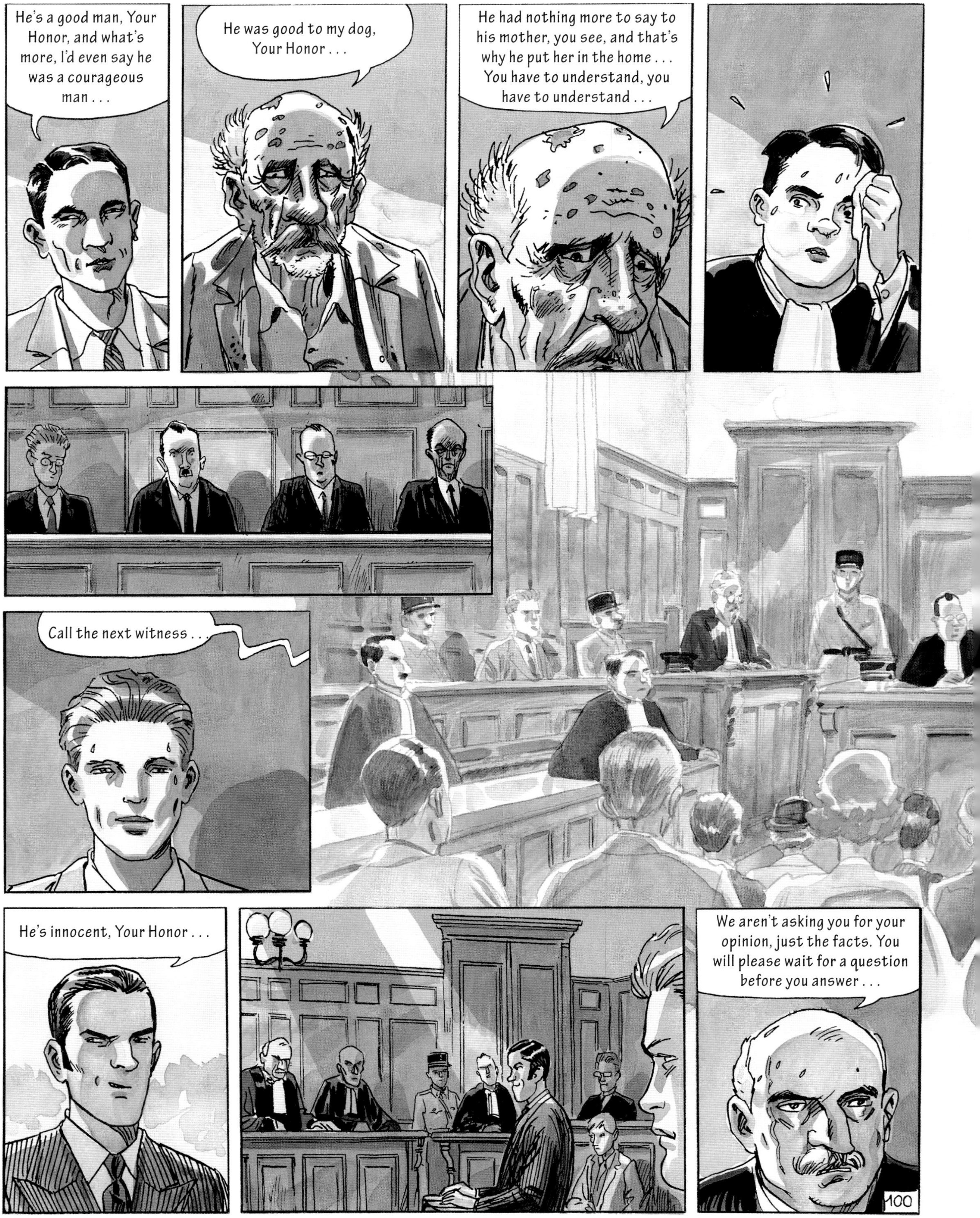
He's a good man, Your Honor, and what's more, I'd even say he was a courageous man . . .
He was good to my dog, Your Honor . . .
He had nothing more to say to his mother, you see, and that's why he put her in the home . . . You have to understand, you have to understand . . .
Call the next witness . . .
He's innocent, Your Honor . . .
We aren't asking you for your opinion, just the facts. You will please wait for a question before you answer . . .
100

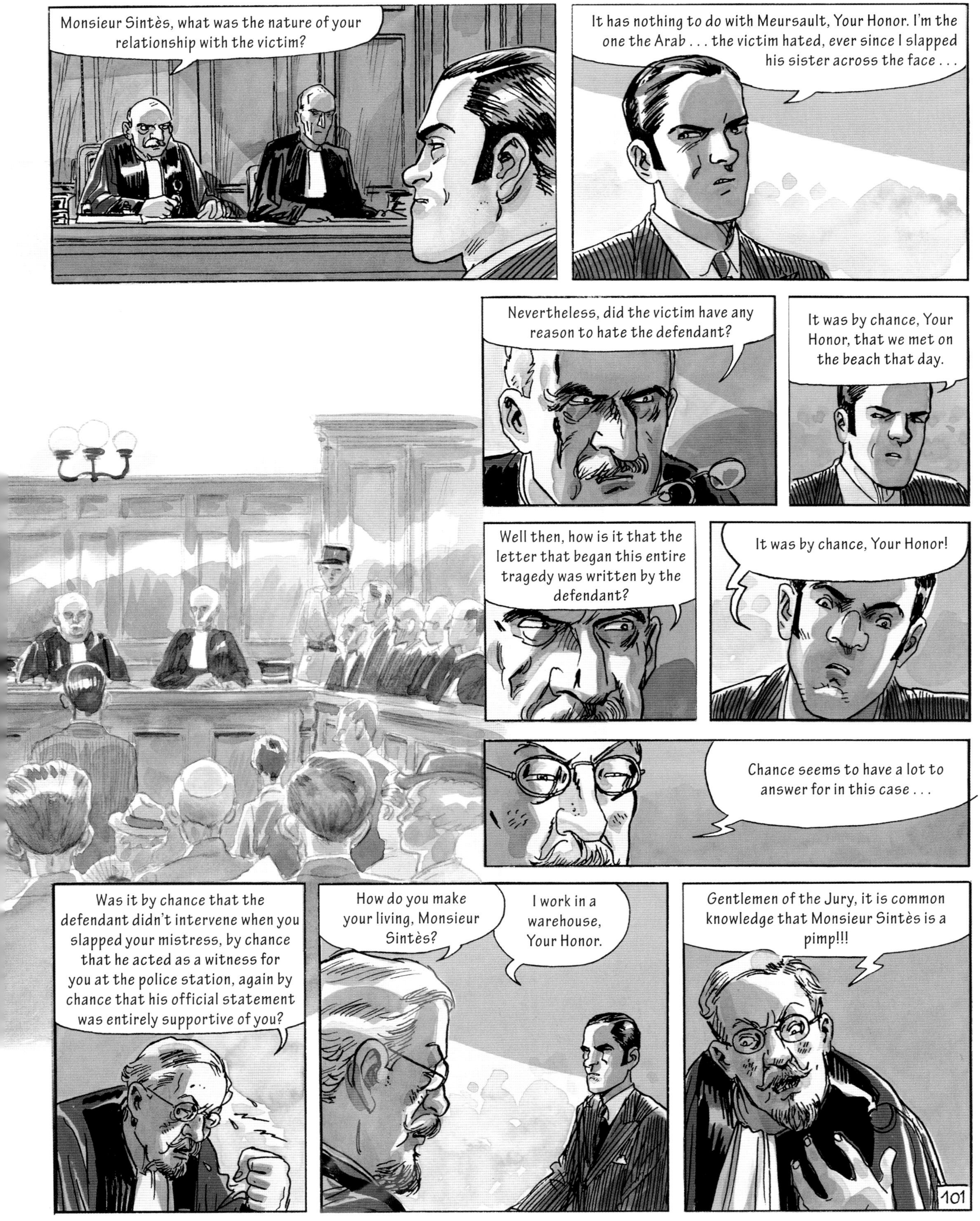
Monsieur Sintès, what was the nature of your relationship with the victim?
It has nothing to do with Meursault, Your Honor. I'm the one the Arab . . . the victim hated, ever since I slapped his sister across the face . . .
Nevertheless, did the victim have any reason to hate the defendant?
It was by chance, Your Honor, that we met on the beach that day.
Well then, how is it that the letter that began this entire tragedy was written by the defendant?
It was by chance, Your Honor!
Chance seems to have a lot to answer for in this case . . .
Was it by chance that the defendant didn't intervene when you slapped your mistress, by chance that he acted as a witness for you at the police station, again by chance that his official statement was entirely supportive of you?
How do you make your living, Monsieur Sintès?
I work in a warehouse, Your Honor.
Gentlemen of the Jury, it is common knowledge that Monsieur Sintès is a pimp!!!
101

The defendant is his accomplice and his friend. To tell the truth, this is a matter of a sordid crime of the most shameful order, worsened by the fact that we are dealing with a moral monster! . . .

Objection, Your Honor!

Please allow the Prosecutor to finish.

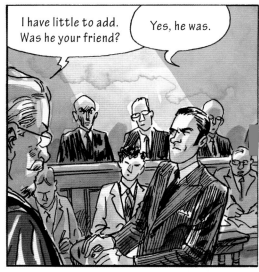

I have little to add. Was he your friend?

Yes, he was.

Is that true?

Yes.

This very man who only days after the death of his mother engaged in the most shameful, debauched behavior, committed murder for the most petty of reasons to settle an unspeakably immoral dispute!

Really now, is the defendant on trial for having buried his mother or for having killed a man?!

HAHAHAHAHA . . .

Only someone as naïve as the honorable defense lawyer could fail to understand how these two events were essentially, emotionally, profoundly connected!

Yes, I accuse this man of having buried his mother with the heart of a criminal!

102

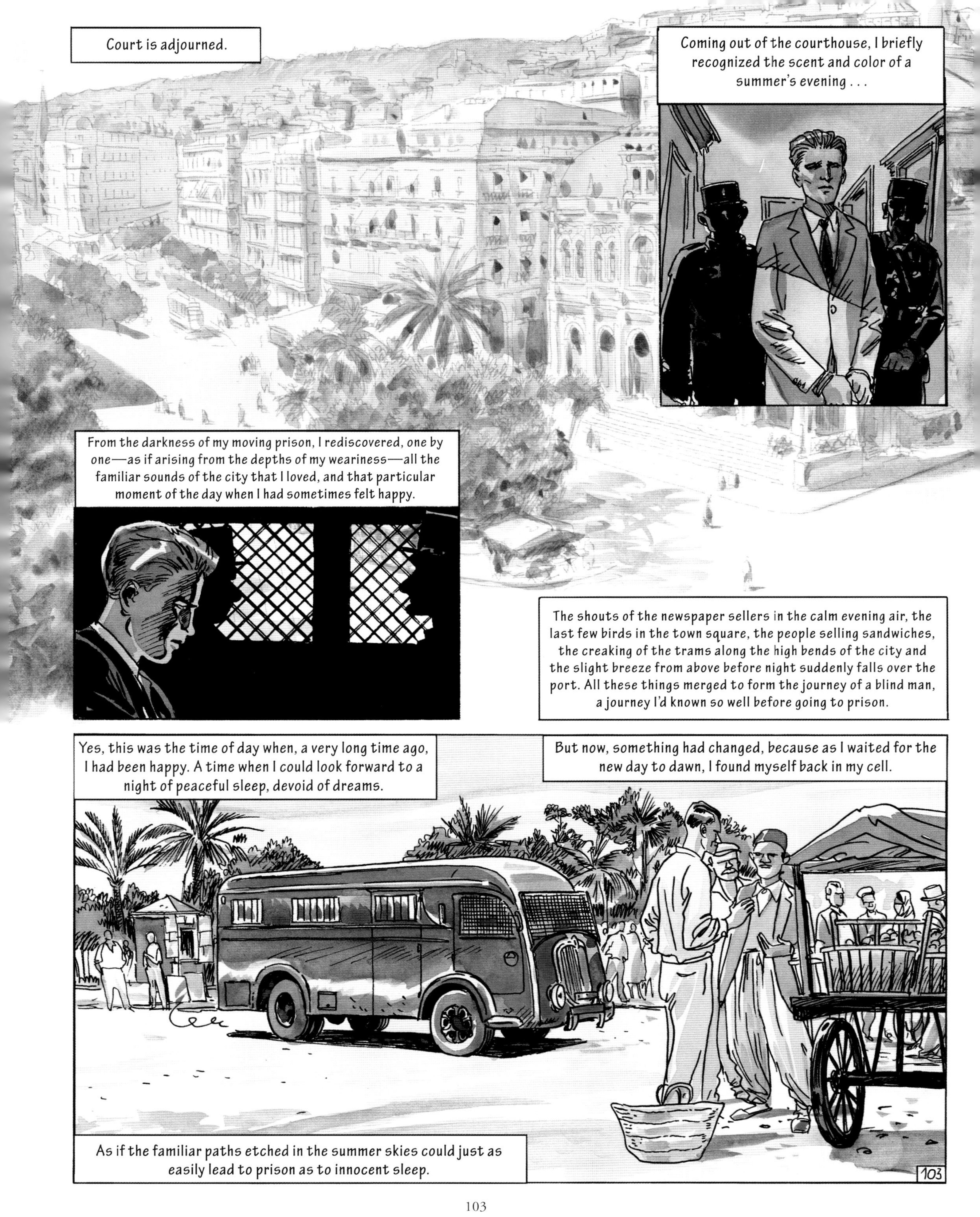
Court is adjourned.
Coming out of the courthouse, I briefly recognized the scent and color of a summer's evening . . .
From the darkness of my moving prison, I rediscovered, one by one—as if arising from the depths of my weariness—all the familiar sounds of the city that I loved, and that particular moment of the day when I had sometimes felt happy.
The shouts of the newspaper sellers in the calm evening air, the last few birds in the town square, the people selling sandwiches, the creaking of the trams along the high bends of the city and the slight breeze from above before night suddenly falls over the port. All these things merged to form the journey of a blind man, a journey I'd known so well before going to prison.
Yes, this was the time of day when, a very long time ago, I had been happy. A time when I could look forward to a night of peaceful sleep, devoid of dreams.
But now, something had changed, because as I waited for the new day to dawn, I found myself back in my cell.
As if the familiar paths etched in the summer skies could just as easily lead to prison as to innocent sleep.
103

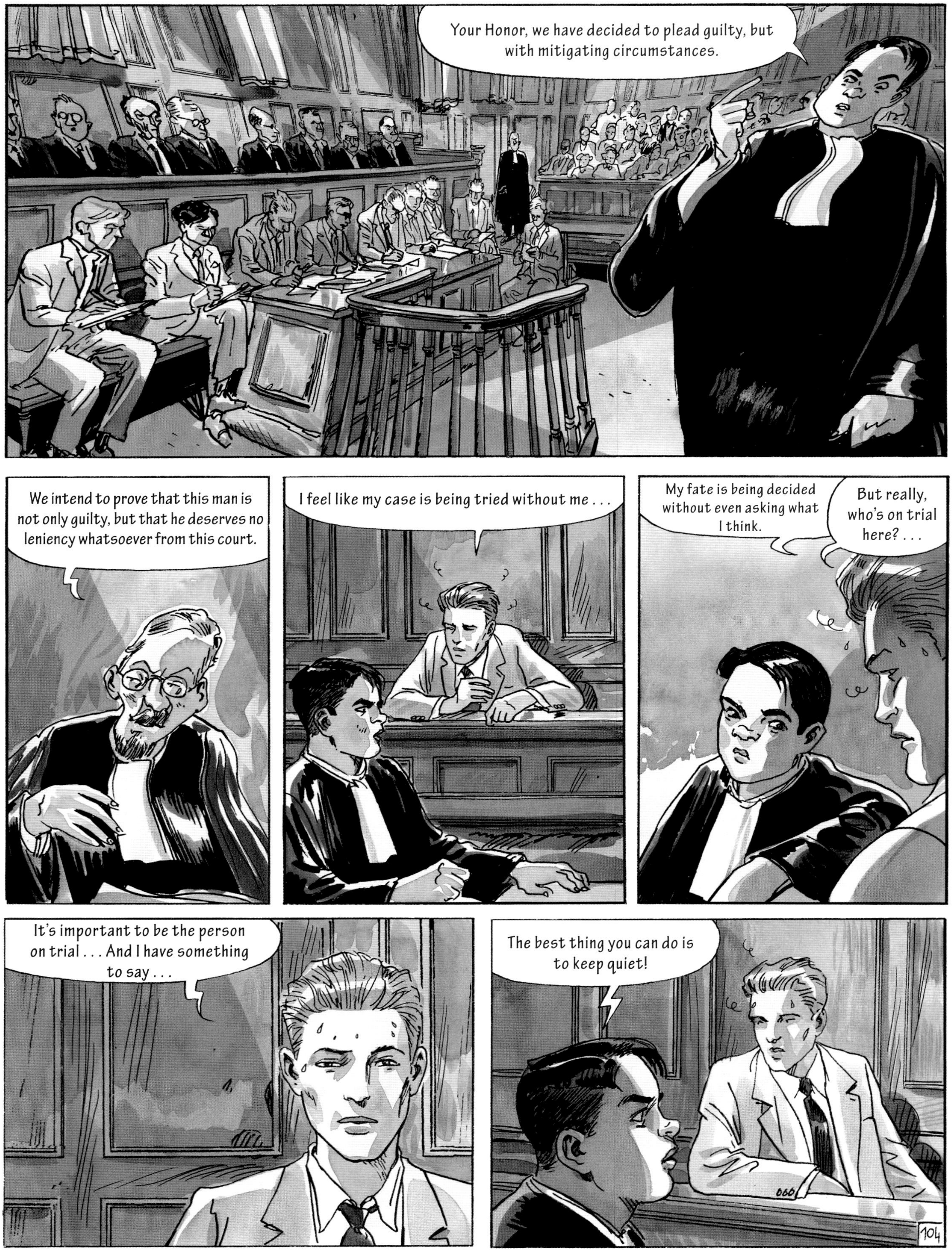
Your Honor, we have decided to plead guilty, but with mitigating circumstances.
We intend to prove that this man is not only guilty, but that he deserves no leniency whatsoever from this court.
I feel like my case is being tried without me . . .
My fate is being decided without even asking what I think.
But really, who's on trial here? . . .
It's important to be the person on trial . . . And I have something to say . . .
The best thing you can do is to keep quiet!
104

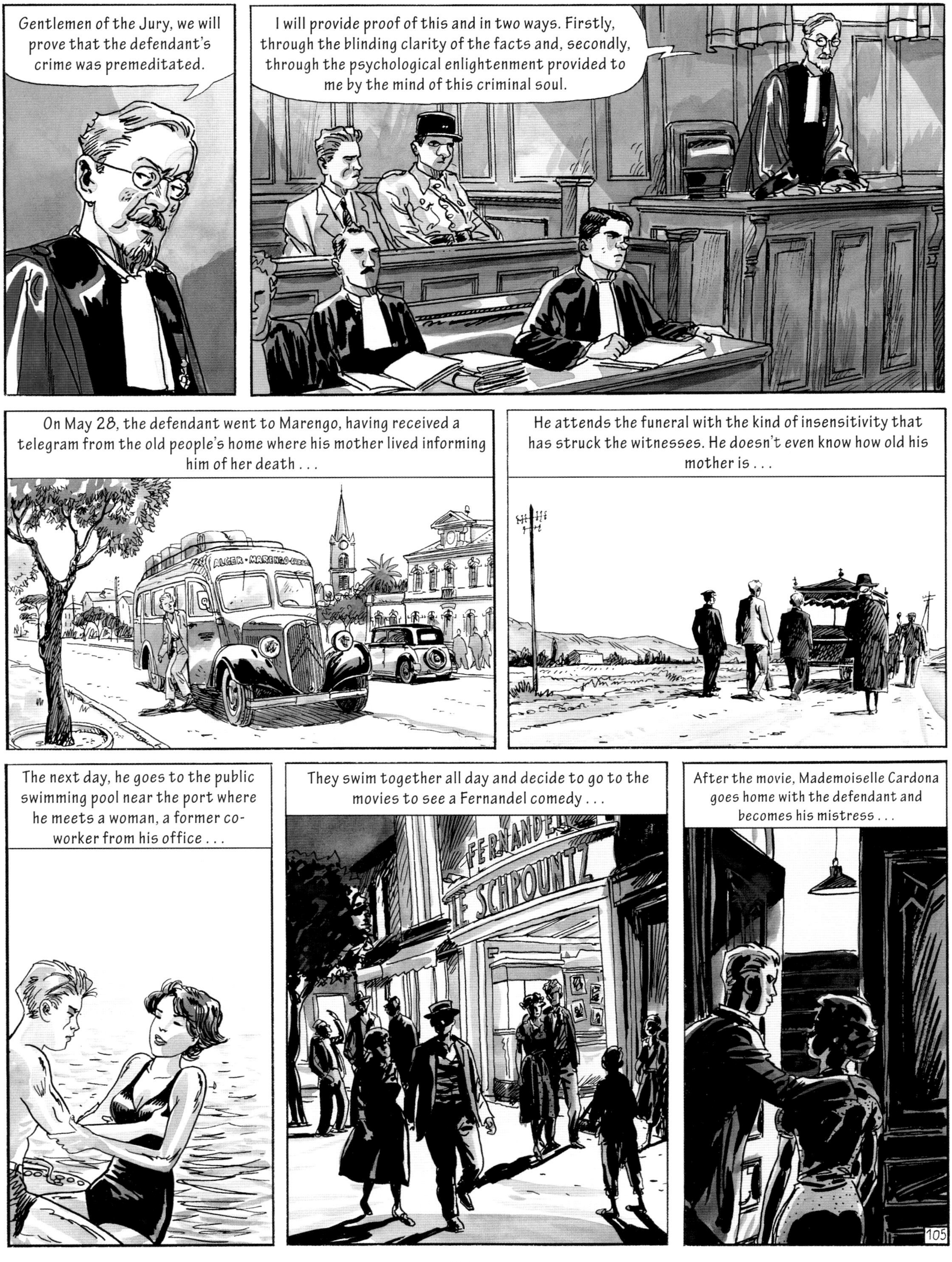
Gentlemen of the Jury, we will prove that the defendant's crime was premeditated.
I will provide proof of this and in two ways. Firstly, through the blinding clarity of the facts and, secondly, through the psychological enlightenment provided to me by the mind of this criminal soul.
On May 28, the defendant went to Marengo, having received a telegram from the old people's home where his mother lived informing him of her death . . .
ALGER · MARENGO
He attends the funeral with the kind of insensitivity that has struck the witnesses. He doesn't even know how old his mother is . . .
The next day, he goes to the public swimming pool near the port where he meets a woman, a former co-worker from his office . . .
They swim together all day and decide to go to the movies to see a Fernandel comedy . . .
FERNANDEL
LE SCHPOUNTZ
After the movie, Mademoiselle Cardona goes home with the defendant and becomes his mistress . . .
105

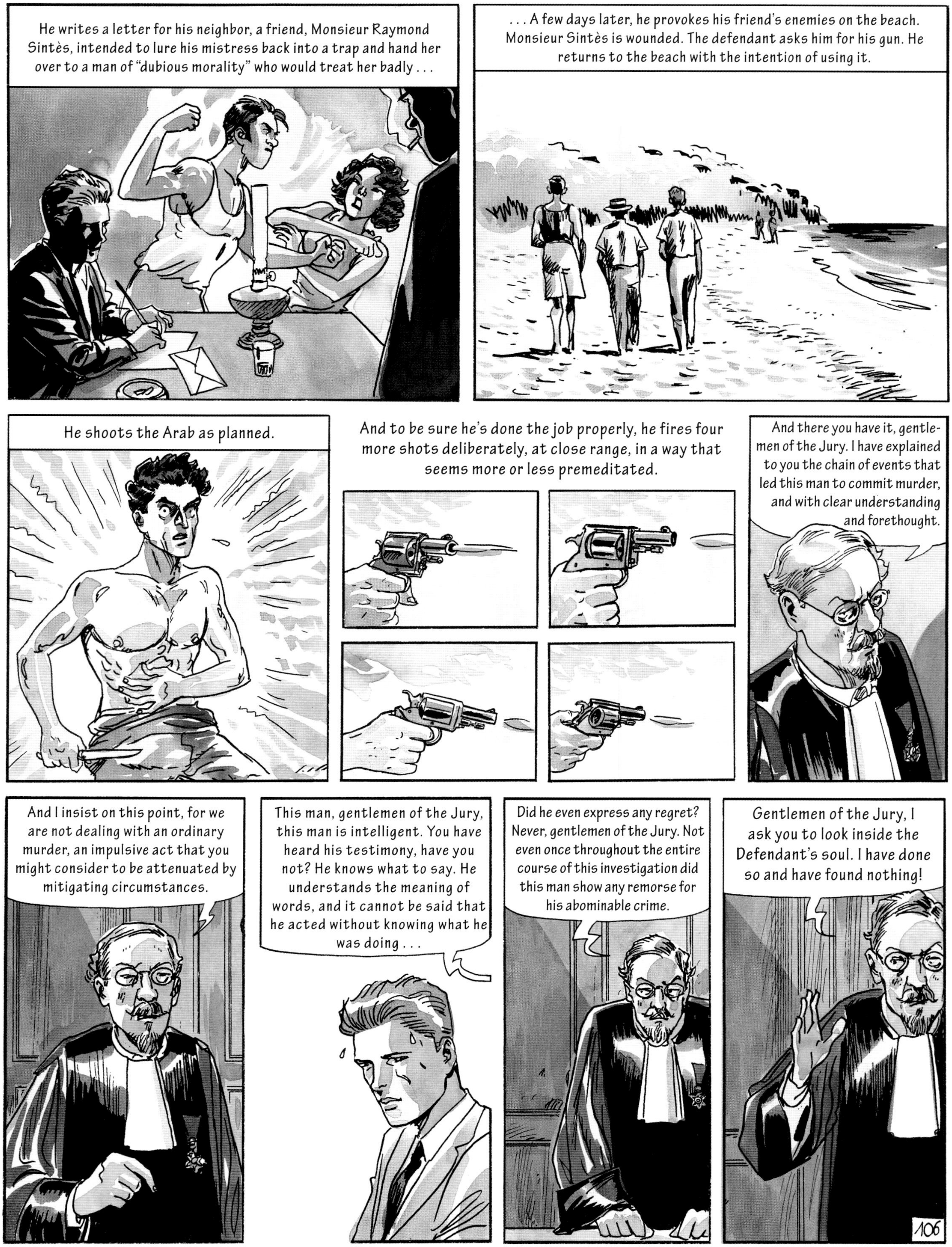
He writes a letter for his neighbor, a friend, Monsieur Raymond Sintès, intended to lure his mistress back into a trap and hand her over to a man of "dubious morality" who would treat her badly . . .
. . . A few days later, he provokes his friend's enemies on the beach. Monsieur Sintès is wounded. The defendant asks him for his gun. He returns to the beach with the intention of using it.
He shoots the Arab as planned.
And to be sure he's done the job properly, he fires four more shots deliberately, at close range, in a way that seems more or less premeditated.
And there you have it, gentlemen of the Jury. I have explained to you the chain of events that led this man to commit murder, and with clear understanding and forethought.
And I insist on this point, for we are not dealing with an ordinary murder, an impulsive act that you might consider to be attenuated by mitigating circumstances.
This man, gentlemen of the Jury, this man is intelligent. You have heard his testimony, have you not? He knows what to say. He understands the meaning of words, and it cannot be said that he acted without knowing what he was doing . . .
Did he even express any regret? Never, gentlemen of the Jury. Not even once throughout the entire course of this investigation did this man show any remorse for his abominable crime.
Gentlemen of the Jury, I ask you to look inside the Defendant's soul. I have done so and have found nothing!
106

. . . In truth, he has no soul. There is nothing that makes a man human, not a single moral principle, can be found in him . . .

Of course, we should not reproach him for this . . .

. . . but where this court is concerned, tolerance, a virtue that in this instance is entirely inappropriate, must give way to the higher, more demanding virtue of justice. Especially when the lack of a soul in a man such as this becomes an abyss in which all of society can be engulfed and destroyed.

Think about his behavior toward his mother!

First he sends her to the old people's home because he can't take care of her.

Then he doesn't shed a single tear at her funeral.

Finally, the next day, he goes to see a comedy with a woman with whom he begins a debauched affair that same night!

Tomorrow, gentlemen of the Jury, this very court will judge the most abominable of crimes: the murder of a father. The mind is repulsed by such a hideous act. I dare to hope that the justice of man will not hesitate to punish it. And I have no qualms when I say that the horror which that crime arouses in me is almost overshadowed by the horror I feel at the indifference of the defendant.

A man who has, morally speaking, murdered his mother, cuts himself off from society in the same way as someone who has actually laid a murderous hand on the person who gave him life. In any case, the first crime paves the way for the second and, in some respects, even legitimizes it.

I am convinced, gentlemen of the Jury, that you will not find that I am exaggerating when I say that the man standing trial is just as guilty of murder as the man who will appear before this court tomorrow.

My duty is painful but I will carry it out without flinching . . .

Yes, gentlemen of the Jury, the defendant has no place in a society whose most essential principles he disregards. He cannot appeal for sympathy when he does not understand the heart's most basic instincts.

I ask you for this man's head!

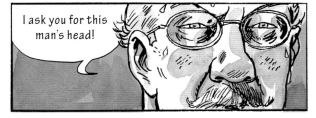

And I ask for it with a clear conscience, for while there have been many times during my long career when I have been obliged to ask for the death sentence, never before have I felt this painful duty so justly counterbalanced or so strongly motivated by my awareness of a higher, sacred power and by the horror I feel when I look at the face of this man in whom I can distinguish nothing that is not monstrous.

107

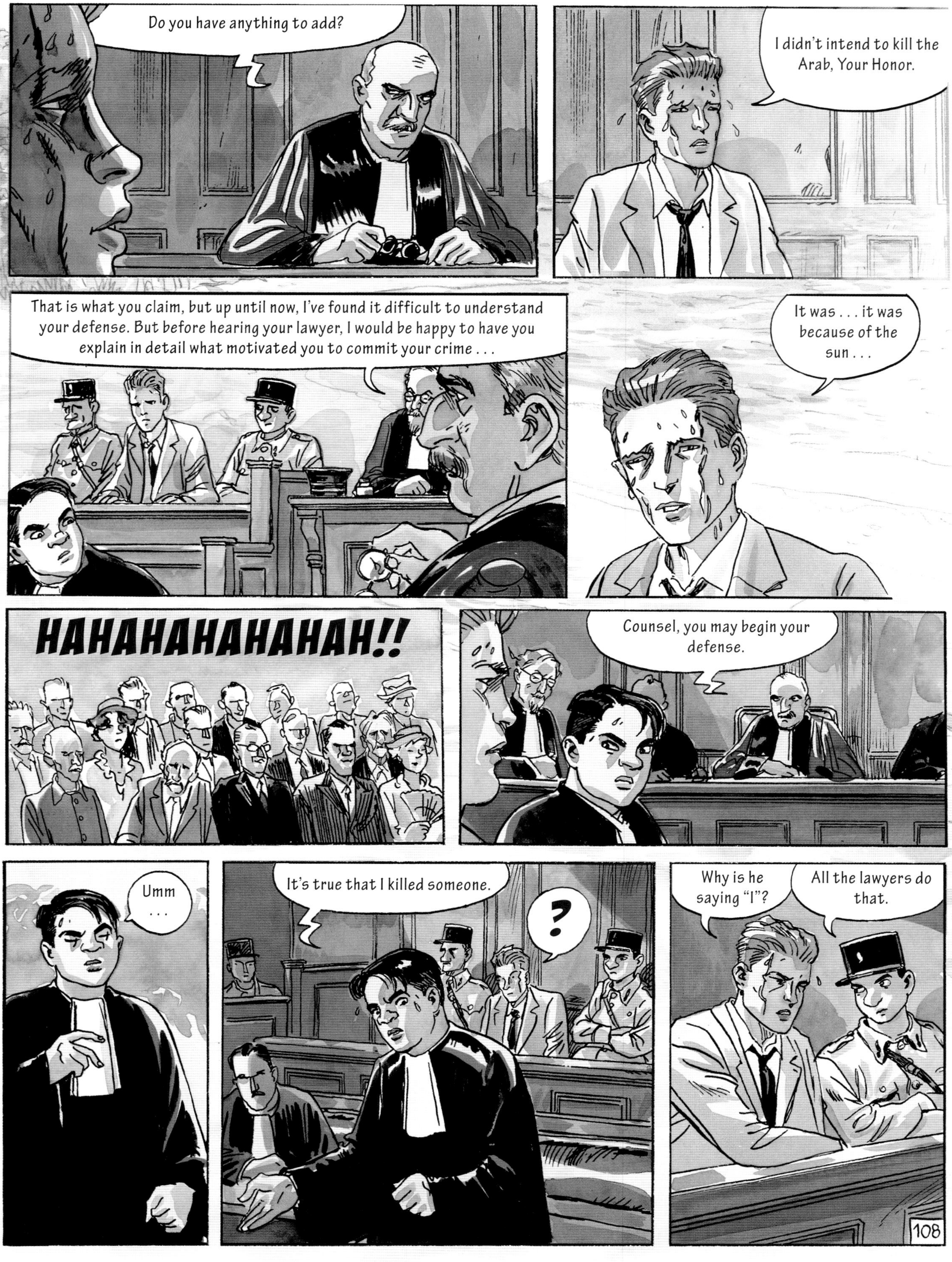
Do you have anything to add?
I didn't intend to kill the Arab, Your Honor.
That is what you claim, but up until now, I've found it difficult to understand your defense. But before hearing your lawyer, I would be happy to have you explain in detail what motivated you to commit your crime . . .
It was . . . it was because of the sun . . .
HAHAHAHAHAHAH!!
Counsel, you may begin your defense.
Umm . . .
It's true that I killed someone.
?
Why is he saying "I"?
All the lawyers do that.
108

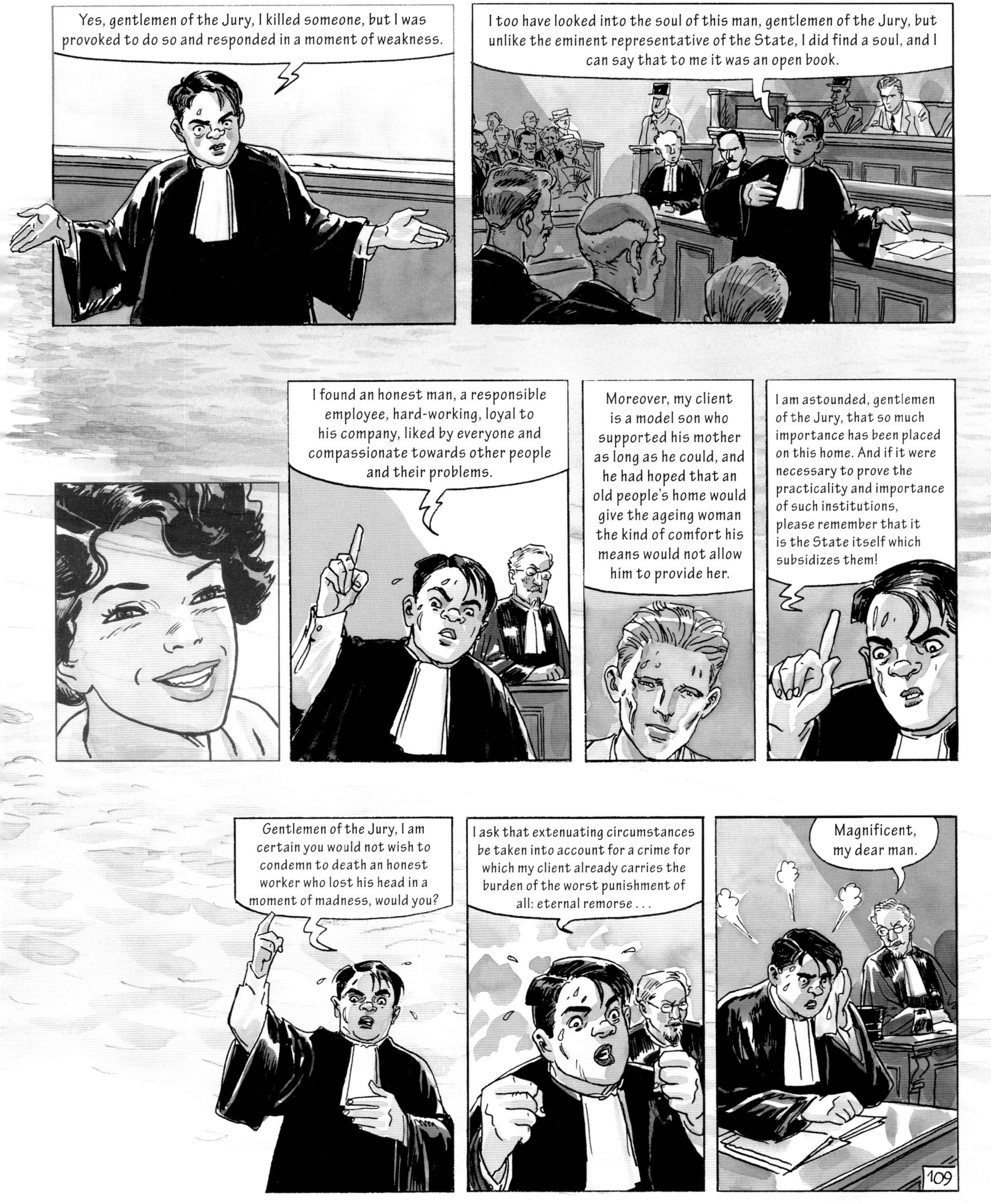
Yes, gentlemen of the Jury, I killed someone, but I was provoked to do so and responded in a moment of weakness.
I too have looked into the soul of this man, gentlemen of the Jury, but unlike the eminent representative of the State, I did find a soul, and I can say that to me it was an open book.
I found an honest man, a responsible employee, hard-working, loyal to his company, liked by everyone and compassionate towards other people and their problems.
Moreover, my client is a model son who supported his mother as long as he could, and he had hoped that an old people's home would give the ageing woman the kind of comfort his means would not allow him to provide her.
I am astounded, gentlemen of the Jury, that so much importance has been placed on this home. And if it were necessary to prove the practicality and importance of such institutions, please remember that it is the State itself which subsidizes them!
Gentlemen of the Jury, I am certain you would not wish to condemn to death an honest worker who lost his head in a moment of madness, would you?
I ask that extenuating circumstances be taken into account for a crime for which my client already carries the burden of the worst punishment of all: eternal remorse . . .
Magnificent, my dear man.
109

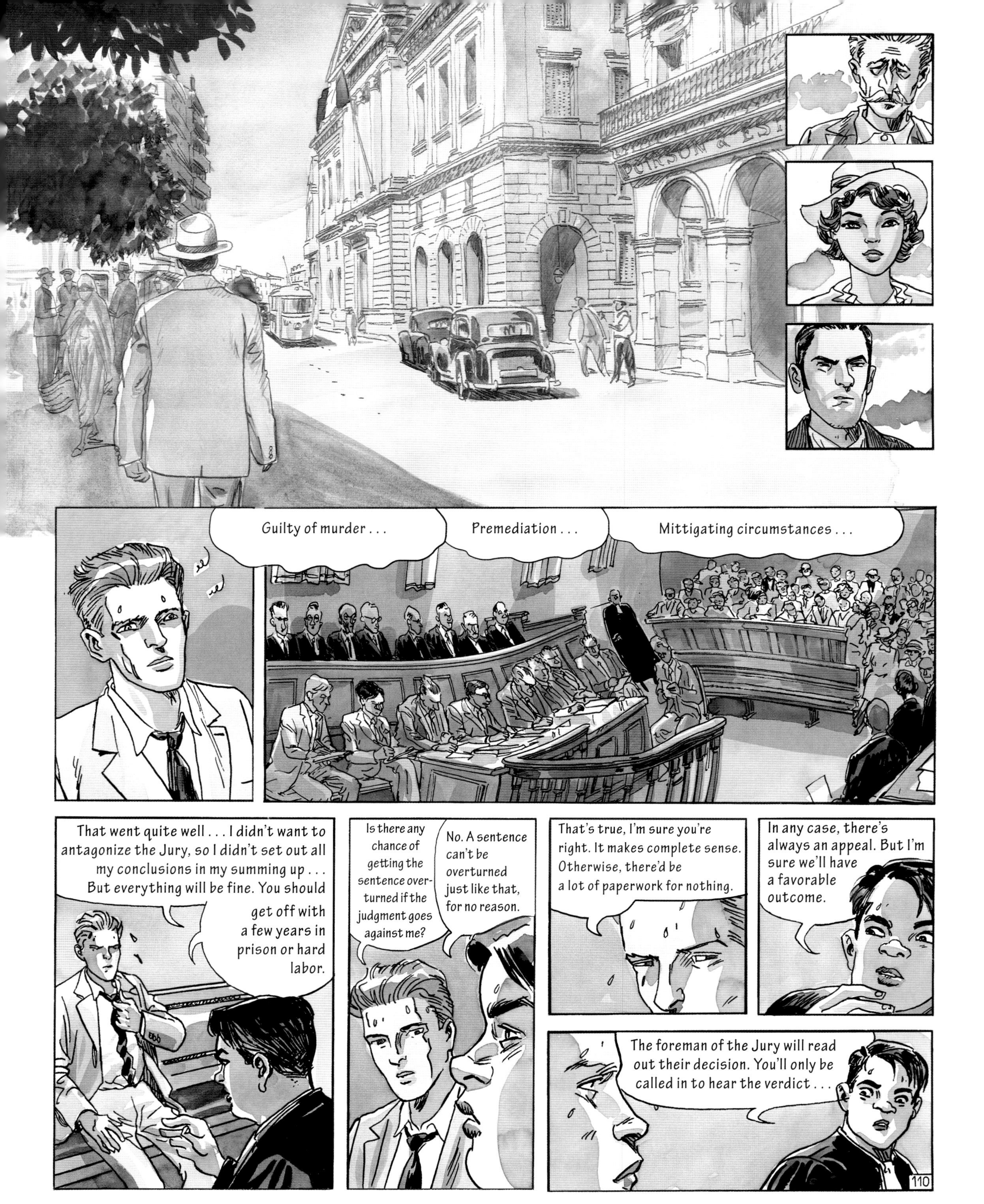
Guilty of murder . . .
Premediation . . .
Mittigating circumstances . . .
That went quite well . . . I didn't want to antagonize the Jury, so I didn't set out all my conclusions in my summing up . . . But everything will be fine. You should get off with a few years in prison or hard labor.
Is there any chance of getting the sentence overturned if the judgment goes against me?
No. A sentence can't be overturned just like that, for no reason.
That's true, I'm sure you're right. It makes complete sense. Otherwise, there'd be a lot of paperwork for nothing.
In any case, there's always an appeal. But I'm sure we'll have a favorable outcome.
The foreman of the Jury will read out their decision. You'll only be called in to hear the verdict . . .
110

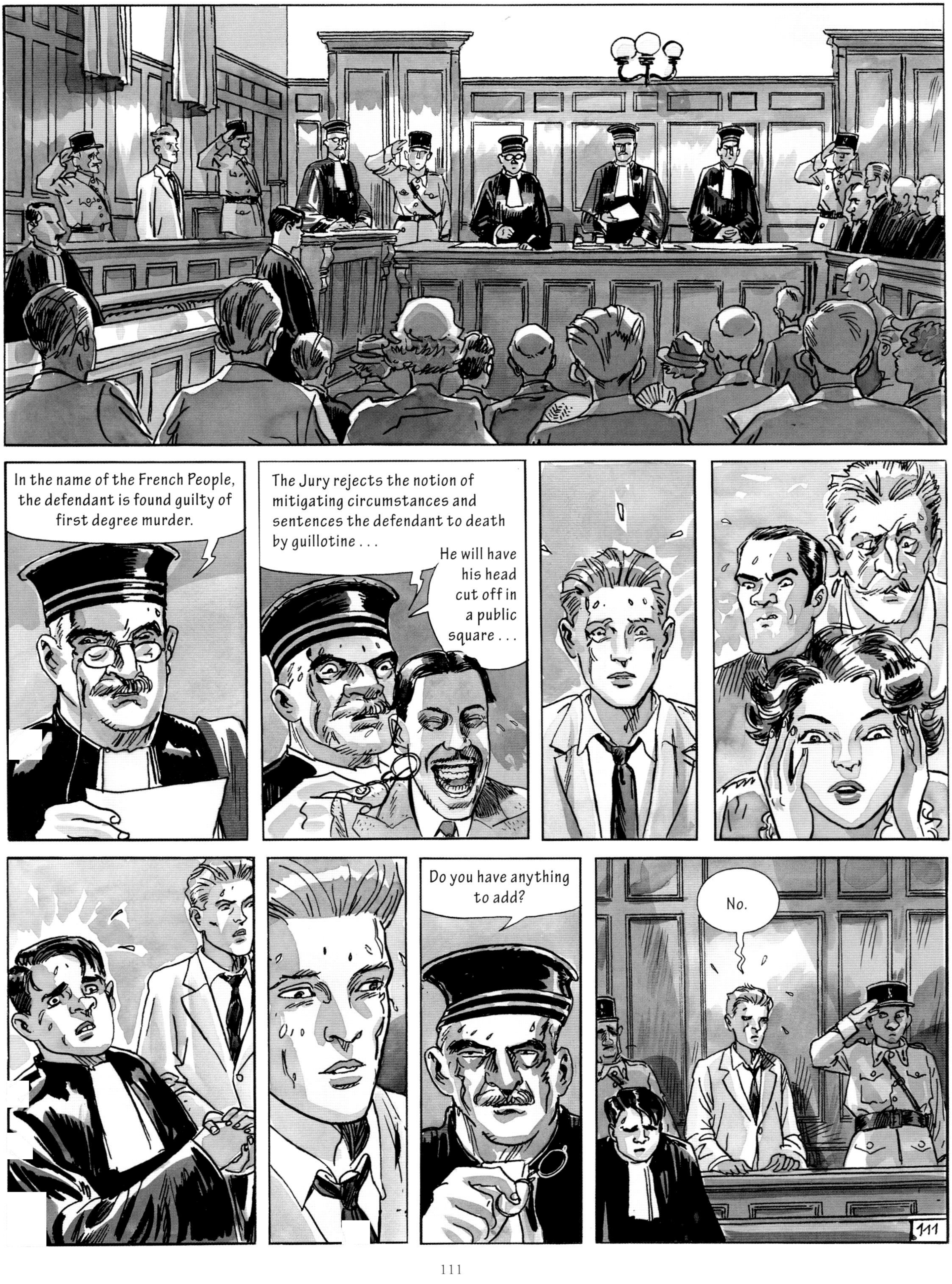
In the name of the French People, the defendant is found guilty of first degree murder.
The Jury rejects the notion of mitigating circumstances and sentences the defendant to death by guillotine . . .
He will have his head cut off in a public square . . .
Do you have anything to add?
No.
111

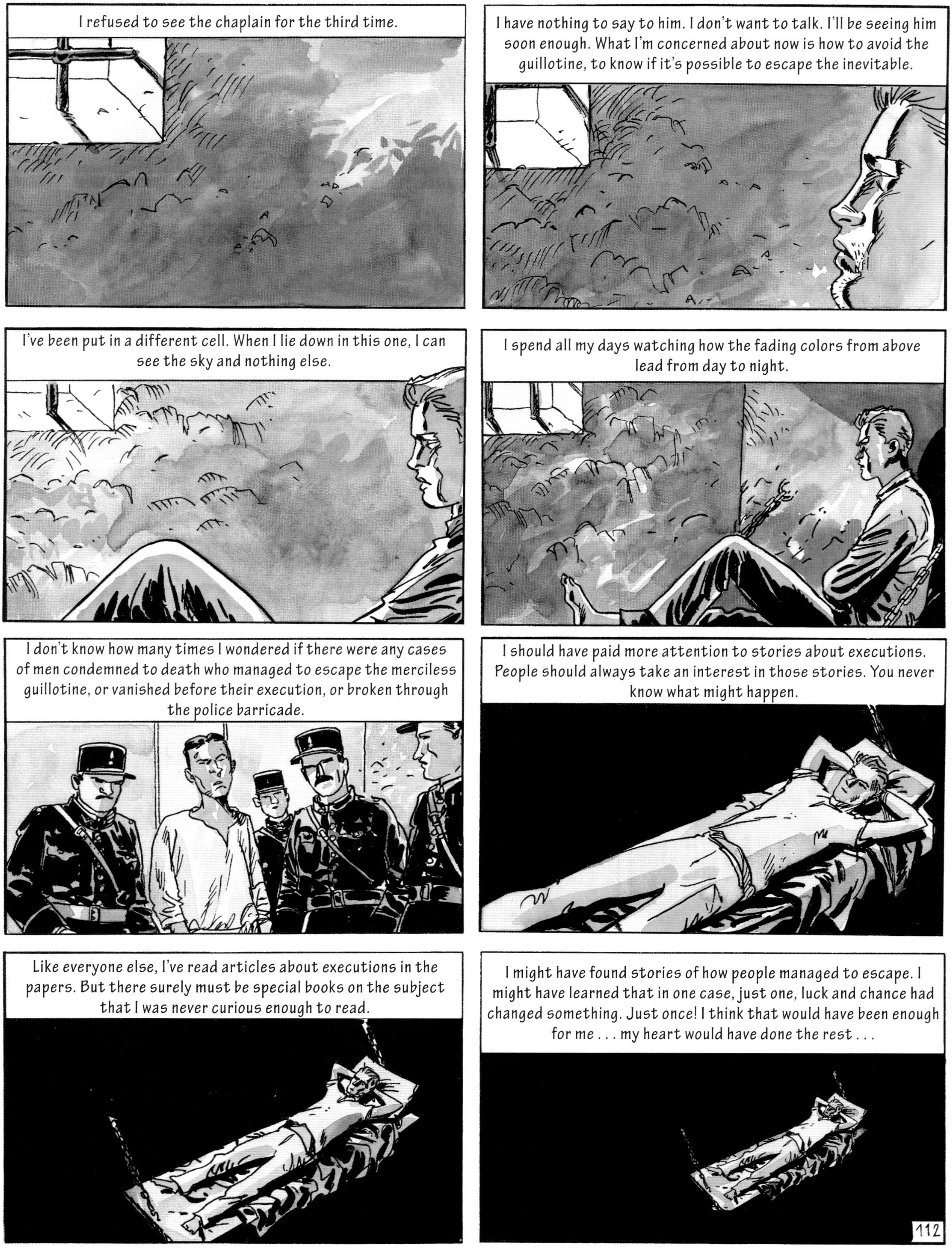
I refused to see the chaplain for the third time.
I have nothing to say to him. I don't want to talk. I'll be seeing him soon enough. What I'm concerned about now is how to avoid the guillotine, to know if it's possible to escape the inevitable.
I've been put in a different cell. When I lie down in this one, I can see the sky and nothing else.
I spend all my days watching how the fading colors from above lead from day to night.
I don't know how many times I wondered if there were any cases of men condemned to death who managed to escape the merciless guillotine, or vanished before their execution, or broken through the police barricade.
I should have paid more attention to stories about executions. People should always take an interest in those stories. You never know what might happen.
Like everyone else, I've read articles about executions in the papers. But there surely must be special books on the subject that I was never curious enough to read.
I might have found stories of how people managed to escape. I might have learned that in one case, just one, luck and chance had changed something. Just once! I think that would have been enough for me . . . my heart would have done the rest . . .
112

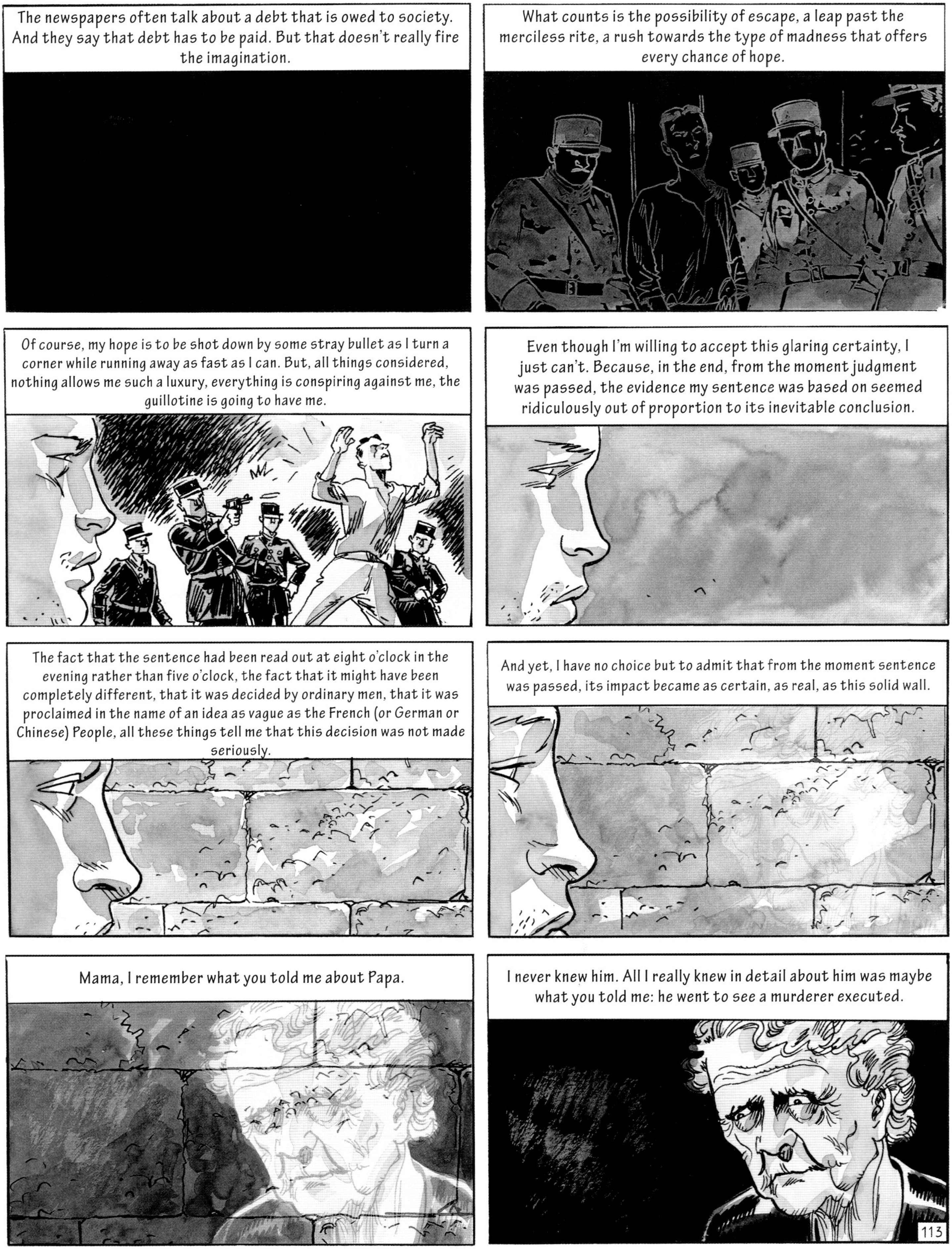

The newspapers often talk about a debt that is owed to society. And they say that debt has to be paid. But that doesn't really fire the imagination.

What counts is the possibility of escape, a leap past the merciless rite, a rush towards the type of madness that offers every chance of hope.

Of course, my hope is to be shot down by some stray bullet as I turn a corner while running away as fast as I can. But, all things considered, nothing allows me such a luxury, everything is conspiring against me, the guillotine is going to have me.

Even though I'm willing to accept this glaring certainty, I just can't. Because, in the end, from the moment judgment was passed, the evidence my sentence was based on seemed ridiculously out of proportion to its inevitable conclusion.

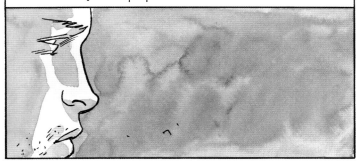

The fact that the sentence had been read out at eight o'clock in the evening rather than five o'clock, the fact that it might have been completely different, that it was decided by ordinary men, that it was proclaimed in the name of an idea as vague as the French (or German or Chinese) People, all these things tell me that this decision was not made seriously.

And yet, I have no choice but to admit that from the moment sentence was passed, its impact became as certain, as real, as this solid wall.

Mama, I remember what you told me about Papa.

I never knew him. All I really knew in detail about him was maybe what you told me: he went to see a murderer executed.

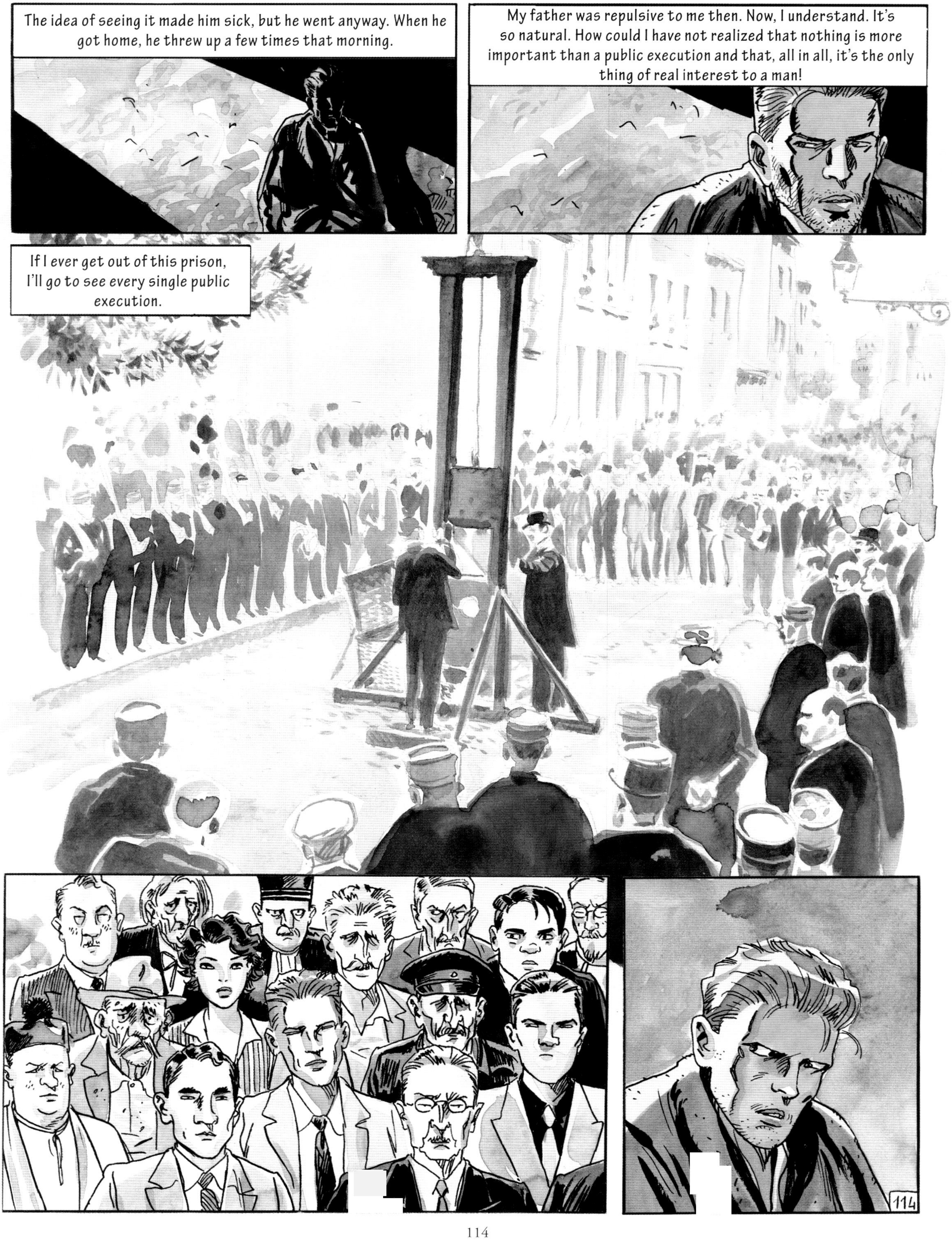
The idea of seeing it made him sick, but he went anyway. When he got home, he threw up a few times that morning.
My father was repulsive to me then. Now, I understand. It's so natural. How could I have not realized that nothing is more important than a public execution and that, all in all, it's the only thing of real interest to a man!
If I ever get out of this prison, I'll go to see every single public execution.
114

Sometimes, I'd think up new laws. I'd change the sentences. I'd realized that the most important thing is to give the condemned man a chance. One chance in a thousand, that would be enough to make things right . . .

I thought it would be possible to find some mixture of drugs that would kill the patient nine times out of ten (that's what I thought: the patient). The patient would know, and that would be a condition.

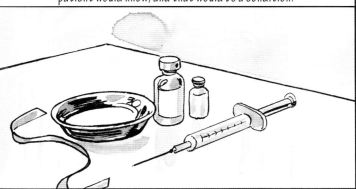

Because after thinking about it a lot, after considering things calmly, I understand what is flawed about the guillotine: there's no chance, none at all. The death of the patient had been decided, once and for all.

If by some bizarre chance anything goes wrong, they just start again. And so, logically, what is really annoying is that the condemned man has to hope that the guillotine will work properly. So the condemned man has to collaborate morally.

It's in his own interest that everything goes smoothly. For a long time—and I don't know why—I thought you had to walk up the steps of the scaffolding to get to the guillotine.

I think it's because of the French Revolution, I mean because of everything I'd been taught or shown about it. But then I remembered a photograph published in the newspapers about a sensational execution.
The guillotine is really set up on the ground, the simplest thing in the world. It's much narrower than I'd imagined.

I hadn't realized this before, which was rather strange. In the picture, I was struck by how well constructed it looked: precision-made, polished, and gleaming. People always have exaggerated ideas about unfamiliar things.

Everything is very simple though: the guillotine is positioned at the same level as the man walking towards it. He walks over to it as if he were going to meet someone. That's also annoying. The imagination could grasp the idea of walking up the steps to the scaffold, ascending to the open skies.

There were two other things I thought about all the time: dawn and my appeal. But I'm trying to be rational and not think about them any more.

I listen to my heart beating. I can't imagine that the sound that has been with me for so long might ever end.

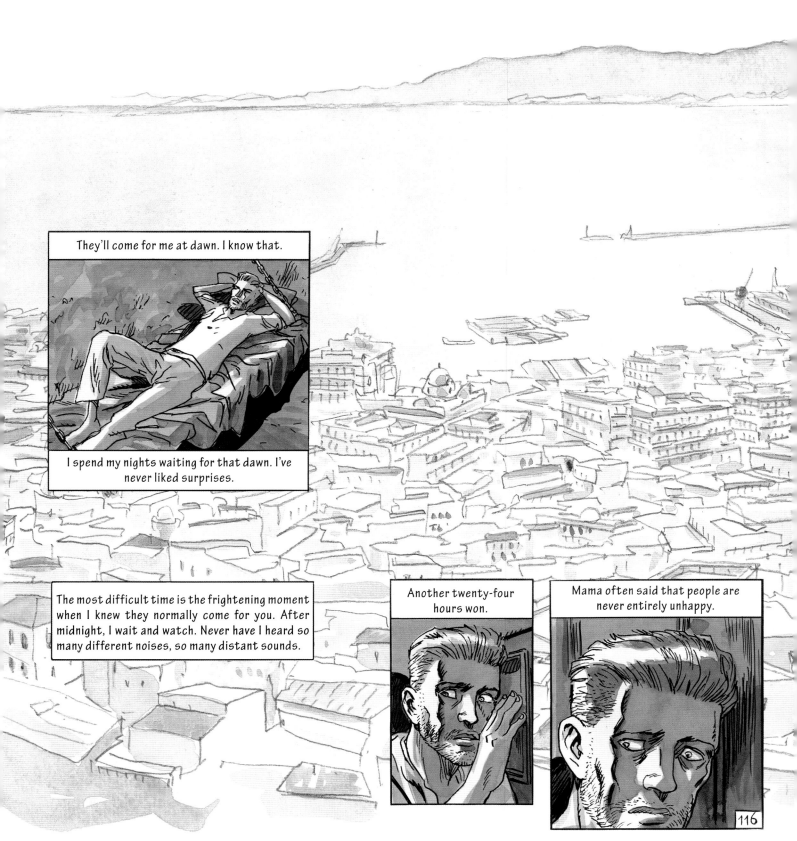

They'll come for me at dawn. I know that.

I spend my nights waiting for that dawn. I've never liked surprises.

The most difficult time is the frightening moment when I knew they normally come for you. After midnight, I wait and watch. Never have I heard so many different noises, so many distant sounds.

Another twenty-four hours won.

Mama often said that people are never entirely unhappy.

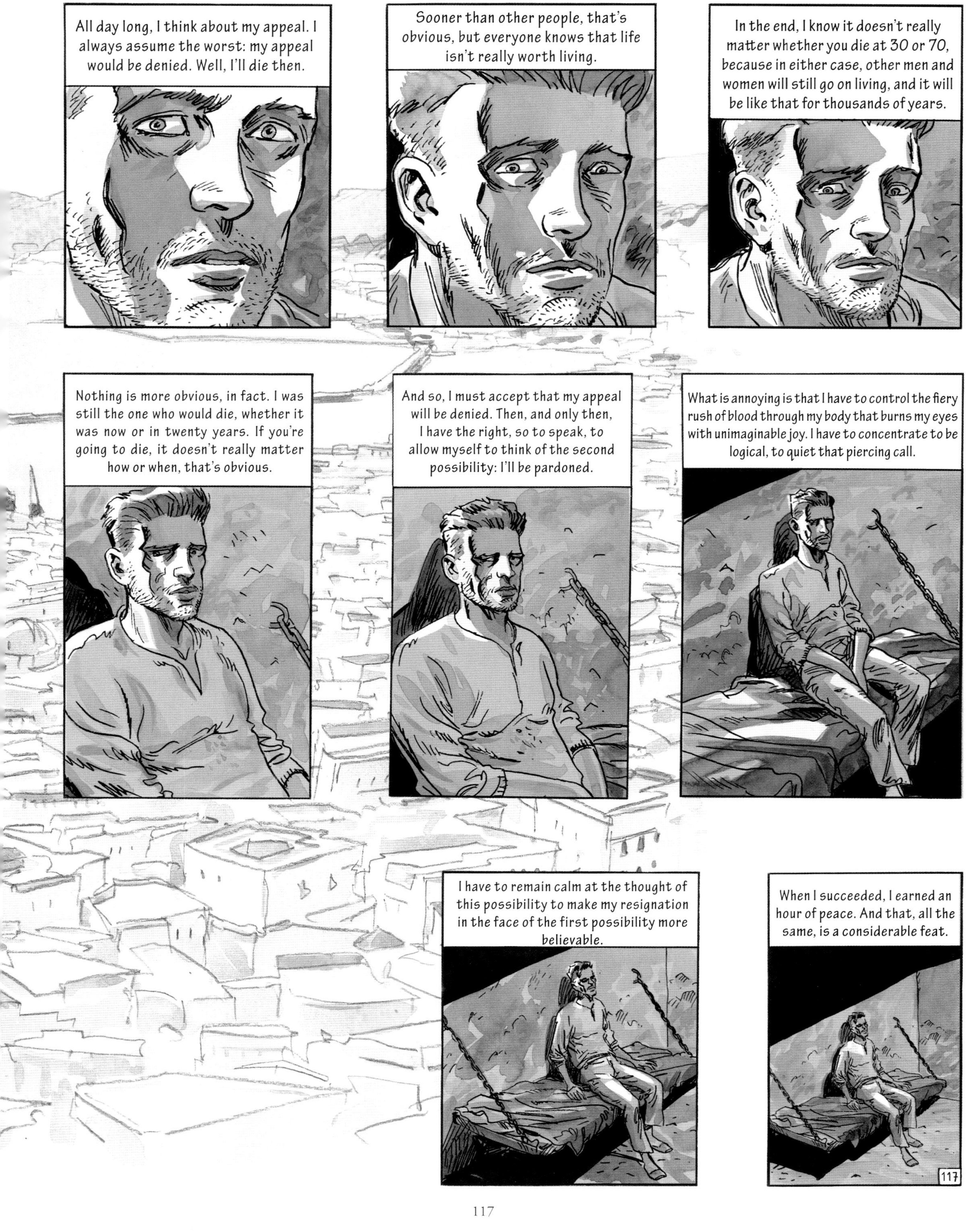
All day long, I think about my appeal. I always assume the worst: my appeal would be denied. Well, I'll die then.
Sooner than other people, that's obvious, but everyone knows that life isn't really worth living.
In the end, I know it doesn't really matter whether you die at 30 or 70, because in either case, other men and women will still go on living, and it will be like that for thousands of years.
Nothing is more obvious, in fact. I was still the one who would die, whether it was now or in twenty years. If you're going to die, it doesn't really matter how or when, that's obvious.
And so, I must accept that my appeal will be denied. Then, and only then, I have the right, so to speak, to allow myself to think of the second possibility: I'll be pardoned.
What is annoying is that I have to control the fiery rush of blood through my body that burns my eyes with unimaginable joy. I have to concentrate to be logical, to quiet that piercing call.
I have to remain calm at the thought of this possibility to make my resignation in the face of the first possibility more believable.
When I succeeded, I earned an hour of peace. And that, all the same, is a considerable feat.
117

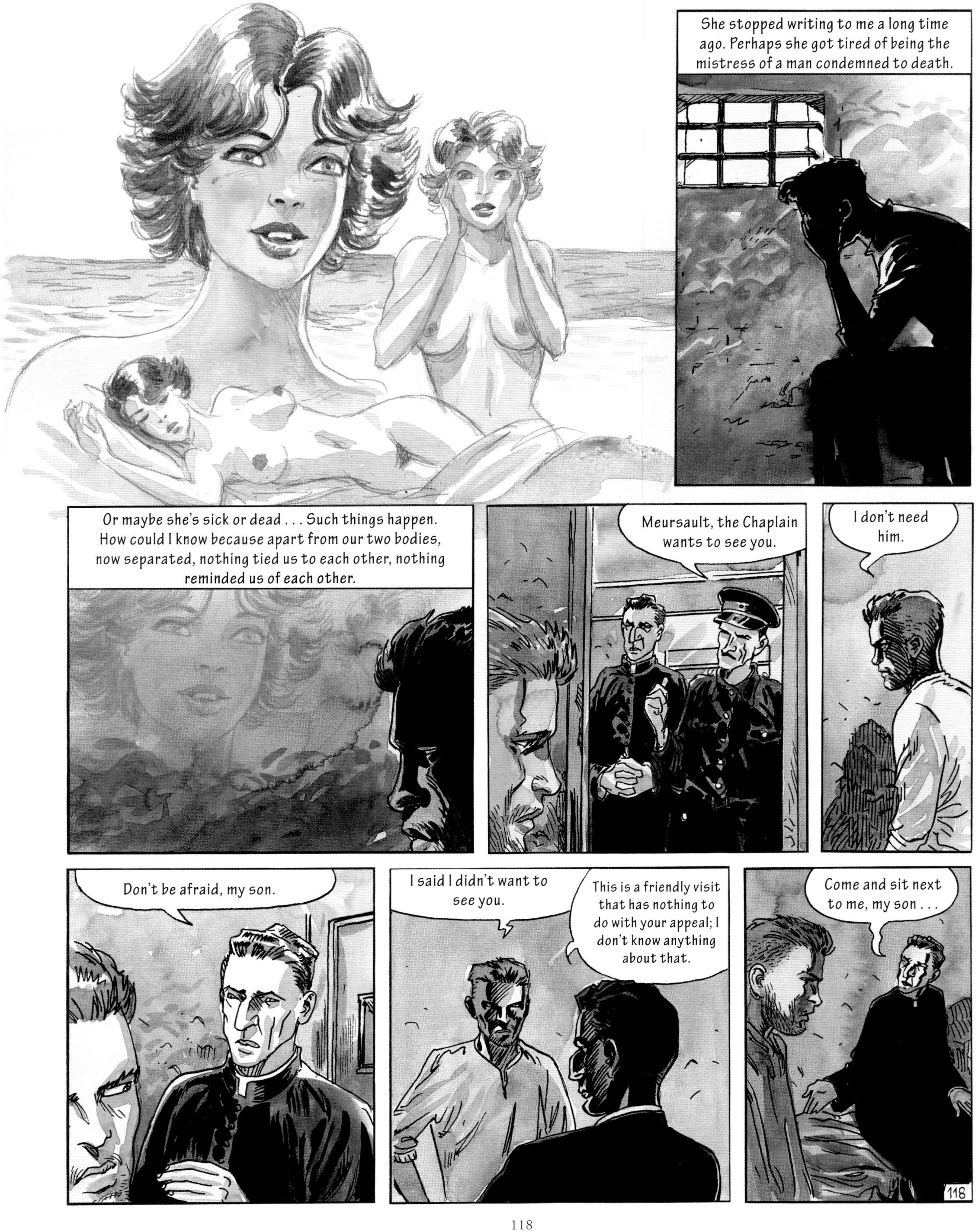
She stopped writing to me a long time ago. Perhaps she got tired of being the mistress of a man condemned to death.
Or maybe she's sick or dead . . . Such things happen. How could I know because apart from our two bodies, now separated, nothing tied us to each other, nothing reminded us of each other.
Meursault, the Chaplain wants to see you.
I don't need him.
Don't be afraid, my son.
I said I didn't want to see you.
This is a friendly visit that has nothing to do with your appeal; I don't know anything about that.
Come and sit next to me, my son . . .
118

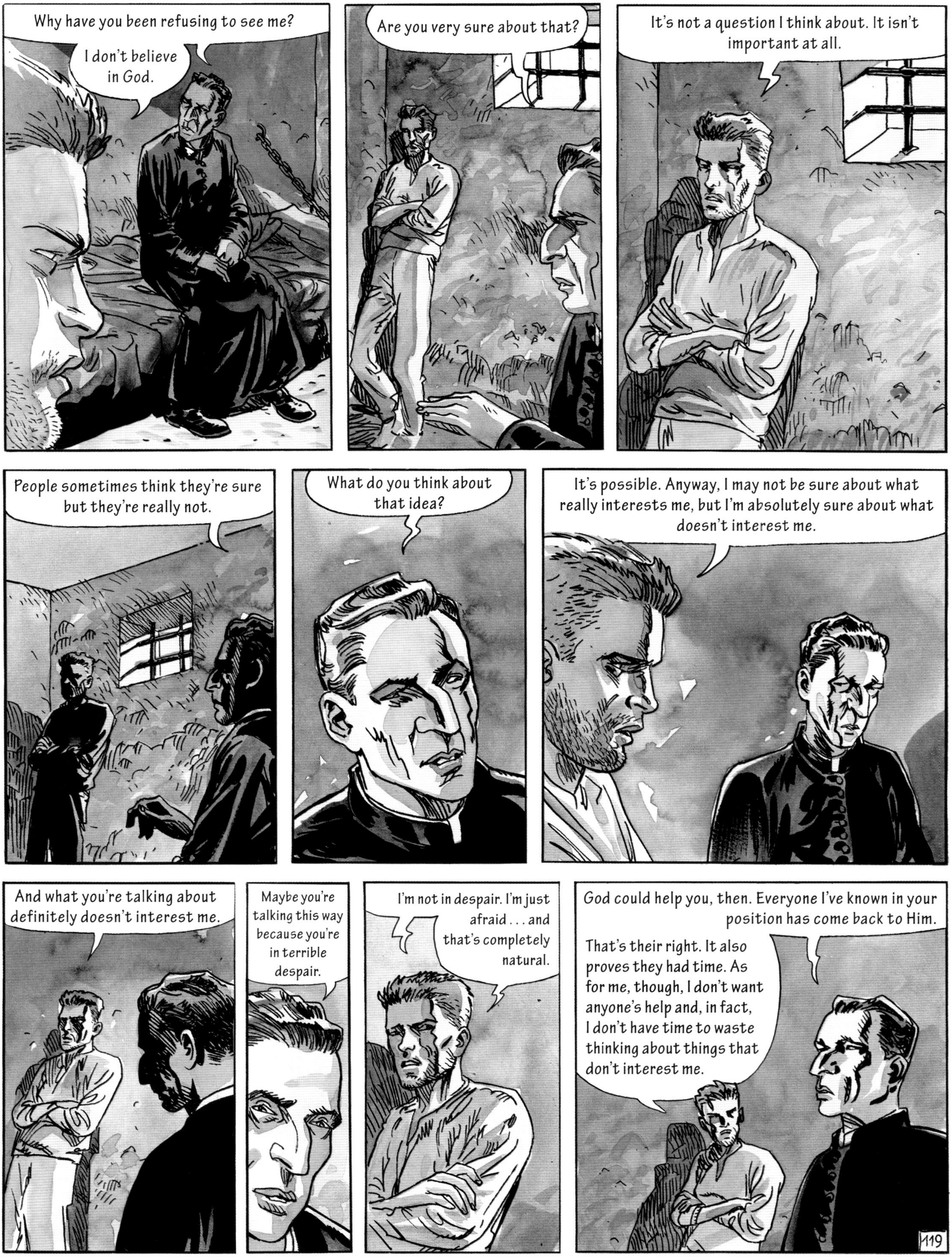
Why have you been refusing to see me?
I don't believe in God.
Are you very sure about that?
It's not a question I think about. It isn't important at all.
People sometimes think they're sure but they're really not.
What do you think about that idea?
It's possible. Anyway, I may not be sure about what really interests me, but I'm absolutely sure about what doesn't interest me.
And what you're talking about definitely doesn't interest me.
Maybe you're talking this way because you're in terrible despair.
I'm not in despair. I'm just afraid . . . and that's completely natural.
God could help you, then. Everyone I've known in your position has come back to Him.
That's their right. It also proves they had time. As for me, though, I don't want anyone's help and, in fact, I don't have time to waste thinking about things that don't interest me.
119

My friend, if you talk this way, it's not because you're condemned to death . . . we're all condemned to death.

It's not the same thing. And besides, that's no consolation.

Of course . . .

But you'll die later if you don't die today. The same question will arise then.

How will you deal with this terrible trial?

Exactly the way I'm dealing with it now.

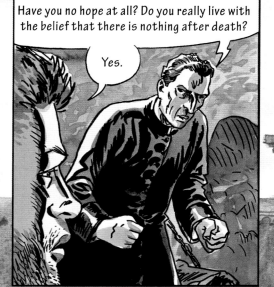

Have you no hope at all? Do you really live with the belief that there is nothing after death?

Yes.

I'm sure you'll win your appeal. But you are carrying a heavy sin and must repent. The justice of man is nothing, but the justice of God is everything.

Yet it's the former that's condemned me.

But it hasn't washed away your sin.

120

I don't know what a sin is. I've just been told I'm guilty. I'm guilty, and I'm paying for it. No one could ask any more of me.

You're wrong, my son, more could be asked of you. Perhaps it will be asked of you.

What do you mean?

You could be asked to see.

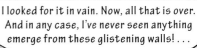

To see what?

Pain and sadness are seeping out of all these stones, I know that. I've never looked at them without feeling anguish. But deep within my heart, I know that even the most despondent of men have seen a divine face emerge from the darkness. It is that face I am asking you to see.

I've been staring at these walls for months. There is nothing and no one I know better in the world. A long time ago, I might have tried to see a face in them. But that face had the color of the sun and the flame of desire: it was Marie's face! . . .

I looked for it in vain. Now, all that is over. And in any case, I've never seen anything emerge from these glistening walls! . . .

May I embrace you?

NO.

Do you really love this world so much?

. . .

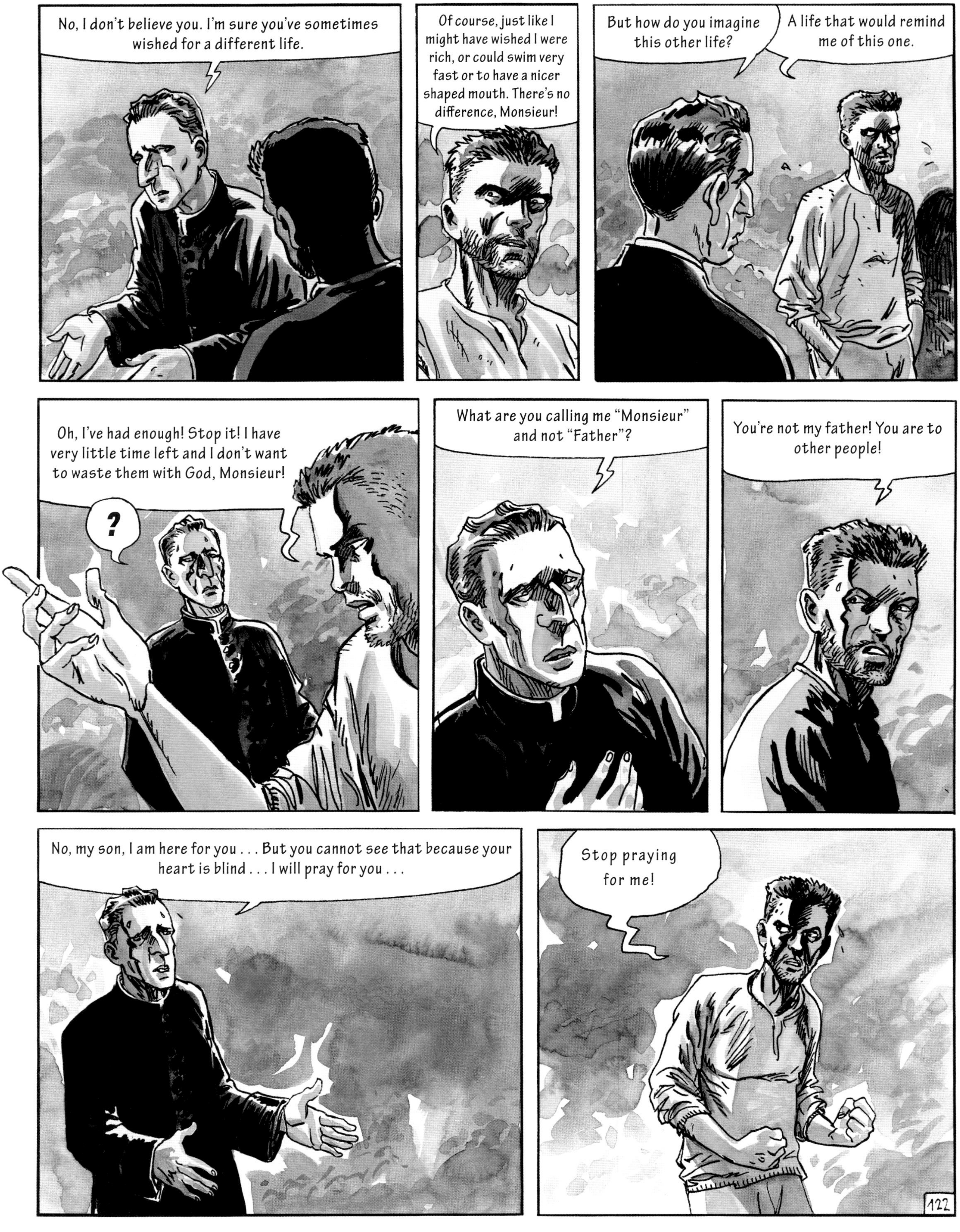
No, I don't believe you. I'm sure you've sometimes wished for a different life.
Of course, just like I might have wished I were rich, or could swim very fast or to have a nicer shaped mouth. There's no difference, Monsieur!
But how do you imagine this other life?
A life that would remind me of this one.
Oh, I've had enough! Stop it! I have very little time left and I don't want to waste them with God, Monsieur!
?
What are you calling me "Monsieur" and not "Father"?
You're not my father! You are to other people!
No, my son, I am here for you . . . But you cannot see that because your heart is blind . . . I will pray for you . . .
Stop praying for me!
122

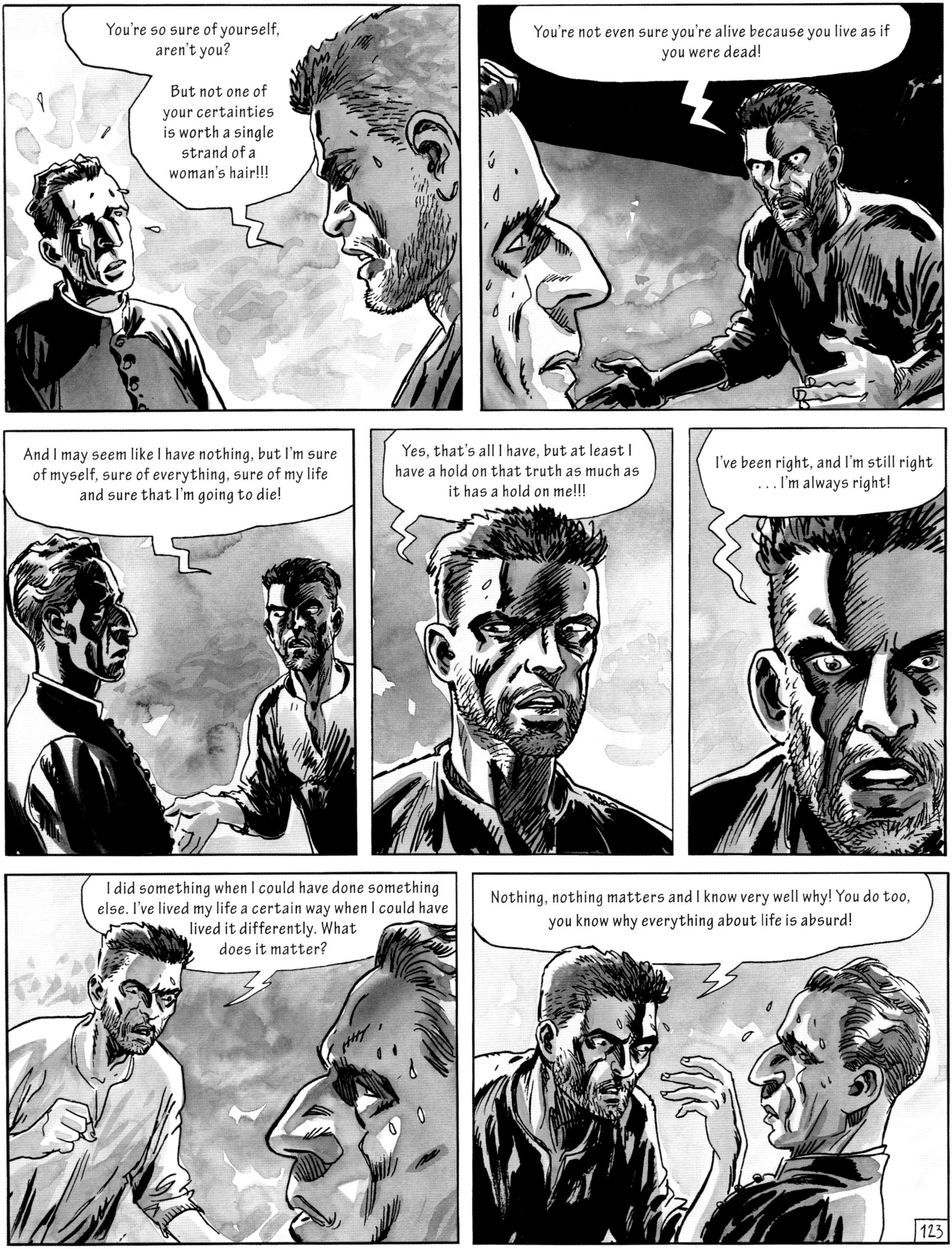
You're so sure of yourself, aren't you?
But not one of your certainties is worth a single strand of a woman's hair!!!
You're not even sure you're alive because you live as if you were dead!
And I may seem like I have nothing, but I'm sure of myself, sure of everything, sure of my life and sure that I'm going to die!
Yes, that's all I have, but at least I have a hold on that truth as much as it has a hold on me!!!
I've been right, and I'm still right . . . I'm always right!
I did something when I could have done something else. I've lived my life a certain way when I could have lived it differently. What does it matter?
Nothing, nothing matters and I know very well why! You do too, you know why everything about life is absurd!
123

Why should the death of other people or a mother's love matter so much?

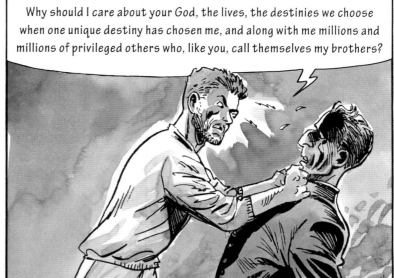

Why should I care about your God, the lives, the destinies we choose when one unique destiny has chosen me, and along with me millions and millions of privileged others who, like you, call themselves my brothers?

Can't you understand, can you really not understand? . . .

Everyone is privileged. Everyone else too would one day be condemned to death.

You as well, you'll be condemned to death!

What did it matter if accused of murder you were being executed for not crying at your mother's funeral? . . .

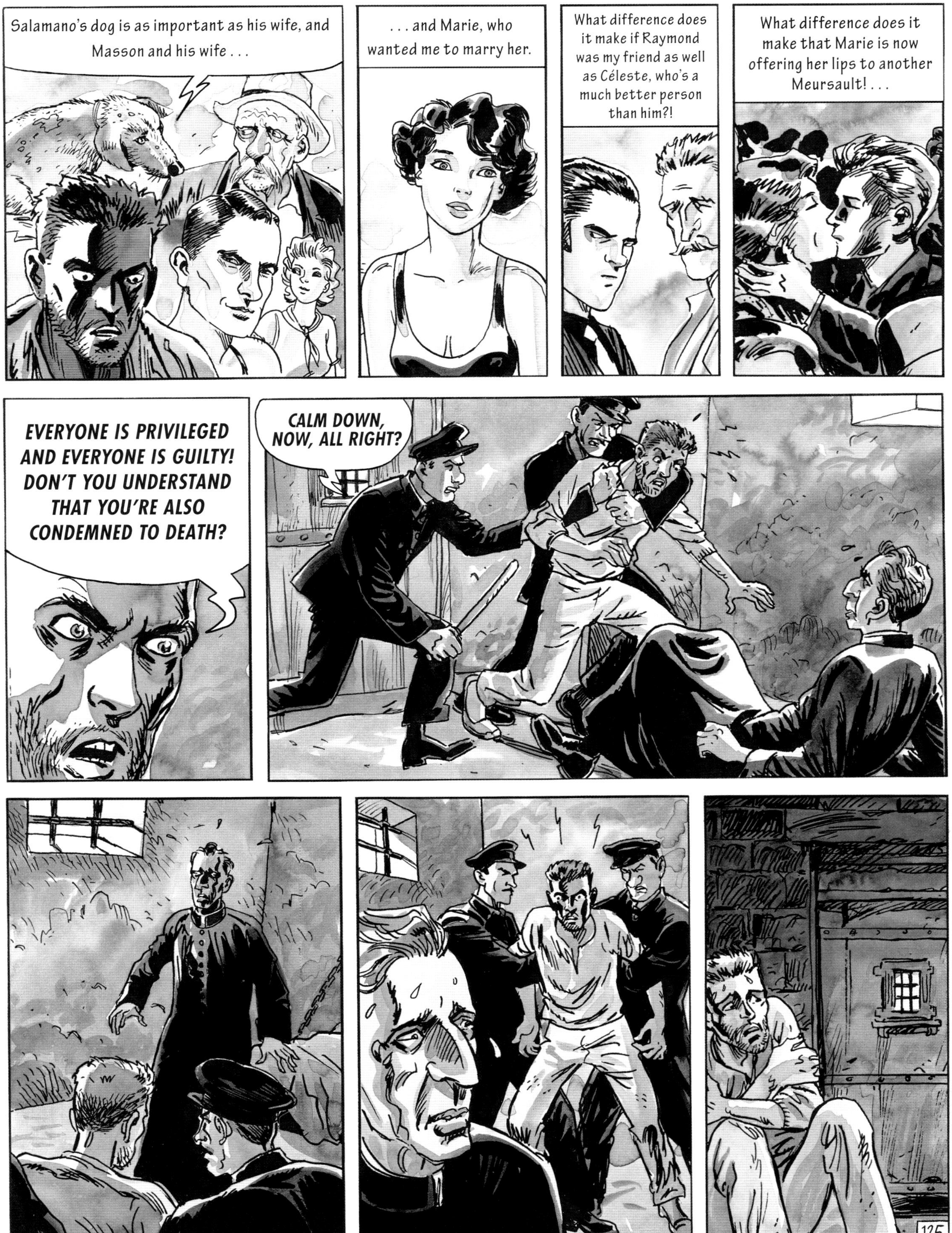
Salamano's dog is as important as his wife, and Masson and his wife . . .
. . . and Marie, who wanted me to marry her.
What difference does it make if Raymond was my friend as well as Céleste, who's a much better person than him?!
What difference does it make that Marie is now offering her lips to another Meursault! . . .
EVERYONE IS PRIVILEGED AND EVERYONE IS GUILTY! DON'T YOU UNDERSTAND THAT YOU'RE ALSO CONDEMNED TO DEATH?
CALM DOWN, NOW, ALL RIGHT?
125

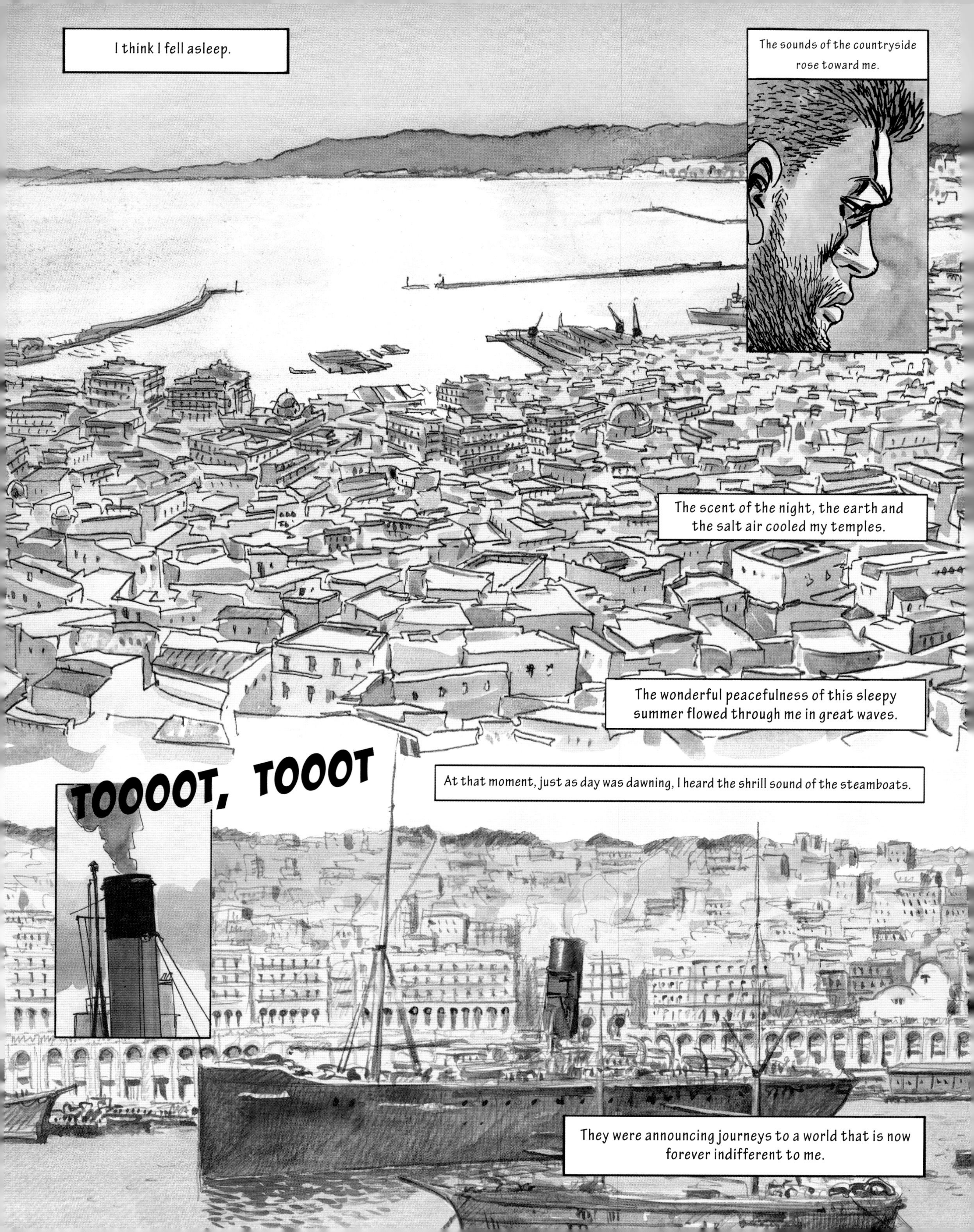
I think I fell asleep.
The sounds of the countryside rose toward me.
The scent of the night, the earth and the salt air cooled my temples.
The wonderful peacefulness of this sleepy summer flowed through me in great waves.
TOOOOT, TOOOT
At that moment, just as day was dawning, I heard the shrill sound of the steamboats.
They were announcing journeys to a world that is now forever indifferent to me.

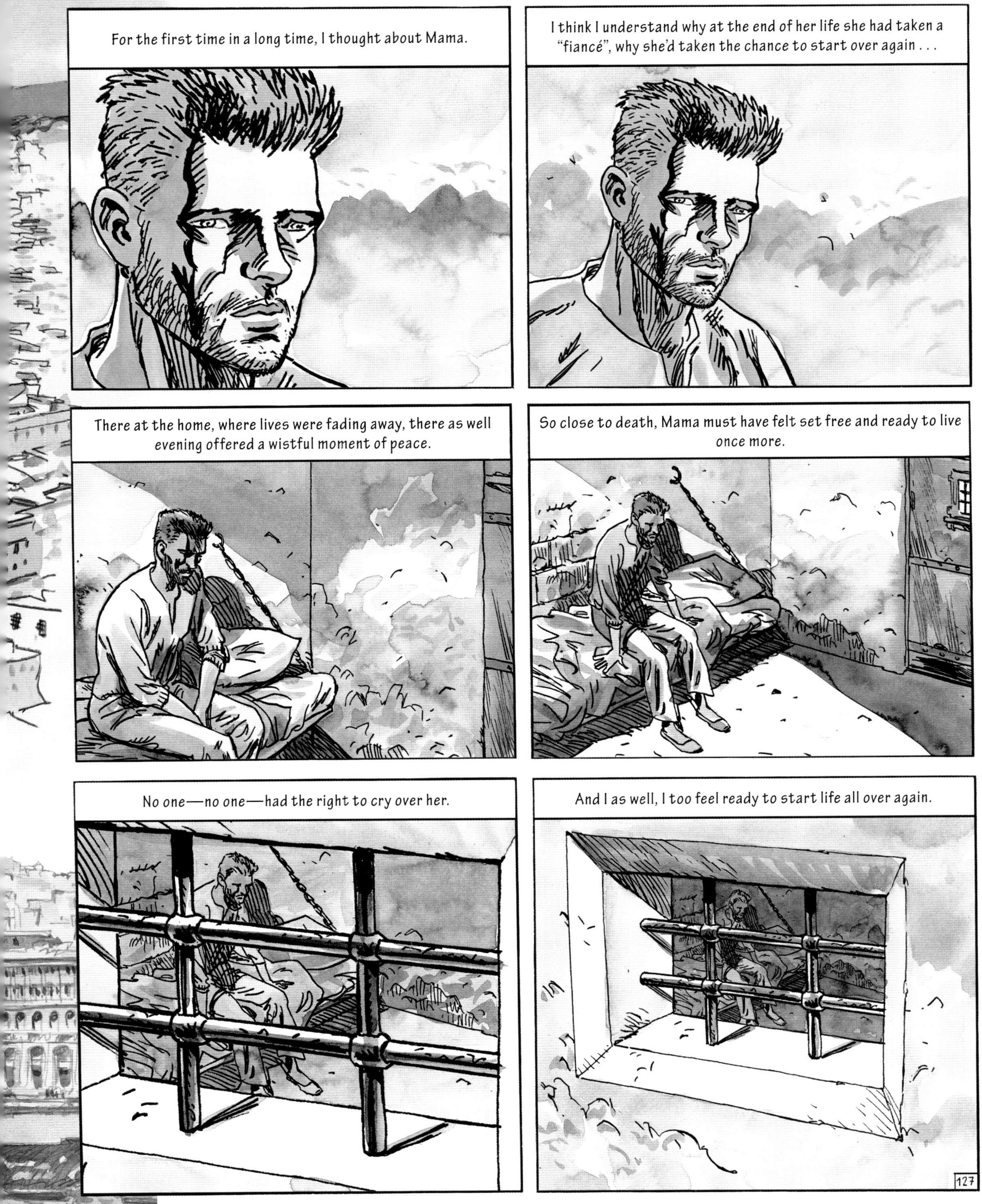
For the first time in a long time, I thought about Mama.
I think I understand why at the end of her life she had taken a "fiancé", why she'd taken the chance to start over again . . .
There at the home, where lives were fading away, there as well evening offered a wistful moment of peace.
So close to death, Mama must have felt set free and ready to live once more.
No one—no one—had the right to cry over her.
And I as well, I too feel ready to start life all over again.
127

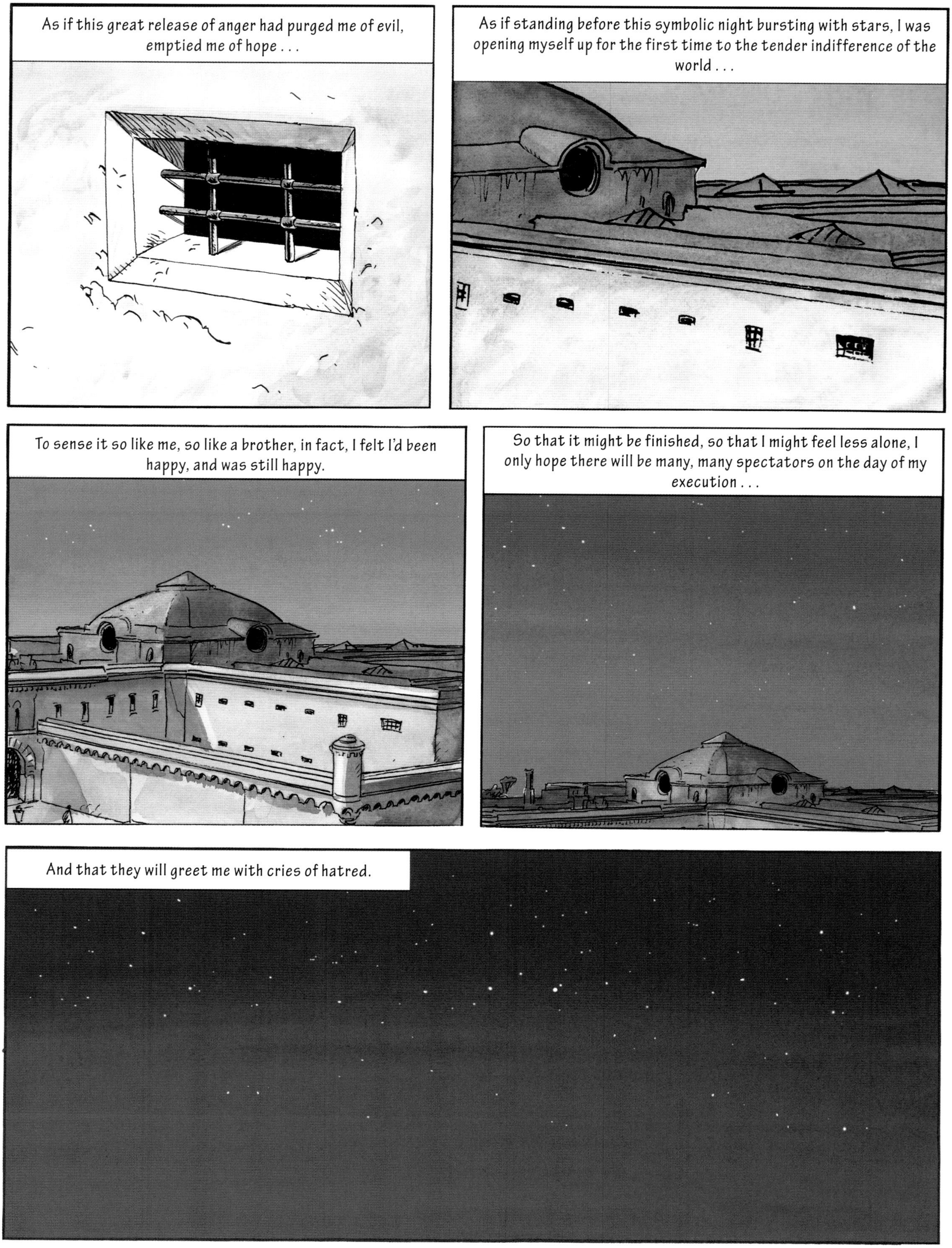
As if this great release of anger had purged me of evil, emptied me of hope . . .
As if standing before this symbolic night bursting with stars, I was opening myself up for the first time to the tender indifference of the world . . .
To sense it so like me, so like a brother, in fact, I felt I'd been happy, and was still happy.
So that it might be finished, so that I might feel less alone, I only hope there will be many, many spectators on the day of my execution . . .
And that they will greet me with cries of hatred.

# ABOUT THE AUTHOR

ALBERT CAMUS was born in Algeria in 1913. During World War II, he joined the resistance movement in Paris, then became editor-in-chief of the newspaper *Combat* during the liberation. A novelist, playwright, and essayist, he is most famous for his novels *The Stranger* and *The Plague*. He was awarded the Nobel Prize for literature in 1957.

# ABOUT THE ILLUSTRATOR

JACQUES FERRANDEZ was born in Algeria in 1955. In 1987, he began his *Notebooks from the Orient*, a series of panoramic portraits depicting the history of the French presence in Algeria, for which he was awarded the Historia Prix Spécial. An indisputable expert on the Algerian question, he adapted Camus's short story *The Guest* as a graphic novel before undertaking this new interpretation of *The Stranger*. His books have been the subject of many exhibitions in France and Algeria.

# ABOUT THE TRANSLATOR

SANDRA SMITH is the translator of all twelve novels by Irène Némirovsky; a new translation of Camus's *L'Etranger* (*The Outsider,* Penguin UK); and *The Necklace and Other Stories: Maupassant for Modern Times* (Liveright). Her translation of Némirovsky's *Suite Française* won the French-American Foundation and Florence Gould Foundation Translation Prize for Fiction, as well as the PEN Book-of-the-Month Club Translation Prize. After ten years as a Fellow of Robinson College, Cambridge, Smith now lives in New York.